# THE COLLOQUIAL STYLE IN AMERICA

# THE

# Colloquial Style in America

RICHARD BRIDGMAN

*New York*

OXFORD UNIVERSITY PRESS

1966

The quotations from *Hello Towns!, Sherwood Anderson's Notebook, The Sherwood Anderson Reader, Poor White,* and *Horses and Men* by Sherwood Anderson are used by permission of Harold Ober Associates, Inc., agents for the Estate of Sherwood Anderson.

The quotations from *Winesburg, Ohio* by Sherwood Anderson are used by permission of The Viking Press, Inc.

The quotations from *In Our Time* by Ernest Hemingway (copyright 1925 Charles Scribner's Sons; renewal copyright 1953 Ernest Hemingway) from *The Short Stories of Ernest Hemingway* (copyright 1938 Ernest Hemingway) and from *You Know Me Al* by Ring Lardner (copyright © 1960 Charles Scribner's Sons) are used by permission of Charles Scribner's Sons.

The quotations from *In Our Time* by Ernest Hemingway are used by permission also of Jonathan Cape Ltd.

The quotations from "Melanctha" (copyright 1909 Gertrude Stein; renewal copyright 1936 Gertrude Stein) from *Three Lives* by Gertrude Stein, from *Lectures in America* by Gertrude Stein (copyright 1935 Alice B. Toklas; renewal copyright 1962 Alice B. Toklas), and from *Selected Writings of Gertrude Stein,* edited by Carl Van Vechten (copyright 1946 Random House, Inc.), are used by permission of Random House, Inc., and by permission also of the Estate of Gertrude Stein.

FOR

DENNY

# CONTENTS

*Epigraphs throughout are from Gertrude Stein*

# ACKNOWLEDGMENTS

John Henry Raleigh, Stanley Cavell, and James D. Hart read versions of this study and kindly assisted me with their suggestions. Albert R. Kitzhaber provided a detailed commentary on the manuscript and, with equal generosity, listened to me talk out some of its many problems. Henry Nash Smith prompted me with his ideas from the beginning; at the same time he never stopped pressing for the clarification of mine. The effect of his calm good will throughout this period is inestimable. For all this help, however distorted in translation, I am most grateful.

The Committees on Research at Dartmouth College and at the University of California at Berkeley provided funds for typing the manuscript on several occasions; and by awarding me a summer Faculty Fellowship in 1964, the University of California enabled me to complete the book. Such assistance was as essential as it was welcome. Once more I express my appreciation for it.

R.B.

THE COLLOQUIAL STYLE IN AMERICA

# Introduction

LITTLE HAS BEEN WRITTEN about national prose style, for there are legitimate doubts that such an entity exists. A few pioneering explorations of American literature have located important image-rivers flowing through its style. References to gardens, to heroic innocence, and to darkness appear insistently enough in nineteenth-century American writing of all kinds to be regarded as transcending the preoccupations of any single writer. They constitute a part of the general literary response to national experience, that is, they form part of the national stylistic landscape.[1] Beyond these studies of images, however, and short of linguistics, only offhand generalizations have been advanced about an American way of using language. Such generalizations commonly superimpose political assumptions upon the literary medium, finding it, for example, "democratic" — hence, obviously, "direct," "hardy," and "casual." The usefulness of such descriptions, which as Richard Ohmann points out "name without explaining,"[2] is easily dismissed; yet, their persistent appearance indicates that readers of American literature feel, even though they cannot substantiate their intuition, that this literature possesses certain distinctive stylistic features. The present study attempts to discover the source of those feelings.

My initial assumption is so broad as hardly to admit dispute: that a change has indeed taken place in American prose style in the last century and a half. Even in the absence of absolute proof (which in stylistic matters is unthinka-

ble) most readers would agree, I should think, that the prose
of Erskine Caldwell, John Steinbeck, William Saroyan, and
J. P. Marquand more closely resembles the prose of Ernest
Hemingway than that of Nathaniel Hawthorne. Conversely,
the prose of George Lippard, Maria Susanna Cummins,
Augusta Evans, Susan Warner, and William Ware has more
affinities with Hawthorne than it has with writers in the current century. The very look of Hawthorne's page differs from
Hemingway's. Its characteristic form is blocklike with dense
and tangled interiors, while Hemingway crosses his page with
thin lines and chips of language, clean and well-lighted. Can
there be any doubt to whom each of the following two sentences belong?

> Beyond that darksome verge, the firelight glim-
> mered on the stately trunks and almost black foliage
> of pines, intermixed with the lighter verdure of sap-
> ling oaks, maples, and poplars, while here and there
> lay the gigantic corpses of dead trees, decaying on
> the leaf-strewn soil.

> We walked on the road between the thick trunks
> of the old beeches and the sunlight came through
> the leaves in light patches on the grass.

If we add similar quotations from lesser writers in both cen-
turies, the difficulty of attribution does not appreciably increase:

> She bent down on the velvet moss, while the green
> leaves of the shrubbery encircling her on every side,
> and the thick branches of trees, meeting overhead in
> a canopy of verdure, made the place seem like a
> fairy bower of some olden story.

> On one side of the road was forest, healthy-looking
> pine and elm, dark trunks looking almost black
> against the pale, milky-green of the new foliage.[3]

Now I would agree that for some purposes style cannot be discussed apart from the context in which it operates. Hawthorne's desire to create a sinister impression for the specific story "Ethan Brand" helped to determine the diction he selected. But style is both initiated by the artist and imposed upon him, so that when Hawthorne chose "darksome verge" and "gigantic corpses" to construct an atmosphere of fatality, he drew upon a vocabulary no longer available to Hemingway. Quite aside from his peculiar training and cast of experience, the writer bears the impress of a communal past and he walks through a shared present, which partially overrides individual volition. This study tries to keep both the social and the personal sources of style in mind, that is, to determine what problems and what solutions were virtually forced upon the writer by his time and to give an account of what the writer deliberately contributed to help bring about this general stylistic change.

If one accepts provisionally the existence of a change in American prose style, then the next pertinent question is, when did it begin? Recently the date 1884 has been advanced from several quarters, most succinctly by Ernest Hemingway: "All modern American literature comes from one book by Mark Twain called *Huckleberry Finn*." [4] As early as 1913 H. L. Mencken was championing Mark Twain: "I believe that he was the true father of our national literature, the first genuinely American artist of the blood royal." [5] Later, William Faulkner agreed, saying: "In my opinion, Mark Twain was the first truly American writer, and all of us since are his heirs, we descended from him." [6]

This critical admiration has not extended to Mark Twain's work as a whole, nor to his literary theories (such as they were), nor to his practical criticisms. One book alone has drawn the praise. Whatever the merits of Mark Twain's other writing, and whatever the weaknesses of *Huckleberry Finn,* everyone — literary hacks, artists, and critics — agrees

that the style of this single book has had a major effect on
the development of American prose. Herman Wouk, for example, recently proposed that Mark Twain "established at a
stroke the colloquial style which has swept American literature, and indeed spilled over into world literature." [7] T. S.
Eliot placed Mark Twain with Dryden and Swift as one of
those writers "who have discovered a new way of writing,
valid not only for themselves, but for others." [8] Lionel Tril-
ling felt that "as for the style of the book, it is not less
than definitive in American literature. The prose of *Huckleberry Finn* established for written prose the virtues of
American colloquial speech." [9] Most enthusiastic of all has
been Bernard DeVoto's assertion: "In a single step it made a
literary medium of the American language; the liberating
effect on American writing could hardly be overstated." [10]

DeVoto's claim is an attractive one, but does not seem to
me historically justified. I believe we have come to accept a
false view of the ease with which writers profited by Mark
Twain's example. The stylistic possibilities suggested by
*Huckleberry Finn* were ignored, misunderstood, cynically
exploited, and finally developed (with painful slowness) into
durable form. Moreover, one cannot overlook the importance for style of several nationalistic impulses which initiated the idea of a colloquial prose long before Mark Twain's
book appeared.

The literary relations of colonial America and the mother
country are familiar enough. Seventeenth-century Americans
drew sustenance directly from English sources, many of them
having been born and educated there. Any differences in the
standard styles of the mother country and of the colonies are
attributable to the special conditions imposed by the American wilderness and the special preoccupations of the colo-
nists. English examples determined changes in colonial style,
as in the eighteenth century when American magazines
pirated Augustan poems from their British counterparts and

editors encouraged imitations of Waller, Dryden, and Pope. The major American figures maintained the continuity of the English tradition. As Stuart P. Sherman pointed out, "We can distinguish the styles of Franklin, John Adams, and Webster from one another, but not, with any assurance, from that of some British contemporary." [11] Similarly, of early nineteenth-century novelistic style, Leo Marx has commented: "If we ask what is different about German writing, we know very well the first answer to expect: it is written in German. But the language of Cooper is not all that different from that of Scott, and with Cooper's generation the boundary between British and American literature remains uncertain." [12] Only after the achievement of political independence did any significant movement toward the creation of an indigenous literature appear in the United States.

The first surge toward literary independence concentrated more upon content than upon form. Critical battles were joined, for instance, over whether Niagara Falls possessed the intrinsic dignity of Westminster Abbey. Although on some peripheral formal matters, spelling in particular, critics had mixed opinions, the arbiters of taste generally agreed that the crudities of American common speech were to be barred from any decent writer's style. Vulgarity in writing had to be fenced in with quotation marks, or clearly labeled as comic and therefore not to be taken seriously.

Still, a need was felt for a new style in the United States. The theoretical motive for it was to achieve a literary independence commensurate with the political independence already won. So Noah Webster proposed in 1789: "We have . . . the fairest opportunity of establishing a national language . . . in North America, that ever presented itself to mankind. Now is the time to begin the plan." [13] The literature of the New World was to reflect its republican ideals. Practically, the pressure for a new style came from the already existing components of that new style in popular speech. Americans shared, especially on the frontier, basic experiences that required a vocabulary not precisely equivalent to that considered standard in England. "It is remarkable," said Captain Marryat in 1839, "how very debased the language has become in a short period in America. . . . They have a dictionary containing many thousands of words which, with us, are either obsolete, or are provincialisms, or are words necessarily invented by the Americans." [14] The sense of regional uniqueness extended far enough in the early 1800's to produce a *Kentucky English Grammar*. It was not altogether a joke for Sam Slick to comment, "I never seed an Englishman yet that spoke good English." [15]

The linguistic situation in the United States was historically unique. Romantic, nationalistic, and practical pressures impelled American writers to evolve a new means of expression out of the casual discourse of the nation. There, if anywhere, "American" was to be heard. Not that the American language was a new language, distinct from English. Compared to the gross differences which existed between French when it was first being adapted for serious literary use and the Latin from which it was derived, the distinctions between American informal speech and standard literary English were subtle. There was a spoken language in the United States with a natural way of using it (American), and there was a literary language with an accepted way of using it (English). In many respects these overlapped, and yet they were far from identical.

Making a literary vehicle out of the spoken language was more easily conceived than executed. Logically, it seemed to require the sorting out of native elements already present in the standard literary style, and then their reblending with other elements hitherto excluded from the printed page. But how was one to assemble an indigenous vocabulary? And what would it sound like in operation? The most obvious answer was to transfer the speech of an American

(whatever that was) to the printed page, the chief consideration being verisimilitude. At first, the writer's ear had to furnish the evidence against which he could check and improve
his mimetic powers. Only after various regional and social
dialects had been learned and dialogue had been sufficiently
refined were enough conventions available to permit stylization. This process of establishing a literary imitation of colloquial speech and then polishing it resembles the gradual
stylistic refinement of language in the English Renaissance
theater, a recent study of which, after describing the primitive heartiness of the early theater's popular style, designated
the problem facing the next generation of playwrights: "To
assimilate this raw speech into an organized style that would
lend itself to more complex uses without, in the process, losing its vitality and its close kinship with the spoken word." [16]

The fundamental question for all those working with the
vernacular was how to eliminate the taint of vulgarity and of
humor that normally accompanied popular speech. Taking a
long view of the nineteenth century for a moment, one can
trace the vernacular's increasing acceptance in the familiar
descriptive terms "prose humor," "local color," and "realism." They signal the progressive flooding of the literary
world with a common speech that for more and more readers
is accepted as a literary norm. What was enjoyed with
condescending amusement before the Civil War was encouraged after the war for its vivacious authenticity, then
later as the literary manifestation of a militant attitude toward
life.

Mark Twain's use of a boy as narrator in *Huckleberry
Finn* provided American writers one important entry to the
language and homely particulars of American life. In that
story we hear no condescending adult voice by which Huck
can be judged insufficient. His idiom is the standard. And because Huck is a boy, not only is his language natural to
him, but his attitude toward the world of particulars around

him is one of unremitting interest. His quiet concentration upon all that surrounds him invests the commonplace world with dignity, seriousness, and an unforeseen beauty that radiates through the very words he uses. An adult is tainted with stylistic original sin — double vision, awareness of tradition, vanity. Huck's style is prelapsarian in its innocence and single-minded directness. That is its excellence, but its limitation too, for although Huck saw deeply, his was a narrow vision. After the example of *Huckleberry Finn* writers had to learn how to overcome the limits of his restricting viewpoint.

As others have since, Mark Twain met the problem by avoiding it. In his subsequent work he either imitated *Huckleberry Finn* or he regressed to a mixed style where, like his admirers Stephen Crane and George Ade, he deliberately encouraged incongruities for their easy irony. Somewhat later Ring Lardner found a provisional solution. By using an illiterate ballplayer as his narrator, he managed to extend the range of experience of the vernacular voice, yet conserve its linguistic naïveté. The handicaps of this approach, however, were all too evident. Sherwood Anderson tried yet another tack, making simplicity in language a doctrinal virtue. But despite an abundance of faith, he lacked the technical control that could protect him from writing simplistic parodies of himself. All in all, the thoroughly puzzled American writers could not disentangle a stable idiom from the vernacular. Merely to recognize the importance of Mark Twain's contribution was not to understand how to adapt his example to the uses of a general American prose style. Although *Huckleberry Finn* was in the sky, the day remained cloudy.

By the last quarter of the century, technical improvements in the management of both dialect and standard dialogue necessitated the move toward stylization, toward a distinctive and cohesive mode of writing. Since perfect accuracy of reproduction in dialect was neither possible nor artistically de-

sirable, at a certain point of sophistication the dialect writer
was obliged to change his goal: rather than verisimilitude, he sought to achieve verbal artfulness. His attention
shifted from the world "out there" to the prose surface. In
order to free colloquial constituents from their naturalistic
bondage, the writer had to form new literary conventions, an
uncertain process with many a retreat and no clear success.
Henry James produced work of special pertinence for solving
the stalemate in which the realists like Mark Twain found
themselves. He wished to give the impression in his narrative
prose of a mind at work, to reveal the slow progress and con-
voluted recapitulations of thought. Having already produced
a form of dialogue that for all its external simplicity bore a
heavy psychological burden, James set to work some of the
techniques he had developed for dialogue to produce a
stylized version of the mind talking. The results sufficiently
intrigued him that for a time he exaggerated them to see
what further possibilities they might afford his prose style.
Radical punctuation, fragmented expressions, and odd ver-
balisms resulted. James's practice supplied answers which
Mark Twain's camp of vernacularists needed, the medium
of transmission being Gertrude Stein.

With her abstract exercises in writing, Gertrude Stein
drew the basic features of colloquial language out into the
open, magnifying and underlining them. Although it was not
precisely her intention, she offered colloquial language as
free as possible of a subject matter, thus concentrating the attention of the student of style upon pure manner. The in-
struction provided by both her precepts and her copious
examples helped Ernest Hemingway create a definitive style
based upon the American colloquial tradition. In his first
years as a writer we can watch him experimenting with the
narrator whose presence ostensibly legitimizes the presence of
the colloquial mode. He later concealed and sometimes with-

drew the narrator, but at the same time he tinkered with his prose so that, whether the narrator were present or not, it retained its colloquial base.

On the basis of this summary then and in spite of genuine reservations about the possibility of discussing a national prose style, I believe one can still affirm the following propositions with some confidence:

1) American prose style changed significantly between 1825 and 1925.
2) On the whole the change was toward greater concreteness of diction and simplicity in syntax.
3) The change was initiated primarily in dialect pieces and in fictional dialogue.
4) Toward the end of the century writers became increasingly conscious of the techniques of colloquial writing.
5) These techniques were then stylized to accentuate the following characteristics of colloquial style:
   a) stress on the individual verbal unit,
   b) a resulting fragmentation of syntax, and
   c) the use of repetition to bind and unify.

If one asks once more how Hemingway's prose and the prose of the twentieth century differ from that of Hawthorne and *his* century, the briefest answer would argue the greater verbal simplicity of the modern style. Long words are eliminated or infrequently used, and then as deliberate contrasts. The sentences themselves are shorter. What was hinged and stapled by semicolons in the earlier prose is broken up into a series of declarative sentences in the later. Fewer details are provided, and those offered are precise and concrete. References to a cultural and historical past are stripped away, and the haze of emotive words is dispelled. Primary colors are accented. The immediate material world claims all the reader's attention. The result is a sharp, hard focus. Hemingway's prose is not the ultimate prose by any means, but its lean, artful sufficiency based upon a vernacular diction and a colloquial manner had to be achieved before it could effloresce into more intricate structures.

Since this study traces a movement in colloquial prose that progressively simplifies and concentrates verbal expression, it may occur to the reader that some Southern writers have employed an oral style that is fundamentally expansive and opulent in nature. Although Southern writing can be as laconic as other American colloquial prose, it also indulges in that public oratory we habitually associate with the Southern politician, and which we often hear in the prose of Thomas Wolfe and William Faulkner, of Robert Penn Warren and William Styron, and even, ironically, of James Baldwin. Such prose, which is not embarrassed by the oratorical flourish, can be accommodated to the historical process which this study describes, for the oratorical mode shares the characteristics of the colloquial. Its exclamations, repetitions, uncertain backings and fillings, accumulations of synonyms, and rhetorical emphases all originate in the extemporaneousness of speech, the spontaneous jetting of language that maintains its equilibrium by constant movement forward rather than by a poised interrelationship among stable elements.[17]

Except for this last point concerning Southern writing, the propositions advanced in this introduction are elaborated and documented in detail in the chapters to follow. I hope I have offered enough evidence in them to convince the reader until he has had an opportunity to test my conclusions for himself, but not so much as to oppress him. Abuse of the reader being the cardinal sin of stylistic studies, I have tried to alleviate such distress by liberal use of italics and small capitals in order to emphasize significant points in extended quotations. One other procedural note: inasmuch as fiction writers were more open to new techniques than were the essayists committed to maintaining genteel standards in the American monthlies, my stylistic examples are drawn almost

exclusively from fictional prose. Also, since colloquial language must initially issue from a specific speaker or be prac-
ticed in dialogue, fiction provided a medium for speech that
expository prose of the nineteenth century rarely could. This
is not, however, to deny an analogous easing of expository
style in the period under investigation.

# ONE

# Parts of Speech

"Gradually the written language says something and says it differently than the spoken language."

*Everybody's Autobiography*

I

SPEECH AND WRITING enjoy an intimate and not altogether separable relationship, but the two forms of verbalization do differ importantly in their physical performance and reception. When one speaks, the listeners hear the words almost as soon as they are uttered. It makes a stylistic difference that words pass more quickly from mind to sound to ear than they do from mind to paper to eye. The extra time required to transcribe sound symbols in visual form can be annoying, especially when the words are flowing rapidly, but it also provides intervals of indeterminate length for making verbal decisions, a luxury not readily available to the speaker. The writer is more conscious of his words than the speaker. Not only can he alter his vocabulary and syntax in his head as he proceeds, but once the word is written, he can change it, move it about upon the page, or strike it out.

There are, to be sure, written speeches, and these may be marked by a high degree of artifice. If the speaker has prepared his speech in advance, he may then read it to the audience from the text, or he may deliver it from memory. But unless the speaker is the most dogged writer imaginable, his speech will differ somewhat from normal written prose. The speaker experienced in the special problems of the platform will acknowledge that his audience is absorbing his message by ear. For modern literate man this activity is more difficult than reading, since listeners are unlikely to visualize words as they listen to a speech, whereas readers frequently not only see the words, but also hear them as they read. This means that because two senses are concentrated on the words, reading is a fuller process than listening. The visual appearance of the word and its sound make their impact simultaneously. The listener, however, absorbs the speech only by ear, and, even if his visual attention is fixed upon the speaker, he may be distracted. For this reason, the experienced speaker will simplify his syntax and repeat or restate key ideas as an aid to comprehension. When Mark Twain prepared a reading from *Huckleberry Finn,* he added italics to guide his verbal emphases and he repeated phrases. One portion originally read: "That was so — I couldn't get around that, no way. That was where it pinched." In his prompt copy Mark Twain changed it to: "That was *so* — yes, it was *so* — I couldn't get around *that,* no way. *That* was where it *pinched."* [1]

The speaker may also insert rhetorical questions, deliberate pauses, even apparent lapses of memory, all to make his speech sound dramatic and "alive." Moreover, the speaker may depart from the written form of his speech through spontaneous interpolations. If the speaker has memorized his speech, he may substitute one phrase for another during his delivery, or he may change the order of his syntax as he speaks, not always consciously. And, whether he reads from a prepared text or delivers a memorized speech, he may add comments as his memory is jogged into some new perception, or in response to the audience's reactions. When this happens, if the interpolation is of any length, the rhythm of his delivery will normally change noticeably. Everyone knows the experience of watching a speaker look up from his manuscript, begin to grope for words, and finally express himself rather loosely. The rhythm and often the diction of the extemporaneous speech changes. That change in rhythm is as noticeable as a shift in gear. This particular gear, which normally serves to get one around town, is called the colloquial. Because this term and its companion, the vernacular, are critical ones for the revision of literary norms that has occurred in America, they merit some special attention.

As a fact of usage, *vernacular* normally appears as a noun and *colloquial* as an adjective — a helpful distinction to begin with. The vernacular is the substance, the verbal clay to be shaped. One way in which that clay is shaped in speech and in writing is designated colloquial. The colloquial manner determines what the words will look and sound like in context and what they can do.

Beyond such basic statements, these two terms resist definition. The vernacular is difficult to distinguish from standard English once one acknowledges that it is more than the difference between "an old dog" and "a venerable canine." When, in Cooper's *The Prairie,* Obed Batt identifies Paul Hover as "a collector of the *apes,* or bee," then asks, "Do I use the vernacular now, — am I understood?" (ch. 11), he is not lapsing into vulgarity, but moving from the specialized jargon of the scientist into the daylight of ordinary discourse. Moreover, vernacular changes with the company. The informal vocabulary used by the educated man in his profession is blended with new words when he goes to a hardware store or a cocktail party. One does not descend to the vernacular so much as one moves laterally across different phases of it. Any word used with sufficient frequency as to become generally familiar gains access to the vernacular insofar as the vernacular is defined as a nation's common fund of language.

But other connotations adhering to the vernacular obscure its identity. For example, a recent and widely disseminated definition of the vernacular reads as follows:

> English vernacular formerly referred to the native, spoken language—as opposed to the literary lan-

guages of Latin or Norman French. It now usually
means Nonstandard and perhaps Informal English,
the native homely, spoken language as contrasted
with Formal or literary English, usually with the
implication that the vernacular has more vitality
and force.[2]

Such a definition shows how sociological assumptions are imposed upon language. The idiom marked by formality and
appearing in print is "standard." However, the definition
continues, it is usually thought to be less forceful than the
vernacular. For the vernacular to be regarded as possessing
more force and vitality than standard English is perhaps a triumph of democratic sentiment, but it is no great advance
over the opposite nineteenth-century assumption that the
lower strata of society made animal noises (that is, spoke the
vernacular) while the upper, educated classes emitted angelic
harmonies (standard English). If one attempts to particu-
larize the general description of the vernacular offered by this
modern definition, one may find it difficult to imagine a "native homely, spoken language," for such a description reflects
nostalgia for a rural simplicity no longer, if ever, available.
While the definition is emotionally accurate, it is practically
useless.

The vernacular, like "normal" and "standard," is finally an
abstract compound whose elements cannot be directly identified. But even though the vernacular never literally exists on
any given page, its influence as a conception is still powerful.
Its magnetism draws the writer in a general direction. Men
live by their beliefs, however removed from substantive reality those beliefs may actually be. Belief in the reality of heaven
will alter one's behavior just as the belief that one's language
should be "the natural, instantaneous coinage of our
thought"[3] will alter one's prose.

In the nineteenth century, standard diction was distinguished qualitatively, not quantitatively. It represented a

euphemistic ideal rather than a national norm. But that decorous ideal was no more standard in the sense of being widely and regularly used than any other jargon or dialect. It, like the others, constituted but a portion of the English language as a whole, with the special distinction of being certified by those then in power. Power does determine standards though, and for this reason the vernacular as it appeared in early nineteenth-century literature did have some identifiable characteristics. Because its spokesmen were invariably of the lower class, used regional dialects, made frequent grammatical blunders, and were largely preoccupied with country matters involving violence and cloacal humor, it appeared that the vernacular was essentially a vulgar medium.

But the national mood altered over the century, and the alteration caused a redefinition of "standard." The change is not completed yet, as the famous dispute over the permissiveness of *Webster's Third New International Dictionary* may remind us. For the aristocratic temperament, standard is prescriptive: at its worst, it represents a dialect that has succeeded, guarded against interlopers by intricate passwords. The democratic inclination, however, is to make standard descriptive: the standard is statistically determined, as it were, for its features are understood to be the mass norm. "A nation's language is a very large matter," said Mark Twain. "It is not simply a manner of speech obtaining among the educated handful; the manner obtaining among the vast uneducated multitude must be considered also." [4] If the vernacular is not regarded as inevitably vulgar, but merely as ordinary, then it is clear that as the nineteenth century wore on, ordinary language became increasingly identified with an ever-broadening middle class. As the speech of that class was reproduced with greater fidelity, the basic identity of the vernacular as it appeared in literature changed. During the transition from prose humor to local-color writing, such raw objects and activities as privies, decaying corpses, dog fights, kicking, butting, and gouging were gradually replaced by more acceptable yet homely details of everyday life. The American writer tapped a diction which was neither evasively decorous nor violently coarse, yet one which was familiar to him and to his readers. So even as serious literature was absorbing the vernacular, the nature of the vernacular itself was undergoing a change. And whereas in the nineteenth century a very real distinction could be made between the vernacular and standard diction as they were used in prose, in the twentieth century the vernacular had virtually become standard.

While the *idea* of the vernacular was of the very greatest importance in the evolution of American prose style, the mercurial indeterminacy of its actual existence lessens its usefulness as an identifying feature of that style. The crucial determinant is not which word is used so much as how it is used. The disposition of words has already been identified as colloquial, but how in fact shall that disposition be recognized? The answer most ready at hand is to define the colloquial mode as any prose written as if it were spoken by someone. To this, one must add that the presence of a narrator is no guarantee that the result will be colloquial, just as, conversely, the basic features of colloquial writing may appear even without an announced narrator. Those colloquial features are derived from the psychology of speech; and of speech itself it can be said that it turns often and rarely observes neat sequences of thought. Having been submitted by the operating mind to only the hastiest preliminary organization, talk moves through a series of discursive units observing a logic of its own. The speaker digresses to chase a will-o'-the-wisp into the thickets of private association, or is distracted from what he took to be his main line of thought by the challenges of his listener. Dead spots occur in talk which have no purpose other than to sustain the rhythm and hold the floor while the speaker locates the next set of ideas. Improvisation requires on-the-spot adjustment to increase its effectiveness. All of these result in the rhetorical maneuvering which constitutes the colloquial situation. Such maneuvers eventually find their way into prose, where some are swiftly discarded while others are seized upon and stylized. The characteristics that ultimately identify the colloquial style — stress, fragmentation, and repetition — are not in themselves unique to it. But in aggregate and in heavy concentrations, they do signal a major and identifiable style. Because of the importance of these colloquial features, their sources and the nature of their occurrence need to be examined in greater detail.

II

Several observers have noted that modern American prose appears to give unusual prominence to single elements within its sentences. Harold Whitehall, expanding his sense of the difference between American and British English, wrote:

> In the most typical American writing, sentences seem to be constructs in which the key words function as isolated counters of expression . . . [while] in British English, individual words, even the key words, seem to be far more submerged into the larger syntactical units of expression. The sense hovers over the whole phrase or sentence, not over the word. . . .[5]

Malcolm Cowley also described the colloquial American style as composed of sentences which focused on a key word. That word, he thought, gained its conspicuous position by appearing repeatedly in a context of flat assertions made with simple, monosyllabic words.[6] More recently, Northrop Frye has distinguished three basic rhythms of verbal expression: that of verse with a regularly recurring pattern of speech; that of prose based upon the unit of the sentence; and that of ordinary speech, which he regards as centered upon a short phrase which contains the essential idea or word upon which the speaker is concentrating. The surrounding verbal sounds, he believes, "are largely rhythmic filler." [7] Frye, Whitehall, and Cowley all agree that there is a certain style of verbal communication, especially associated with North America (although Frye is establishing universal categories), which emphasizes single words or phrases at the expense of the larger verbal structure. The jewel is displayed against a plain, featureless background; the pearl is located in the formless viscosity of the oyster. What accounts for this colloquial propensity for outlining and elevating single words?

Some vernacular words had always drawn more than normal attention to themselves as words, often abetted by the writer's attitude toward their informality. When writers first began to introduce questionable diction into their prose, they quarantined it with quotation marks, or put it in italics to emphasize its alien identity, or introduced it with a phrase that designated its origin and dissociated the writer from intimacy with it. John Neal, whom one twentieth-century critic has called "the first in America to be natural in his diction," [8] prided himself on the colloquial vigor of his language. In a series of articles he wrote during 1824 and 1825 for *Blackwood's Magazine* on the subject of American writers, Neal remarked: "We have continued, as we began — using *low* words, unless they were wholly beneath us, whenever the subject required it; whenever they were more suitable, expressive, or vigorous, than *high* words." [9] But as late as 1869, in his autobiography, *Wandering Recollections,* Neal still formally set off his colloquial expressions:

> He had written, or *made,* as he termed it, an article for the "North-American Review."

> I had to put up with a "glittering generality" as we politicians would call it.

> When a boy, I was always a bungler, not being sure of hitting a barn-door — I might say of *fetching* a two-story house.

> Most of us tried our hand at what our secretary called *ex-trumpery* speaking.

> I came to be talked about as rather an "ugly customer." [10]

The writer's attitude toward his vernacular material can give it the double prominence that anything reaches which, in addition to being odd, is declared odd. Neal's behavior is altogether typical of many writers who were attracted to the vernacular yet unwilling to commit themselves wholly to it. Whether rhetorical or typographical, procedures such as Neal employed in 1834 caged the vernacular and, by caging it, drew attention to it:

> With this, the hunter "squared himself, and sot his triggers," fully determined either to hunt the disputed game, or be vanquished in combat.[11]

Deep-seated social attitudes are reflected in this use of quotation marks with the vernacular. Certain words, like certain clothes, schools, and professions, are proper for the educated and others are not. On a reduced scale, such quarantining of the vernacular resembles the humorist's frequent use of a frame of standard English to enclose vernacular stories. The presence of a literate narrator to introduce the vernacular speaker permitted the reader to enjoy colorful informality, yet be assured that the hierarchy of social values still stood, that the vulgar were still under control.

On such occasions, the robust candor of the vernacular threatened the legitimacy of standard literary English. For example, when George, the educated narrator who normally introduces Sut Lovingood's tales, has translated a passage of Sut's "English," Sut bursts out: "Now why the devil can't I 'splain myself like yu? I ladles out my words at random, like a calf kickin at yaller-jackids; yu jis' rolls 'em out tu the pint, like a feller a-layin bricks — every one fits. How is it that bricks fits so clost enyhow? Rocks won't ni du hit." [12] Even as Sut expresses his exasperation with the clumsiness of his diction, he is exposing standard prose to criticism. Rocks make up the vernacular world — hard, individual, rough, heavy, intractable. Bricks are a product of an organized social world. That is why they fit so well. They are manufactured, artificial, uniform, and capable of being manipulated without difficulty. And when a rock appeared in a brick wall, even if it was not formally set off, its very incongruity drew the reader's attention to it. Vernacular life offered details simply alien to standard prose, whether from the diction of steamboating, bear-hunting, or courting, or such idiomatic expressions as "I'm married folks," or the metaphorical comparison, "green as a jimson weed." Even as the power of the printed obscene word attests, the mind is arrested by the appearance of a word it has not seen before, however familiar it may otherwise be. In an extreme way, the shock of four-letter words suggests the power of the vernacular term encountered for the first time in a normal context.

Misspellings also emphasized individual words by so disguising them that, even if the words were not newly encountered, they were encountered for the first time looking as they did. The motives for misspelling varied, and as we shall see in the following chapter, it makes a difference whether the writer's goal was accuracy or buffoonery. Sometimes the word is spelled phonetically by a semi-literate writer: *fite, enuf, jist* or *jest, strate.* At other times the malformation is not an error in spelling, but reproduces a dialect pronunciation, although sometimes one cannot distinguish naïve phonetic literalness from scientific accuracy, since the spellings *larn, fellers,* and *sartain* could result from ignorance or a wish to represent the sounds. Barbarisms are also spelled "correctly" in the sense that their rendering accurately represents usage: *onst* (once), *seed* (seen), *hearn* (heard). Such errors resemble those misspellings where the actual construction of a word is mistaken. Sometimes in these cases plain distortion takes place — *norate* for *narrate;* sometimes folk etymology is at work — *cowcumbers* for *cucumbers;* sometimes malapropisms occur in which the known word is inadvertently substituted for another: "Tha found him requitted of murder, but tha found him gilty of salt an batter." [13] Finally, there are occasional instances of the kind of revelation associated with the portmanteau economy of the language of *Finnegans Wake.* So Huck Finn describes one of the subjects taught by the duke and the king as "yellocution" (ch. 31).

These vernacular tricks with language arouse various responses in the reader: superiority, amusement, curiosity, the pleasure of mimetic recognition. The point, however, is that the reader's mind is more than normally engaged by the actual structure of the vernacular word, and, depending upon the nature of the disguise it is given, the adjustment necessary to translate it may be quite complicated. *Norate* is no word, *cowcumber* is a partially familiar one, *salt an batter* are familiar words in the wrong context, and *yellocution* is at once no word and a neologism superior to the proper one. The effort to understand in each of these instances accentuates the word itself.

In the more rudimentary stages of vernacular writing, the disguised word is not only misspelled, but italicized as well so that none may miss the joke. When an ailing woman is told by her doctor that she must be cupped on the sternum, she shrieks, "What! . . . you cup me on de *starn!*" A rural matron reassures a traveler spending the night in her home that he may undress without trepidation: "You can un*kiver* now, stranger; I'm *married folks*, you ain't afeard o' *me*, I reckon!" An appeal for a drink of whiskey is rendered: "Colonel, let us have some of your *byled* corn." In short, comic punch lines contain punch words, and the blow is always a vernacular one.[14]

If one major preoccupation of those using the vernacular

was to render the words as they actually sounded, another was to determine what those words meant. This again focused attention on the single word. Sometimes this was done quite baldly, as when Cooper in *The Prairie* refers to "the brown and party-colored livery of the fall," then footnotes it: "The Americans call the autumn the 'fall' from the fall of the leaf" (ch. 8). As late as 1887 in *Zury* Joseph Kirkland was doggedly defining his vernacular terms:

> "Chuck-holes" is the expressive Western name for the short, sharp depressions which use makes in unworked country roads.

> The "prairie flowers" (blue gentian) gave to the whole award a tinge of pale azure.

> "Puncheons" or "slabs" are the side-cuts from logs squared for sawing.[15]

Overt definition also frequently occurs in the narrative itself when opposed points of view come into conflict. With at least an upper and a lower linguistic world recognized in the United States, a good deal of inter-translation was necessary. Sometimes the genteel narrator served as the interpreter, either furnishing a paraphrase of the vernacular, or actually defining the troublesome word. Sut Lovingood's heavy dialect required frequent explanation. George was his sympathetic but sometimes puzzled interlocutor:

> "What have you been doing, Sut?"
> "Helpin tu salt ole Missis Yardley down."
> "What do you mean by that?"
> "Fixin her fur rotten cumfurtably, kiverin her up wif sile, tu keep the buzzards frum cheatin the wurms."
> "Oh, you have been helping to bury a woman." [16]

Only after Sut has provided several ugly versions of his activity can George understand and translate his idiom into acceptable decency. Sometimes the translation proceeds in the other direction, from standard down to coarse. Sut, for example, tells of a young blacksmith so smitten with love "he splotch'd his whiskers wif foam," whereupon he is asked:

> "What was the matter with this Mr. Mastin? I cannot understand you, Mr. Lovingood; had he hydrophobia? . . ."
> "What du yu mean by high-dry-foby? . . ."
> "A madness produced by being bit by some rabid animal. . . ."
> "Yas, hoss, he hed high-dry-foby *orful,* an' Mary McKildrin . . . hed gin him the complaint." [17]

The one occasion when George, the representative of normality, lapses into a sentimental idiom occurs, appropriately enough, when he begins to recount a youthful escapade. Hypnotized by nostalgia, George soon reflects: " 'Tis strange how faithfully memory paints the path and places belonging to our boyhood — happy, ragged, thoughtless boyhood." Sut knows that George's memory is anything but faithful, so as George muses on about "the Bluff with its triple echo . . . the Dardis lot, and its forbidden grapes . . . the old church and its graveyard," all stock ingredients of sentimental fiction, Sut exclaims, "Oh, komplikated durnashun! That hain't hit. . . . Yu's drunk, ur yure ashamed tu tell hit."

The actual incident in George's "happy, ragged, thoughtless boyhood" involved terror, violence, and a repellent conclusion in which young George splashes through an uncovered privy hole. Sut being familiar with the incident calls for a drink. "Arter I'se spunged my froat, I'll talk hit all off in English, an' yu jis watch an' see ef I say 'echo,' ur 'grapes,' ur 'graveyard' onst." Again, a specific dictional critique brings an uncustomary stress to bear upon individual words.[18]

The interchanges between Sut and George involve gross alternatives. Their misunderstandings and disputes over dic-

tion were a staple of comic writing so long as dialects existed
in the United States. But as the nineteenth century progressed, this same process of criticism and redefinition began
to take place within the arena of the norm. Henry James
dramatizes innumerable clashes over words and the tone
in which they are used:

> "I don't like the way you say that," she declared.
> "It's too imperious."
> "I beg your pardon if I say it wrong. The main
> point's to give you an idea of my meaning."

The linguistic issue here is no longer the crude one of decorum facing vulgarity. Now the most familiar of words come
under scrutiny. One's words stand for one's experience, and
as one's experience changes, the words one uses become
crucial.

> "Did you ever hear anything so quaint?"
> "So 'quaint,' my dear?"

As standards and the certainties that bolster them disinte-
grate, the meaning of words becomes less certain. The
lengthy fencing matches between Henry James's men and
women represent their attempts to define themselves and
their companions by defining what they say.

> "You're old enough, dear Miss Miller, to be talked
> about."
> Daisy wondered to extravagance. "Talked about?
> What do you mean?"

The defining impulse, which concentrates upon the word, is
integral with the stylistic shift toward the colloquial.[19]

Definition, whether explicitly carried out or accomplished
by translation or by the confrontation of two conflicting
meanings for a single term, is but another way for words to
achieve abnormal prominence. Still another occurs in lists of
things. Lists define by proximity, by implicitly comparing

similarities and contrasting differences. Lists, possessing little visible organization, are common in American vernacular writing. The natural sequence of objects as they are found in life or in the unconscious associative processes of the mind of the narrator determine the order in which the items of the list will be named.

Sut Lovingood describes the contents of an overturned cupboard:

> Pickil crocks, preserves jars, vinegar jugs, seed bags, yarb bunches, paragorick bottils, aig baskits, an' delf war — all mix'd dam permiskusly. . . .[20]

Lacking awareness of any principle of imposed order, Sut lists things as they appear — "dam permiskusly." But what then constitutes the special interest of each item in such a list? I can discern three answers, each peculiar to the vernacular tradition. First, the things in themselves are colorful and unfamiliar to conventional literature. Second, the distorted spelling forces extra attention on the word to decipher and to hear it. To object that the added attention required is so minimal as to be meaningless is, I think, to underestimate the sensitivity of man as a reading mechanism. Like the other irregularities common to the colloquial situation, such as italics, incomplete phrases, alliteration, repetition, word play, each misspelling makes an impression on the mind. The third distinctive feature of the list is its artful juxtaposition of things for humorous effect. Humor — and emphasis — can be achieved by placing the dandy in a frontier setting. So here Sut's list is principally composed of receptacles for foods and medicines, but he ends with Delftware smashed together with the more homely containers — crocks, jars, jugs, bags, bottles and baskets — to make a pottery version of the prim schoolmar'm suddenly thrown into the crude violence of the far West.

At the end of the century Mr. Dooley contributed another

list that interests us in the same way as does Sut's list. Its
terms, odd, misspelled and ironically juxtaposed, lead to a satiric climax:

> An' th' invintions — th' steam-injine an' th' bicy-
> cle an' th' flyin' machine an' th' nickel-in-th'-slot ma-
> chine an' th' Croker machine an' th' sody fountain
> an' — crownin' wur-ruk iv our civilization — th'
> cash raygisther.[21]

The atomizing effect of such a list is increased because the
conjunctions serve not only as connectors but also as buffers.
In the Dooley example, the reiterated "an' th' " separates the
items visually as well as aurally. The conjunctions establish
an exclusive territory for each noun. The effect is that of a
line of people on a darkened stage, each in turn being caught
by a spotlight. Or, reading such a list resembles watching a
long freight train pass by, the items being the cars, the conjunctions the couplings. Each item is independent, yet joined
to the whole. The conjunctions are also unifiers in their unobtrusive and monotonous way. As the separate cars roll by,
an underlying rhythmic beat is felt. The variety of a list is
notable, yet there is a basic regularity to it which can be
worked by the skilled writer. In the following sentence from
*Huckleberry Finn* Mark Twain repeats "I took" three times,
then discards "I," in the next unit, and finally discards
"took" to move into a crescendo of physical items:

> *I took* all the coffee and sugar there was, and all
> the ammunition; *I took* the wadding; *I took* the
> bucket and gourd; *took* a dipper and a tin cup, and
> my old saw and two blankets, and the skillet and the
> coffee-pot. (ch. 7, italics added)

In lists of physical objects, and in sentences like this where
the verbs are muted, things are displayed in themselves. They
do nothing; they are merely available for inspection as ob-

jects at rest. Such static displays also heighten the importance
of the individual word.

The compound sentence characteristic of colloquial prose
is basically a list — a list of actions. The vernacular speaker
offers those actions in an unsubordinated series, just as he
does physical objects. He seems to display only the crudest
awareness of how the actions are related, not because of stu-
pidity, but because he literally recounts the events in the
order in which they occurred. This focuses attention upon
the single unit of action as it is caught and isolated between
commas and conjunctions. One can observe the increased
technical proficiency with which the compound sentence is
managed by beginning with the irregular extravagance of an
1843 dialect story, then moving to the fluent simplicity of
*Huckleberry Finn* in the 1880's, and finally to the deliberately angular rhythm of a Hemingway sentence written in
the 1930's. First, "Mike Hooter's Bar Story":

> Torectly I see Ike take down the ole shooter, AND
> kinder kersamine [examine] the lock, AN' when he
> done that, he laid her on his shoulder, AND shook
> his fist at the bar, AND walked towards home, AN' the
> bar he shuk his fist, AN' went into the cane brake,
> AND then I cum off.[22]

Then Huck Finn:

> I went out in the woods AND cooked a supper, AND I
> had about made up my mind I would stay there all
> night when I heard a *plunkety-plunk, plunkety-
> plunk,* AND says to myself, horses coming, AND next
> I hear people's voices. (ch. 8, capitals added)

And finally, a Hemingway drifter speaks:

> I could see her floating plain AND I hit the glass
> twice with the wrench hard AND I heard the noise
> clink in my ears BUT it wouldn't break AND I had to
> come up.[23]

Such compound sentences originate naturally in the psychology of the colloquial situation. Because the speaker lacks the time to distribute the events in synthetic categories, he produces a linear sequence, moving from event to event, observing democratic equality in the arrangement of his clauses. The most repeated phrase in *Huckleberry Finn* is "by-and-by" which is no more than a vernacular alternative to "and then. . . ." Actions enumerated but barely related constitute the basic sentence of the colloquial style.

The enumeration of events is but the last of the many ways we have discovered in which the psychology of speech separates and emphasizes the single word and phrase. The word may be deformed for dialectal accuracy. It may represent an instance of word-play, a malapropism, or a pun. The word may be drawn from unfamiliar jargon, or it may be coined for the occasion. It may be italicized, repeated, defined, discussed, or argued about. Moreover, the colloquial prose surface is fragmented by the cut-and-thrust of dialogue, by the rhetorical emphases of one speaker, and by the groping hesitancy of another. And, as the stylization of colloquial prose continued, its ground was cleared of the underbrush of qualification. The subject-verb-object relationship was made as direct as possible, and then, with the burden on each word heavier than ever before, each word took on an added importance. But even as individual words achieved increased independence, the basic unifying elements among them also emerged into prominence.

### III

The propensity of colloquial prose to fragment is compensated for by its innate repetitiveness. It is true that instances of repetition occur in all writing, but not to the degree that they do in colloquial prose. The colloquial writer will retain, and at the pitch of stylization even cultivate, repetition. It begins in the simplest possible way, with single letters and syllables — "a-quaking and shaking" — and extends on up through full independent clauses — "She loved to fish. She loved to fish with Nick." [24] The repetitions are visual and semantic as well as aural. Their source often appears to be below the level of consciousness, although in the later stages of colloquial writing, heightened technical awareness diminishes the incidence of inadvertent repetition.

Repetition often turns up when the action is crucial, or where the writer-speaker is in some way thoroughly engaged. With the mind diverted, one combination of letters summons up a similar combination. Extemporaneous speakers such as the revivalist depend upon the repetition of phrases to hold the audience, but they themselves become mesmerized by the rhythms of their speech. "Oh, come to the mourners' bench! come, black with sin! (*amen!*) come, sick and sore! (*amen!*) come, lame and halt, and blind! (*amen!*) come, pore and needy, sunk in shame! (*a-a-men!*) (*HF,* ch. 20). Here meaning plays a distinctly secondary role to patterned noise.

Any kind of distraction or mutiny of the intellectual monitor may increase verbal echoes. A journalist keeping a day-to-day account of the deliberations of the U.S. Senate describes "Cordell Hull's very hush-hush huddle." [25] The stupor of fatigue and narcotics in which Norman Mailer testifies he revised *The Deer Park* may be responsible for such phrases as "men lacquered with liquor" and a "painful jail of jealousy." [26] Or, to take a quite different example, Beatrix Potter's first story of Peter Rabbit displays unmistakable sound associations not present in her other work, probably because she improvised the original story in a letter to a child. So, the onomatopoetic sound of a hoe determines the verb that follows: "the noise of a hoe — SCR-R-RITCH, SCRATCH, SCRATCH, SCRITCH. Peter SCUTTERED underneath the bushes." When Peter emerges, his vantage point calls up the next verb: "He came out, and climbed upon a WHEELBARROW, and

PEEPED over." [27] The improvisation, haste, and distraction evidenced in these quotations constitute an integral part of the colloquial situation.

We can never determine absolutely what the author's state of awareness was at the time of composition, but the distinction between conscious and unconscious sound association can be demonstrated in three passages from Harriet Beecher Stowe's "The Minister's Wooing." When Mrs. Stowe writes,

> They fussed and fuzzled and wuzzled till they'd drinked up all the tea in the teapot,

one is confident that she deliberately encouraged the alliteration for the reader's amusement. But in a second sentence marked by a high incidence of the letter "p," one cannot ascertain with any confidence how conscious the alliteration was:

> Huldy . . . showed 'em her pantries, and her cakes, and her pies, and her puddin's, and took 'em all over the house; and they went peekin' and pokin' . . .

Finally, when Mrs. Stowe catalogues some flowers to lend color rather than humor to her story, the syllable "-ar" dominates her list. But it seems improbable that she deliberately assembled the unobtrusive internal rhymes:

> Huldy planted marigolds and larkspurs, pinks and carnations . . . and trained up mornin' glories and scarlet runners round the windows. [28]

The repeated syllable either emanates from the unconscious or represents a case of sheer coincidence.

Fits of alliteration and other sound repetitions and associations may be brought on then when the writer is more preoccupied with the imagined experience than with the surface of his prose. This is no more than to say that instances of repetition arise more often in speech than in writing, and

more often in colloquial writing than in other prose. The
writer may be excited, he may be pleasurably relaxed, he may
be writing in a hurry, but the result will be an increase in
sound associations. Henry Nash Smith has pointed out that
"when Mark Twain is working up a rhetorical effect, he re-
sorts to conspicuous alliteration ('winding rivers, and weary
wastes')." [29] Mark Twain alliterates not only when he himself is straining for an effect, but also when circumstances
strain his character Huck Finn. When the crowd disinters
Peter Wilks, Huck's tension heightens the alliteration, the
rhyme, and the repetition of whole words:

> So they *dug* and *dug* like everything; and it got aw-
> ful *dark,* and the rain *started,* and the wind *swished*
> and *swushed* along, and the lightning came *brisker*
> and *brisker.* . . . At last they got out the coffin and
> begun to un*scr*ew the lid, and then such another
> *cr*owding and *sh*ouldering and *sh*oving as there was,
> to *scr*ouge in and get a *s*ight, you never *s*ee. . . .
> (ch. 29, italics added)

Rhetorical control for the colloquial writer begins in repetition and controlled variation. Even as he jettisons conventional arrangements for his prose, he begins to build new
ones in his own medium. The listing of food at a Tennessee
frolic is threaded through with the sound "uh."

> The SUPPER is made UP by the fellers; every one
> fetches SUMTHIN; SUM A lick of meal, SUM A middlin
> of bacon, SUM A hen, SUM A POSSUM, SUM A PUNKIN,
> SUM A grab of taters, or a pocket of peas, or dried
> apples, an SUM only fetches a good appetite and a
> skin chock FULL of particular deviltry.[30]

The effect is one of casually managed variety. The serpentine
sentence, made up like this one of a series of separate images,
each of which emerges to take on a peculiar brilliance, the
whole unified by the droning regularity of the narrator's tone

and supplemented by the alliterative rhythm, is common to
the colloquial.

> Well, the eyes KEP COMIN' CLOSER and CLOSER, and
> gettin BIGGER and BRIGHTER, and the fust thing I
> know'd ther was a whole grist of 'em all follerin'
> right after the fust ones, and DODGIN' up and DOWN
> in the DARK like they was so many DANCIN' DEVILS.[31]

Even when the repetition is not exact, one word conjures
up a compatible partner. Threaded throughout *Huckleberry
Finn* are such phrases as

> squirming and scrouging
> moaning and mourning
> sobbing and swabbing
> fretted and sweated
> thinking, and wrinkling
> warmed up and went warbling and warbling
> chipping in a little Scripture (chs. 21, 23, 25, 31, 31,
> 29, 28)

Mark Twain's sensibility responded with unusual acuteness
to the stimuli of sounds, especially in this book. These minute repetitions and a thousand others constitute the musical
murmur of Huck's voice. From time to time it breaks into
overt but diversified repetition. The form of

> dug and dug

and

> brisker and brisker

is varied by the comma in

> he drank, and drank;

and by the italics in

> and begged and *begged*

and

well, go on, *go* on;

and it lengthens into

and listened, and listened, and listened

as well as

always moving back, and back, and back

and

told me to say it *again,* say it *again,* say it *again!*
(chs. 29, 29, 6, 25, 27, 40, 21, 28)

As some of these quotations suggest, the eye makes associations, too. In the phrase, "It STOOD on her BACKSTOOP, minus
a HOOP," [32] one passes from the "stoo-" in *stood* to its visual
repetition in *stoop;* then on to the aural repetition of "-oop"
in *hoop.* In *Huckleberry Finn* the "oh" sound is mixed
with the "ow" look:

. . . besides some TOW. I TOTED up a LOAD, and went
back and set down on the BOW of the skiff to rest.
(ch. 6, capitals added)

Nor need the associations literally repeat. They may only
approximate the original. Consider these three sentences from
*Huckleberry Finn:*

It was all grass clear to the canoe; so I hadn't left
a track. I followed around to see. I stood on the
bank and looked out over the river. All safe. (ch. 7)

Can there be any doubt that "all grass" produced "all safe"?
Or when Huck sees a canoe "riding high like a duck," does
not that observation of aquatic wild life give rise to the figure
of speech with which he describes his next action? — "I shot
head first off the bank, like a frog" (ch. 7).

The associations may reveal a pictorial or semantic connection as well as a visual or aural one. The vision of a log calls
up the idiom "fit to split" when Mike Hooter finds him-

self in a state of high amusement: "I never see ennything so funny in all my life! There was I layin' down behind er log, fit to split. . . ." [33] A newspaper reviewer of the novel *Candy* observed that although it had "sold like hotcakes," any public discussion of its subject necessarily called for "fudging." [34] Another reviewer of a biography of Lord Alfred Douglas fittingly enough referred to a "pugnacity, marked by the Queensberry rules." [35]

The level at which such associations are created may often be below what we would deem conscious; so in fact may be their reception. But the point is that all of these various repetitions and associations go to make up the unity of form in colloquial prose. They join company with the frequent occurrence of co-ordinating conjunctions, which Walt Whitman sometimes brought to the fore in his verse.

I believe in those wing'd purposes,
And acknowledge red, yellow, white, playing within me,
And consider green and violet and the tufted crown intentional
And do not call the tortoise unworthy because she is not something else,
And the jay in the woods never studied the gamut, yet trills pretty well to me,
And the look of the bay mare shames silliness out of me.[36]

Compare this with a sentence from *Huckleberry Finn,* similarly arranged:

Then she got to talking about her husband,
And about her relations up the river,
And her relations down the river,
And about how much better off they used to was,
And how they didn't know but they'd made a mistake coming to our town, instead of letting well alone —
And so on and so on,
Till I was afeard *I* had made a mistake coming to her to find out what was going on in the town;

But by-and-by she dropped onto pap and the murder,
And then I was pretty willing to let her clatter right along.
   (ch. 11)

These co-ordinating conjunctions furnish the beat for long colloquial sentences. The sense may wander, the meaning may cloud over, and clarification may never come (since cloudiness is the truest vision of the moment), but underneath it all pulsates that monotonous, barely noticeable rhythm of the conjunctions, sufficiently dependable to sustain equilibrium and to provide the confidence and comfort that go with it.

The resemblance between Whitman and the colloquial prose writer is no more coincidental than the frequent references to the poetic quality of modern American prose. When the distractions of the abnormal, the clownish, and the awkward handling of the colloquial manner were eliminated, what remained was a highly rhythmic prose with frequent internal rhyme and alliteration, making concentrated statements with concrete images. In the first flush of colloquial stylization, the following sentence from Hemingway's "My Old Man" was the rule rather than the exception:

"He won't win," George says very low, leaning over and buttoning the bottoms of his breeches.[37]

Colloquial writers had to become aware of the repetition inherent in their prose and of what use they might make of it. In the process of stylizing the colloquial traits learned in dialogue, American writers seized on repetition to restore a coherence threatened by that fragmentation which was in turn produced by the stress of individual words and phrases. The way of fragmentation led toward incoherence, the way of repetition toward verse. Discretion and practice were needed to reach a prose compromise. But before studying the negotiations that achieved that compromise, I should like first to consider the historical motives for cultivating the colloquial voice and its early routes into literature.

# Nineteenth-Century Talk

> So the only way the Americans could change their
> language was by choosing words which they liked
> better than other words, by putting words next to
> each other in a different way than the English way,
> by shoving the language around until at last now
> the job is done, we use the same words as the English
> do but the words say an entirely different thing.
>
> *Wars I Have Seen*

I

BENJAMIN FRANKLIN reflected the old colonial mentality
when he reassured David Hume, "We shall always in America make the best English of this Island [Great Britain] our
standard." [1] Well into the nineteenth century many Americans continued to look to England for a stylistic guidance, which the magisterial British quarterlies provided in
abundance. Their first rule read: American idioms flaw
prose. "We wish, if possible," said the *Annual Review* in
1808, "to stem *that torrent of barbarous phraseology,* with
which the *American* writers threaten to destroy the purity of
the English language." Such indignation sometimes yielded
to complacency, as when the *Eclectic Review* assessed an
American author: "For an American the composition is tol-
erable; but [he] has a good share of those words and phrases,
which his literary countrymen must, however reluctantly, re-
linquish before they will rank with good writers." [2] In spite
of these entrenched arbiters, and almost in spite of themselves, Americans discovered their attitudes toward their lan-

guage were changing. Even while colonial vulgarities were under attack, they expanded irresistibly, and the expansion necessarily affected style.

Three sources supplied the motor force for a native style in the United States: romantic individualism, nationalistic pride, and practical necessity. The egalitarian fervor of a newly independent nation on a barely explored continent infected writers with a desire for a new means of literary expression. Romanticism in particular provided a change in mood appropriate for the development of a vernacular prose style. It championed the worth of the individual, the dignity of common speech, and the special value of spontaneity. If the individual were superior to the accumulated wisdom of society, then he need not follow the traditional way of doing things. In literature this meant that he need not obey conventions, nor learn a special diction thought to be appropriate for literary uses; nor need he feel obliged to defer to a cultural past by salting his prose with knowing references. "I never shall write what is now worshipped under the name of *classical* English," declared John Neal in 1828. "It is no natural language — it never was." [3] What Neal called "classical English" the innovators equated with the dialect of a corrupt aristocracy, whose polished prose presupposed a leisure the American yeoman could not afford.

Romantic preference for the language men speak was peculiarly adaptable to the Jacksonian era. So long as only a very small segment of the population produced and consumed literature, it was expedient to identify the vernacular (literally, the idiom of the home-born slaves) as vulgar. But when men became theoretically equal, then the connotations surrounding the vernacular began to change. Speech itself exemplified naturalness, for it relied upon intuition to guide it rather than preconceived forms. To speak extemporaneously was to open a passage to reality. "Fie on that eloquence which makes us love itself and not its matter,"

Montaigne wrote, and Emerson commended him for it. "I know not anywhere the book that seems less written. It is the language of conversation transferred to a book" ("Montaigne; or, The Skeptic").

Many American writers might share Emerson's enthusiasm for "the language of conversation," but the problem of transferring it to a book continued to puzzle them. Lowell also admired Montaigne and drew the epigraph of *The Biglow Papers* from him: "J'aimerois mieulx que mon fils apprinst aux tavernes à parler qu'aux escholes de la parlerie." ("I'd much prefer that my son learn to speak in the taverns than in elocution school.") Lowell's entry to the vernacular was the Yankee dialect, but that hardly represented the sound and rhythms of the continually widening middle class. The writer who sought to render its idiom faithfully was thrown upon his own wits, for he possessed no literary model to guide him. The conventions of ordinary speech were not easy to come by. Until they were, aesthetic independence had not been achieved, only proclaimed. For the moment, Americans were liable to invoke the abstract political watchwords of a yeoman republic in order to describe the attributes of style they were seeking: honesty, manliness, simplicity. At the same time they made it known what they were against, for in the absence of native tradition, negative definition was a useful and necessary way of proceeding.

Attacks upon neo-classicism were symbolically attacks upon the Mother Country and upon the conservative elements in the United States. Samuel Johnson functioned for a time as a stylistic bogey-man, since he stood for sesquipedalian prose, an authoritarian dictionary, and open contempt for the barbaric wilds of America, where "there is little to be observed except natural curiosities." [4] Hugh Henry Brackenridge made a typical attack when he charged: "The English language is undoubtedly written better in America than in England, especially since the time of that literary dunce, Samuel

Johnson, who was totally destitute of taste for the *vrai naturelle,* or simplicity of nature." [5] As a competing lexicographer, Noah Webster frequently criticized Dr. Johnson and English ways. Unlike what "the modern stile of writing would made us beleev," he wrote in 1790, utilizing his theory of phonetic spelling, "elegance iz most generally found in a plain, neet, chaste phraseology." [6] Natty Bumppo later expressed analogous sentiments when he praised the meat of a bison's hump: "Cut more into the centre of the piece; there you will find the genuine riches of natur'; and that without need from spices, or any of your biting mustard, to give it a foreign relish" (ch. 9).

No foreign relish necessary. In the campaign for an indigenous style, nationalism was as important a force as romantic individualism. While election crowds in 1840 were crying, "Down with Van Buren with his English carriage, English horses, and English driver," [7] an American review declared, "The country is tired of being be-Britished." The be-Britishment referred to was literary; it involved "having our thinking done in London, our imagination fed only with food that is Londonish, and our matters of feeling illustrated and described only by London associations, tropes, and similitudes." [8] Similar complaints flowed from other quarters. John Neal had raised the issue of American literary subservience a decade earlier. "Our best writers are English writers, not American writers. They are English in everything they do . . . in their dialogue, speech, and pronunciation." [9] Francis Parkman typically believed such imitation debilitated the national character. "The highest civilization of America is communicated from without instead of being developed from within and is therefore nerveless and unproductive." [10]

Americans believed they possessed the potential for great achievement. This the physical grandeur of their continent suggested so compellingly that Oliver Wendell Holmes felt obliged to satirize the grandiose conception of the American poet as "a very Niagara of a fellow with a mouth like the Mississippi." [11] When Evert Duyckinck inquired, "From a people simple, brave, devout, what are we not to expect when these energies shall be turned in the direction of the National Literature," [12] he but rephrased the perennial question: in what direction did the National Literature lie? If the filial subservience of the colonial past had meant weeding Americanisms out of one's prose, then logically, independence meant the cultivation of one's weedy virtues. But no one was yet prepared seriously to raise weeds. That crop flourished only in prose humor. Therefore, much of the early stylistic activity continued to be negative in character — destructive, not constructive — in the hope that the elimination of London tropes and similitudes would leave a residue genuinely American. To this end some writers campaigned forcefully in the 1830's for a blessedly clear issue — the elimination of the skylark and the nightingale from literature. "For us," Longfellow said, "they only warble in books. A painter might as well introduce an elephant or a rhinoceros into a New England landscape." [13] The positive equivalent to this purge was inclusion of the robin, the raccoon, and the katydid in one's prose. "Sky-lark! pooh! who would rise at dawn to hear the sky-lark, if a cat-bird were about, after breakfast?" [14] But such minimal adjustments failed to satisfy the demand for a more specifically native style.

Practical considerations joined romanticism and nationalism in the campaign. When Cap remarks in *The Pathfinder,* "This sounds religious, perhaps, or like a book of poetry, but it does not sound like common sense" (ch. 25), he speaks on behalf of every American who, suspicious of abstractions, prides himself on his self-sufficient practicality. The only standard is effectiveness. Does this style work? Does it get things done? Does it move parishioners? Sell books? Win the lawsuit? Get the bill through Congress? Similarly, the advantages of education were respected when they led to practical achievement. Sam Slick's evaluation of the merits of the school curriculum set the pattern early:

> As for Latin and Greek, we don't valy it a cent; we teach it; and so we do painting and music, because the English do, and we like to go ahead on 'em even in them are things. As for reading, its well enough for them that has nothing to do, and writing is plaguy apt to bring a man to States-prison. . . . Cyphering is the thing — if a man knows how to cypher, he is sure to grow rich.[15]

The pragmatic temper was especially strong on the frontier. There the exigencies of daily life made aureate diction ludicrous, if not downright dangerous. The comic relief in Cooper's *The Prairie* is provided by Obed Battius M.D. (otherwise Obed Batt), a pedantic naturalist and "fellow of several cis-Atlantic learned societies" (ch. 6) whose speech is as preposterously artificial as his wig. Even he recognizes that upon occasion, "I must speak in the vernacular, to be comprehended" (ch. 11).

Except for hidebound pedants, most people recognized that differences in American and English usage were necessary. Americans had new things to name and new situations to cope with, for which the English mode was not precisely suitable. Henry James was appalled by the burden placed upon the English language. No language, he thought, had "known any such ordeal, any such stress and strain, as was to await the English in this huge new community." [16] It was inevitable that a growing disparity should be noted between a prose based on a diction and syntax delicately adjusted to the needs of an insular people for over a thousand years, and the idiom used in the streets, fields, and forests of North America. This idiom was more then just renovated diction, just as any language is more than its lexicon. The fluent, peculiarly timed, and uniquely accented compound known as a language has its specific harmonies. "We are like the Chinese," said Sam Slick. "They have two languages, the written language and the spoken language. . . . That's gist the case with us; we have two languages, one for strangers, and one for ourselves. . . . You must larn the American language, if you want to understand the American people." [17]

Learning that language was tantamount to learning who one was. The mystery was compelling, and for writers its solution was mandatory.

II

American writers learned how to reproduce the unique qualities of speech in a special arena fenced in by quotation marks. The preferences in diction, the syntactical habits, the tonal range of the national speech all were located and polished in literary dialogue. Here, in the overt imitations of Americans speaking, writers prepared the way for the stylistic revolution to come at the end of the century, since the changes that took place in dialogue inevitably affected the narrative prose surrounding it.

Dialect writers in particular made rapid progress toward the colloquial manner. Because it was understood that they dealt with the vulgar side of society, no social inhibitions blocked or distorted their imitations of speech. The dialect character could be expected to say almost anything in virtually any way he pleased. The problems his creator faced were technical in nature. By contrast, the writer dealing with the genteel reaches of society found himself enmeshed in problems of manners as well as of technique. These considerations confused his attempts to achieve colloquial verisimilitude. Genteel speech constituted a basic symbol of moral elevation and social dignity. As a consequence, a remarkable disparity seems to have existed between the way the middle and upper classes actually spoke and the literary versions of their speech. Questions of decorum interposed themselves between the writer's actual experience of normal talk and his rendering of it.

In addition, a formidable technical puzzle confronted the writer, the complexity of which may be difficult to comprehend without some sympathetic reflection. What *do* citizens whose speech is undistinguished by racial, regional, or occupational jargon sound like? Their speech possesses identifying features, but they are subtle ones, not the blatant distortions of dialect. The very abnormality of the word *hoss* calls up the colloquial situation in a way that *horse* can never do. When it is joined to a grammatical irregularity — "Yo' hoss done bit me" — the illusion of speech is complete. But American writers were not yet attuned to the subtler distinctions of normal speech, let alone able to reproduce them in writing. Their incessant complaints indicate how frustrating this deafness proved to be. Fenimore Cooper fretted over "the poverty of materials" available to him as a novelist. "I have never seen a nation so much alike in my life." [18] Hugh Henry Brackenridge, wishing an American Sancho Panza for his novel, *Modern Chivalry,* explained in 1804 that he could not find one: "The American has in fact, yet, no character; neither the clown, nor the gentleman. So that I could not take one from our own country; which I would much rather have done, as the scene lay here. But the midland states of America, and the western parts in general, being half Ireland, the character of the Irish clown will not be wholly misunderstood. . . . On the Irish stage, it is a standing character; and in the theatre in Britain, it is also introduced. I have not been able to do it justice, being but half an Irishman, myself, and not so well acquainted with the reversions, and idiom, of the genuine Thady, as I could wish. However, the imitation at a distance from the original will better pass than if it had been written, and read, nearer home. Foreigners will not so readily distinguish the incongruities; or, as it is the best we can produce for the present, will more indulgently consider them." [19] When Brackenridge says that the American has "no character" he means to a great extent "no linguistic identity," no verbal handle by which his character can be grasped. For this reason, he availed himself of an Irishman, a type for whom rudimentary physical, social, and linguistic conventions were already established. Teague O'Regan spoke a dialect that Brackenridge could reproduce with reasonable success.

In the 1820's, John Greenleaf Whittier responded similarly to the same problem of how to locate a normal idiom. To express himself as the Robert Burns of western Massachusetts, the young Whittier literally imitated Burns's Scots dialect. "Odds leddy! then ye've lost your veil; / But dinna let your spirits fail; / What though the auld thing onward sail / A mile or twa. . . ." [20] In the absence of any American voice recognizable as natural, even one's own, dialect must have seemed relatively easy to hear and to imitate.

But only relatively easy, for the American dialects required time to perfect. In the beginning the slightest hint of dialect was sufficient to gain the reader's assent. Walter Blair points out that at the opening of the century English anecdotes were adapted for American audiences by the addition of a local idiom here and there.[21] A few touches of dialect represented the whole complex of speech signals. They radiated their influence over the surrounding language, making it appear authentic, however false in fact the reproduction was.

A Yankee peddler of 1831 illustrates such early crudeness. "Try a leetle on't mister . . . or maybe you'd like a box of yer own — some call it a new sort o' tooth-paste with more varter in't than nineteen sea-hosses." [22] It is doubtful that "leetle," "varter," and "hosses" belong in the same dialect. They must be regarded as generic distortions. The writer simply identifies his peddler as a Yankee, carries out some rudimentary violence upon language, and then expects the results to be accepted as authentic. The strategy is re-enforced by contrasting the Yankee's speech with a gross Negro dialect. "O, yessa massa," groans a Negro who has been treated with the Yankee's medical nostrum. "Him peel berry moodch nicealy; tankee massa." The very contrast provided by the Negro's mumbling helps to verify the Yankee's dialect. It differs from that of the Negro, it is not formal speech, and the author says it comes from a Yankee: ergo, it *is* Yankee. The century's gradual increase in technical expertise is reflected in James Russell Lowell's dissatisfaction a generation later with the prototypical Yankee dialect character, Sam Slick, for Lowell calls his dialect "a complete falsification of Yankee modes of speech." [23]

Technical ignorance alone was not responsible for the defectiveness of early dialect exercises. The writers and their audience were simply indifferent to over-all impressions. Consistency lacked the importance it was to assume later for both the realists and those seeking aesthetic unity in their prose. Although Fenimore Cooper's linguistic sensitivity was much maligned by Mark Twain, the fact is that his observations of how psychological conditions affect language were frequent and acute. The carelessness appeared in his execution. In *The Pathfinder,* for example, Cooper discusses the speech of two Scotsmen who have been transplanted by the British army into the American wilderness. Both, observes Cooper, "ran into the Scotch or avoided it, as they approached or drew away from their younger days, in the dialogue" (ch. 10). This insight, whether valid or not, attests to a genuine concern for the problem of tongues. Cooper, however, is negligent about implementing it, for his dialogue does not accurately embody his psycho-linguistic generalization.

Norris W. Yates points out that a similar tolerance for inconsistency in speech permitted, in a single story written in

1848, one Negro character to employ both the heroic
idiom of sentimental fiction and low darky chatter. When flee-
ing for his life the slave cries, "Hounds of hell! you shall never
have my sinews to sell for gold." But when at last he wearies of
being a fugitive, he lapses into this: "God bless you, massa! —
don't you know me? Take Simon home — he's tired of being a
free nigger." [24] The point is that in its place each idiom was
aesthetically satisfying, and over-all consistency was simply irrelevant. I am not arguing here for the necessary superiority
of consistency, but I am suggesting that, for an American prose
style based on native speech rhythms to develop, the writers
and their readers had to become sensitive not only to the details that made up the language they sought to approximate
but also to the over-all harmony of their medium.

A late practitioner of the art of dialect-writing, James
Whitcomb Riley, distinguished two basic approaches to it:
"First as a writer bringing to bear all the art he possesses to
represent the way some *other* fellow *speaks* and second as a
Hoosier farmer might *write*." [25] The essence of the first and
more common approach was phonetic accuracy. As indicated
earlier, dialect began with a few verbal tags. The Yankee, for
example, was identified by the vowel sound "-eou" substituted for "-ou." Typically: "Say yeou . . . I smell the yellow fever all reound." [26] But by the time of *The Biglow
Papers,* James Russell Lowell announced that he had reproduced the Yankee dialect with scrupulous accuracy. He had
been familiar with it since he was a boy, Lowell said, and had
continued to study it as an adult. He touched on the problem
of reproducing the sound of speech. "A word more on pronunciation. I have endeavored to express this so far as I could
by types, taking such pains as, I fear, may sometimes make
the reading harder than need be." [27]

Lowell's remark suggests the necessary limits of accuracy in
reproducing dialect. Uncompromising dialect is exasperating
to read. Deciphering it exhausts the attention so rapidly that

the short work is virtually the exclusive domain of dialect — the humorous anecdote, the tall tale, the elaborate practical joke. An Uncle Remus novel is unthinkable. If *Huckleberry Finn* is the first full-length American narrative told in dialect, it is because the dialect in that book is minimal. Huck's idiom is on the edge of colloquial normality and much more available than, say, the forbiddingly tangled dialect of Sut Lovingood. The greater the phonetic accuracy, the greater the patience needed to read it, so that the conscientious artist eventually reaches a point of seriously diminished returns in refining dialect. His next step would place him in the realm of linguistic science. Even Lowell restrained himself from using perceptions that were still possible to reproduce with a conventional alphabet. "By studying uniformity I have sometimes been obliged to sacrifice minute exactness." He provides a sample of a subtlety he was aware of, but did not attempt to include: "*For* is commonly *fer* (a shorter sound than *fur* for *far*), but when emphatic it always becomes *for* as "wut *for*." [28] Lowell sacrifices such perceptions in the name of "uniformity," or in other words, for the sake of that aesthetic unity that invests a readable work of art, as opposed to a scientifically accurate accumulation of particulars without pleasurable order. This points up a basic fact of dialect practice. Even as finesse in reproducing the sound of speech develops, so simultaneously must the art with which that speech is rendered. Intensification of the illusion of reality is inseparable from the intensification of artifice. This truth ultimately turned those writers interested in American speech away from further refinement of dialects and toward the problems of rendering colloquial normality.

Dialect writing was also restricted in the United States because so few strong dialects actually existed.[29] Late in the century, the cities with their immigrant populations provided some new ones, especially the Italian and Jewish. But while some writers undertook to conquer and exploit such dialects, others, having reached the limits of refinement in one dialect, turned to the more subtle characteristics of speech. How, for example, does dialect change under different psychological conditions? In *Maggie,* Stephen Crane provides competent answers, as when he works with a lower-class New York dialect, then overlays it with alcohol, so that the pronunciation undergoes a progressive deterioration:

> Don't try pull man's leg, but have a good time! Dass right! Dass way teh do! Now, if I s'ought yehs tryin' work me fer drinks, wouldn' buy notting! But yer right sort! Yehs know how ter treat a f'ler, an I stays by yehs till spen las' cent! Dass right! I'm good f'ler an' I knows when an'body trea' me right! [30]

Crane's example considers speech from three angles: one, the locale and class of the speaker — urban, lower-class; two, the physical and psychological conditions of the speaker — drunk and pleased; three, the time of the speech, for with the passage of time, the alcohol causes more slurring. "Good f'ler" eventually becomes "goo' f'ler," a notation of a delicacy simply not possible fifty years earlier when in a single sentence a Negro could be reported as saying "berry moodch," and "berry mudch." [31] Crane's technical subtlety demonstrates the heightened awareness achieved at the end of the century, not only of the psychological nuances of the situation being described, but also of the technical means by which these nuances might be reproduced.

### III

From its inception, dialect, — what Henry James called "a hatful of queer pieces," — frequently played the clown.[32] Because it violates an accepted norm, very little effort is required to animate dialect's comic energies. The direction those energies flow depends upon how the dialect is employed, but the important point for the present argument is that, whatever idiom is made the butt of the contrast, linguistic sensitivity inevitably profits. Incongruity was natural to this disoriented nation. The radical dissonance of the copy of Milton's poems Parkman saw with a pistol resting on it, or the pianos abandoned in the alkali dust of the Oregon trail were the rule in American life rather than the exception. American names frequently embodied in miniature this imbalance by linking elegance with plainness. Olympus Pump, Orson Dabbs, Archimedes Pipps, Miss Celestian Scraggs, Montezuma Dawkins, and Orion Mudge are some fictional examples, Orion Clemens and Ulysses S. Grant real ones.[33] One humorist explained the rationale in the parental American mind for naming an offspring Theodosius Spoon (otherwise T. Spoon): "A sonorous handle to one's patronymic acts like a balloon to its owner," but "an emaciated, every-day, threadbare cognomen — a Tom, Dick and Harry denomination — . . . must keep a man at the bottom." (Neal, *Charcoal Sketches*, p. 116)

Dialect, like the plain family name, is liable to appear grotesque when coupled with standard prose. The norm accentuates and ridicules its queer ways. As one of the correspondents of *The Spirit of the Times* remarked, "The way the natives sometimes talk here is amusing."[34] Anecdotes involving characters speaking dialect were customarily framed with conventional prose. A bemused gentleman would set the scene before he exhibited his odd specimens:

> The writer sat alongside the driver one morning, just at the break of day, as the stage drove out of Blackberry; he was a through passenger to Squash Point. It was a very cold morning; in order to break the ice for a conversation, he praised the fine points of an off horse. The driver thawed:
> "Ya-as; she's a goot hoss, und I knows how to trive him!" It was evidently a case of mixed breed.[35]

The door of the lawyer's office opened, there
pressed forward the tall, gaunt figure of a man, a
perfect model of physical power and endurance, a
western flatboatman. The lawyer heeded not his
presence, and started as if from a dream, as the harsh
tones of inquiry grated upon his ear, of,
"Does a 'Squire live here?"
"They call me so," was the reply, as soon as he
had recovered from his astonishment.
"Well, 'Squire," continued the intruder, "I have
got a case for you, and I want jestess." [36]

If the linguistic contrast were not already abundantly clear,
the narrator was liable to underline it:

"Nan, sort a turn them thare chickins."
And thus, the cabin lady kept on doing up her
small stock of English into Hoosierisms and other
figures.[37]

The frame of conventional prose established an invidious
comparison that was sustained by interchanges between the
dialect animal and the genteel man. The polite inquiries of
the interlocutor heightened the dialect rudeness.

"Say yeou, which of these things slips up fust?"
"What?" said I.
"Which of these things slips up fust?"
"Do you mean which steamboat goes up the river
first?"
"Yes, I'll be darned if I don't." [38]

Yet, the undeniable vivacity of the vernacular idiom over-
rode any condescension. In 1858 a eulogist of the editor of
*The Spirit of the Times,* where much of the dialect literature
appeared, located in its pages the source of a new prose:

William T. Porter . . . brought out a new class
of writers, and created a style which may be de-
nominated an American literature — not the au-

gust, stale, didactic, pompous, bloodless method of
the magazine pages of the day; but a fresh, crisp,
vigorous, elastic, graphic literature, full of force,
readiness, actuality and point.[39]

The balance tipped in favor of backwoods dialects especially
when they were brought into the company of academic
jargon, spread-eagle oratory, and genteel euphemisms. So
when Obed Batt, the pedantic naturalist in *The Prairie,* exclaims, "It is a mistake! The animal is not even of the *class,*
mammalia, much less a man," Natty Bumppo's superior response is predictable. "So much for your knowledge!" he answers exultantly. "So much for the l'arning of one who has
looked into so many books, that his eyes are not able to tell a
moose from a wild-cat!" (ch. 17). Natty's criticism of traditional education re-enforces the ever-present contrast between his speech and Batt's. Again and again this kind of
clash can be observed in American literature, with language
serving as the index of distinction. Each such encounter
increases the reader's sensitivity to the faults and virtues of
the contesting idioms. The Boston *Post* found amusement, for
example, in describing Rufus Choate at work in the court-
room. Choate was a florid speaker for whom the squash was
"that luxurious esculent of the tropics," and his baroque
effusions caused his contemporaries to claim that he drove "a
substantive and eight." They also led to the *Post*'s publishing
two columns, one entitled "Poetry by Mr. Choate," the other,
"Prose by the Witness." The contrast between the two columns humorously dramatizes the stylistic dangers threaten-
ing Americans — floridity whirling on one side, vulgarity
snapping on the other:

### Choate

Down to that fatal Monday evening, gentlemen of
the jury, when the client's last lingering hope
flickered like a candle and went out . . .

*Witness*

Wal, all I know is that I come into the room, and
there the first thing I sot eyes on was Al Tirrell a-
sitting in his chair, and he was cocked up ag'n the
corner and he was crying . . .[40]

On occasion, the contesting styles were brought more
closely together; a single person could display a mixture of
the elevated and the vernacular in his speech. A western lawyer opens his plea:

"Gentlemen of the Jury: The Scripture saith,
'Thou shalt not kill'; now, if you hang my client,
you transgress the command as slick as grease." [41]

Similarly, a maid inadvertently travesties the conventions of
sentimental prose by keeping a diary in what she calls
"novel language," which she says "seems to come easier to
me." When she reads from that diary, she uses "a voice somewhat different from her ordinary tones, as if the 'novel language' demanded it:

Chapter Five. The Lonely House and the Faithful friend. Thus was I left alone. None but the two
dogs to keep me com-pa-ny. I milk-ed the lowing
kine and water-ed and fed the steed, and then, after
my frugal repast, I clos-ed the man-si-on, shutting
out all re-collec-tions of the past and also foresights
into the future. That night was a me-mor-able one.

When the maid is obliged to continue her story orally, her
delivery changes radically. The stilted diction evaporates, the
grammar falters, and the scene bursts into life:

There was that wretch on top of the house, a-fixin'
his old rods and hammerin' away for dear life. He'd
brought his ladder over the side fence, where the
dog, a-barkin' and plungin' at the boy outside,
couldn't see him. I stood dumb for a minute, and

> then I know'd I had him. I rushed into the house,
> got a piece of well-rope, tied it to the bulldog's
> collar an' dragged him out and fastened him to the
> bottom rung of the ladder.[42]

Sometimes, the styles, instead of being juxtaposed, actually coalesce, forming a synthesis that makes the conventional seem ridiculous. Typically, Artemus Ward subverts stereotyped phrases by subjecting them to dialect spelling. He also introduces vulgar activity into a scene whose dignity depends upon the careful selection of details.

> 'Twas a carm still nite in Joon. All nater was husht
> and nary zeffer disturbed the sereen silens. I sot with
> Betsy Jane on the fense of her farther's pastur. We'd
> bin rompin threw the woods, kulling flours & drivin
> the woodchuck from his Native Lair (so to speak)
> with long sticks.[43]

Not only does this kind of dialect writing reduce the pretensions of trite conventional words and phrases by clothing them in the outlandish garb of misspelling — "nary zeffer disturbed the sereen silens" — it also forces more than normal attention upon the individual words, for most of them in such a passage must undergo translation to be understood. This necessity keeps attention focused on the surface of words.

The prose of the maid and of Artemus Ward results from what James Whitcomb Riley designated as his second approach to dialect — writing as the character himself might write, pretending to *be* the vernacular character. Rather than seeking to represent how that character speaks, the writer adds a complication. He contracts to imitate the character transferring his oral idiom to writing, thus opening the door to unlimited word-play. The difference in the two approaches is illustrated in *Huckleberry Finn*. Ostensibly Huck writes his own story, but in fact his story is recorded as if he were telling it to someone. So when Tom Sawyer writes a letter warning that Jim is going to escape, Huck calls the letter a "nonnamous" one, a neologism faithfully reproducing Huck's misapprehension of the word "anonymous." On the other hand, the letter itself contains such words as "religgion," "helish," and "leasure," the results of Tom's uncertain spelling (ch. 39). A stenographer would have spelled them correctly, but since Tom is understood to have written the letter himself, the misspellings stand. Therefore, when the writer plays the role of the vernacular character *writing,* the misspellings are no longer employed solely for the sake of phonetic accuracy. If the character is assumed to be only semi-literate, his naïve attempts to reproduce his idiom in writing blunder into comedy.

The possibilities afforded by accidental malapropisms and double entendres naturally attracted the "literary comedians," men like Artemus Ward, Bill Nye, Petroleum V. Nasby, and many others around the middle of the nineteenth century who were committed to the profession of making readers laugh. They violated conventions, not to achieve verisimilitude, but to amuse. As we have seen, dialect is always potentially humorous in its abuse of conventions, but whereas the god of phonetic accuracy confers legitimacy upon the violation, comic misspellings exist for their own sake. No linguistic nor psychological justification can be provided for the various spellings of *diary — dierrea, diarea, diarrhea —* except humor. The phonetic accuracy that produces "bar" for "bear" does not justify them, nor are they the result of that understandable confusion which causes Huck to hear "anonymous" as "nonnamous." The distortion in Josh Billings' sentence, "The duk is a foul" is purely for the pleasure of distortion.[44] Such spelling sustains a general atmosphere of orthographic disorder in the midst of which may appear truly relevant absurdities such as, "Do yoo bleeve the present Congris a rump?" and "Let my Boy Constructor loose!" [45]

Even though all dialect writers deliberately manipulate and reshape words, the literary comedian is the most "artificial" of them all. The mimetic writer invites comparison between his imitation and the external reality of dialect speech: "Yas, George, that ar dockymint am in dead yearnist sartin." The transitional stage imitates the semi-literate writer: "Ait ($8) Dullars Rew-ward." Finally, there is the exploiter whose goal is laughter at any cost: What i kno about pharmin, iz kussid little.[46]

Whatever the dialect writer's commitment was, his work remained fundamentally linguistic. He was obliged to pay scrupulous attention to details that rarely concerned the writer who worked with normal prose. He and his reader had to remain alert for the sound, the look, and the sequence of the dialect words, so mercurial could they be in disguise.

Dialects in themselves never played as central a role in American literature as during this period when a new style was emerging. Although it is true that the frog did not of a sudden reveal himself a prince, a colloquial manner was developing beneath the distorted surfaces of dialect. The colloquial mode could not be reached by simply normalizing dialect. Sound and rhythm are basic constituents of style, and both are lost in translation. Here, for example, is a sentence from the preface to Sut Lovingood's *Tales,* first in Sut's idiom, then in a recent normalized version. Sut is discussing the necessity for a preface to his book.

> Well, ef I must, I must; fir I s'pose the perduck-tion cud no more show hitsef in publick wifout hit, than a coffin-maker cud wif out black clothes . . .

> Well, if I must, I must. For I s'pose the pro-duction could no more show itself in public with-out it than a coffin-maker could without black clothes . . .[47]

The translation loses its internal euphony, the pattern of sound that carries the meaning along: namely, *fir* and *per-*

ducktion (which become *for* and *pro*-duction); *must,* per-*duck*-tion, *pub*-lick and *cud* twice (both of which become *could* in translation) ; and finally *ef, sef,* and *wif* (which change into three different word-endings when normalized: i*f, self,* and wi*th*) . These grotesqueries may be barbaric, but, unlike their flat translation, they are lyrically so. The only route to a normal colloquiality that would not lose the melody of speech was the slow one of modification.

After the Civil War, signs that such a modification was un-der way grew more prevalent. Reasons for this shift are avail-able if we re-examine the potentialities of dialect already con-sidered. Cultivating the comic deformities of dialect for example had severe limitations, and its nineteenth-century heyday passed quickly. By the 'seventies, "the misspelling bee" had largely subsided. Not only were its comic poten-tialities exhausted, but its disappearance was encouraged by the appearance on stage of many of the literary comedians. Artemus Ward, Josh Billings, Bill Nye, and many other lesser figures played before the public the role of the comic charac-ter each had created. Since visual typographical humor could not be communicated orally, these performers had to develop other sources of humor: the incongruities not of dialect spell-ing but of tone, of sudden shifts in mood, of understatement, hyperbole, and anticlimax. These stage monologues were basically familiar, casual, and colloquial. The new emphasis concentrated upon the *management* of vernacular material rather than upon its distortion. A sophisticated presentation of the colloquial manner was learned in public as much as on paper.

Furthermore, as pointed out earlier, the United States really lacked strong, distinguishable dialects. Once one put aside the various first-generation immigrant dialects, one was in the area of the general American buzz. The immigrant dialects always yielded in the second generation to a dialect, which, save for a few local peculiarities in pronunciation and some local idioms, prevailed over most of the country. The mobility of the United States population is generally advanced to explain this pervasive standardization of language. New England Yankees moved into the Northwest, bringing their speech with them, and Southerners went into the old Southwest. The two met and fused in the middle grounds of Tennessee, Kentucky, Illinois, Indiana, Missouri. Although various dialects such as the Indiana Hoosier and the Missouri Pike could ostensibly be identified, in the main this great synthetic central dialect was uniform.

The very familiarity of the vernacular voice made it increasingly appreciated. Readers wanted access to the vernacular world with its verbal ease and color, but without the distractingly irregular dialect surface, which made the act of reading as difficult as picking out an image in a roiled pool of water. Writers responded by moving toward a colloquial center. The realistic novelist Joseph Kirkland announced: "If this lingo, now spoken by some ten millions of people, is to be crystallized, it must be done by taking an average and sticking to it. It is a composite photograph establishing a type. I took it (modified of course) from a country district in Central Illinois." [48] It was discovered that even when the humor was toned down, the vernacular continued to stimulate legitimate interest. Although urban sentimentalization of country pleasures was in part responsible for the local color movement, it was also encouraged because the common speech provided genuine revelations — the pleasures of seeing the old dog in print rather than the venerable canine, and of the pasture, the wagon, and the well.

The public's attitude changed also toward the dialect character. As the reader's father, or uncle, or brother, or even the reader himself, he became a more sympathetic figure. The public wished the stigma of clownishness removed, and so the brassy oddness of dialect was muted, allowing the subtler tones of American speech to emerge. Writers like Hamlin

Garland and Sarah Orne Jewett wrote of essentially domesti-
cated characters and, as a consequence, their dialogue
quieted. The earlier humorists had presented dialect figures
whose activities were consistently broad and violent: they
hunted bears, kicked dogs, gulped whiskey, and danced gals
off their feet. The new rural scene emphasized the calmer existence of farming and housekeeping, a life valued in itself
rather than exhibited as a source of crude amusement. Although some writers continued to pursue the outer reaches of
dialect, the main energy turned from idiosyncratic speech
toward the sound of the ordinary man in the middle of
things.

## IV

At the same time that a minority of writers were exploring
the potentialities of dialect, the majority were slowly revising
their management of dialogue. In dialogue, if anywhere, one
could properly demand to hear the American voice. Where
dialects could be used, they met this demand, but the question of how the ordinary American spoke remained unan-
swered. To answer the question required the establishment
of a characteristic diction (the vernacular) and of a characteristic way of using it (colloquial). Literary change is never
linear, but in general it can be said that this movement began
when dialogue was the servant of the narrative, and that it
continued until narrative prose was dominated by the habits
of dialogue: or, it began with Hawthorne, ended with Hemingway.

Dialogue and narrative are, to a degree, separate domains,
but the two interact upon one another, and as written dialogue changed in the nineteenth century, growing freer,
using shorter and more concrete words in fragmented and
rambling sentences, its very makeup influenced its narrative
environment. Narrative prose yielded slowly to the new

music of speech. To illustrate the genesis of a new norm for American literary speech, we can look at sections of dialogue from four of our major nineteenth-century writers, each of whom represents a particular stage along the way. I begin with a writer whose dialogue functioned primarily to advance the narrative, one of whom a contemporary noted, "There is a curious lack of natural dialogue in Hawthorne's books." [49]

Hawthorne's characters do notoriously observe a uniformity of tone when they speak. So carefully managed is their speech that it lacks irrelevancies, an important consideration in dialogue which purports to record what was heard. When the writer decides to approximate conversation — and as we shall see in a moment Hawthorne leans that way — then he contracts to imitate the vagaries of extemporaneous speech. It is the small, subtle shifts in statement, the changes in emphasis and intonation, the accumulated repetitions, the very threads of banality that ultimately make up the fabric of truth.

This realization dawns much after Hawthorne. He provides us an example of "expository dialogue," dialogue which carries the artist's message without a murmur of complaint. Here is one such passage from *The Scarlet Letter*. With it, Hawthorne surveys the contours of the Reverend Mr. Dimmesdale's inner world:

> "Let her see nothing strange — no passion nor eagerness — in thy way of accosting her," whispered Hester. "Our Pearl is a fitful and fantastic elf, sometimes. Especially, she is seldom tolerant of emotion, when she does not fully comprehend the why and wherefore. But the child hath strong affections! She loves me, and will love thee!"
>
> "Thou canst not think," said the minister, glancing aside at Hester Prynne, "how my heart dreads this interview, and yearns for it! But, in truth, as I

already told thee, children are not readily won to
be familiar with me. They will not climb my knee,
nor prattle in my ear, nor answer to my smile; but
stand apart, and eye me strangely. Even little babes,
when I take them in my arms, weep bitterly. Yet
Pearl, twice in her little lifetime, hath been kind to
me! The first time — thou knowest it well! The last
was when thou ledst her with thee to the house of
yonder stern old Governor."

"And thou didst plead so bravely in her behalf
and mine!" answered the mother. "I remember it;
and so shall little Pearl. Fear nothing! She may be
strange and shy at first, but will soon learn to love
thee!" (ch. 19)

To the objection that *The Scarlet Letter* is a romance and
therefore not susceptible to being criticized for failing to
meet the standards of realism, the proper answer is that Hawthorne is unmistakably straining to catch the rhythms,
pauses, and stresses of speech, but cannot find a way to
render his perceptions. The very presence of eight exclamation marks in sixteen sentences indicates a rudimentary attempt to convey emotion with signs. The lovers are tense,
cautious, yearning, and yet restrained, and all their capped
emotion is signalled by those exclamation marks. So too Hawthorne includes two dashes, the first marking an elaboration,
"nothing strange — no passion or eagerness — in thy way of
accosting her," and the second an ellipsis, "The first
time — thou knowest it well!" Both dashes are meant to sig-
nify that the speech was not formally organized in advance.
The first acknowledges that speech must be allowed to expand at will when necessary thoughts unexpectedly enter the
consciousness; the second that on occasion that which is understood by both parties in the conversation can be eliminated.

Today we are accustomed to probe for meaning beneath

the spoken words of fictional characters. Here though, we will be disappointed I think, or deluded, if we pry out a meaning other than the one the conversation offers. Hawthorne is merely jogging our memory. He recharacterizes Pearl, he reminds us again of the strange antipathy children display toward Dimmesdale, and he recalls two instances when Pearl responded kindly to the minister — all in all a mildly tedious job of recapitulation. The only new information offered, which we could easily have guessed, is that the minister is pessimistic and Hester hopeful about the meeting with Pearl. In proportion to its length, the conversation accomplishes very little, except that within the text it does separate two long paragraphs of narration which describe Pearl's activities in the forest and the complicated emotions that she arouses in her parents. This separative function is not a negligible one, but it hardly exhausts the possibilities of dialogue. Moreover, so lengthy and neat are the conversational exchanges in *The Scarlet Letter* that in form Hawthorne's dialogue can hardly be differentiated from his narrative. The reader moves into Hawthorne's dialogue with little sense of change, save that he has hurdled quotation marks. Each participant is permitted his say *in toto*. So long as the dialogue is ancillary to the narrative, as it is here, the reader moves through its full-length lines with very little sense of change or respite. What we find in Hawthorne's dialogue is the set speech. It does not pretend to display the specific character through any special habits of speech. It does not attempt to suggest geographical, social, or professional influences upon speech. It reveals only minimal interest in how emotions alter speech patterns and none at all in the psychology of the speech situation itself. When Dimmesdale says that Hester cannot think how his heart both dreads and yearns for this interview, we recognize an acute psychological truth in the telling, but we are also aware that the observation is not dramatically conveyed. Hawthorne's is drayhorse dialogue laboring faithfully for the narrative. It says what needs to be said to advance the plot, and very little more.

Inconsistency rather than plodding uniformity was at the center of Mark Twain's spirited attack upon Fenimore Cooper's dialogue. The rules governing literary composition, he remarked, "require that when a personage talks like an illustrated, gilt-edged, tree-calf, hand-tooled, seven-dollar Friendship's Offering in the beginning of a paragraph, he shall not talk like a negro minstrel in the end of it." [50] This sardonic reference to verbal imbalance informs us that Cooper's dialogue must at least display variety, however clumsily handled, and hence that a start toward the metamorphosis of American literary dialogue has been made. Cooper did offer several kinds of speech: like Hawthorne he forced some dialogue to serve as the tool of narrative, outlining the action or setting the scene in whispered conferences between beleaguered companions; he established social merit with mannered interchanges between genteel maidens and their humble servants; he made his comic characters engage in heavy-handed word-play; and he created an elegant patois for his Indians. A reviewer of *The Spy* accordingly praised Cooper's "spirited dialogue" in which he detected a Wordsworthian naturalness, "rich with the direct language of untutored men." But the variety observable in Cooper's dialogue does not conceal the awkwardness (or perhaps it was indifference) of its execution. He offered a wide range of idioms, but was fairly slapdash in their management. He found it especially difficult to settle on a suitable pitch for Natty Bumppo's vocabulary. In a study of Leather-Stocking's language, Louise Pound noted that his basic vocabulary was "narrow and hard-worked," but that on occasion he soared to "Ossianic" heights.[51] Natty's normal speech is a hash of dialect, Biblical simplicity, romantic effusion, old saws, and didacticism. In *The Pathfinder,* for example, we discover Natty reproving a companion for the obscurity of his speech while, in the very act of condemnation, he himself disappears in a tangled thicket of prose:

> "What cheer, Master Pathfinder?" demanded Cap, permitting a voice that was usually deep, loud, and confident to sink into the cautious tones that better suited the dangers of the wilderness. "Has the enemy got between us and our port?"

"Master Pathfinder" is one of those ponderous linguistic incongruities Cooper typically enjoys, but it is difficult to understand why, in answer to the seaman's perfectly plain question, Pathfinder should utter his famous inquisitive grunt, as evocatively mysterious as David's "Selah!" and Turoldus' "Aoi!"

> "Anan?"
> "Have any of these painted scaramouches anchored off the harbor towards which we are running, with the hope of cutting us off in entering?"

Cap's attempt to satisfy Pathfinder with an elegant paraphrase is met with reproof:

> "It may be all as you say, friend Cap, but I am none the wiser for your words; and in ticklish times the plainer a man makes his English, the easier he is understood. I know nothing of ports and anchors; but there is a direful Mingo trail within a hundred yards of this very spot, and as fresh as venison without salt. If one of the fiery devils has passed, so have a dozen; and what is worse, they have gone down towards the garrison, and not a soul crosses the clearing around it that some of their piercing eyes will not discover, when sartain bullets will follow."
> (ch. 4)

Natty's speech wobbles from one realm of usage to another. It is spiced with at least one dialect term, "sartain," as well as the idiomatic usage of "ticklish," and it exhibits a deliberately homely (although patently contrived and somewhat ambiguous) comparison, "as fresh as venison without salt." But these gestures toward realism can be matched with an equal number of locutions out of romantic prose — "direful Mingo trail," "fiery devils," and "piercing eyes." Moreover, the last sentence illustrates what Cooper identified in *The American Democrat* as "the common faults of American language." They are "an ambition of effect, a want of simplicity, and a turgid abuse of terms," to which may be added, Cooper went on, "ambiguity of expression." [52] In the last sentence of Natty's speech, the noun "soul" and the verb "will discover" must both be negated before one can reach a positive assertion. In the last clause, "when sartain bullets will follow," one cannot tell whether "sartain" is an adjective qualifying "bullets" — as the syntax indicates — and therefore meaning in a sardonic way that if any person crosses the clearing, bullets belonging to certain people (that is, Indian bullets) will be fired, or whether "sartain" is perhaps an adverb — for this sense is much the clearer of the two alternatives, in spite of the syntactical oddness — and means that should anyone cross the clearing, bullets are certain to fly.

In order to establish a point of reference for our investigations, we should note the general characteristics of this brief exchange. For the sake of verisimilitude Cooper throws a few sops to the reader. The volume of Cap's voice is specified, there is a temporary failure to communicate between Cap and Natty, and the elevated language of ham is dotted with a few colloquial cloves. But Cooper and his audience obviously felt less need for strict realistic consistency in dialogue than did later audiences. The presence of a number of voices in his novels, compared to the over-all similarity of Hawthorne's characters when they speak, diverted Cooper's readers from a recognition that he possessed no fixed linguistic conception of a character like Natty by which he could monitor his speech. Nor does he care about the integrity of his dialogue in general; that was what exasperated Mark Twain. The sardonic fury of Mark Twain's attack upon Cooper indicates how radically certain techniques of literary craft changed during the century. Writers learned to make dialogue play a dual role — to extend the plot and to solidify the character — and learned to do it without violating the integrity of the character's speech.

Here though, there is no reason to believe Cooper wished us to read this passage with any great care for its language. Although some primitive touches of the colloquial are discernible, the overriding purpose of this dialogue is to offer information essential to the plot: who and where the danger is. The manner in which that information is offered remains a secondary consideration.

The panoramic scale of *Moby-Dick* magnified the problem of establishing speech distinctions in dialogue. To invest Ahab with a verbal dignity commensurate with his grandiose character, Melville gave him an archaic, Old Testament idiom, depending upon the historical presence of Quakers in Nantucket to confer the sanction of probability upon his strategy. Among his lesser characters Melville displayed considerable versatility in composing dialogue. Father Mapple is equipped with a racy but eloquent discourse; the commands and shouts of the mates as they pursue the whales are colorful and animated; Ishmael on several occasions indulges in verbal slapstick; Queequeg speaks a pidgin English; Old Fleece mumbles in the grossest of Negro dialects; and Tashtego rumbles out sounds virtually indistinguishable from the thunder overhead. More important to the present study, however, is Melville's work with the speech of ordinary, more or less anonymous, members of the crew. The forty-third chapter of *Moby-Dick* provides a representative instance; as a cordon of seamen pass buckets of water aft, two of them carry on a brief, whispered conversation:

"Hist! did you hear that noise, Cabaco?"

"Take the bucket, will ye, Archy? What noise d'ye mean?"

"There it is again — under the hatches — don't you hear it — a cough — it sounded like a cough."

"Cough be damned! Pass along that return bucket."

"There again — there it is! — it sounds like two or three sleepers turning over, now!"

"Caramba! have done, shipmate, will ye? It's the three soaked biscuits ye eat for supper turning over inside of ye — nothing else. Look to the bucket!"

"Say what ye will, shipmate; I've sharp ears."

"Aye, you are the chap, ain't ye, that heard the hum of the Old Quakeress's knitting needles fifty miles at sea from Nantucket; you're the chap."

"Grin away; we'll see what turns up. Hark ye, Cabaco, there is somebody down in the after-hold that has not yet been seen on deck; and I suspect our old Mogul knows something of it too. I heard Stubb tell Flask one morning watch, that there was something of that sort in the wind."

"Tish! the bucket!"

The speakers here represent a lower-class norm, for their language is not twisted by dialect, occupational jargon, or verbal acrobatics. Although Cabaco is identified as a Cholo (or civilized South American Indian) and on one occasion exclaims "Caramba!" Melville mercifully spares us a Latin accent. Cabaco's interchanges with Archy are brief, nervous, and dynamic. Melville uses repetition artfully, one instance of repetition being particularly subtle. Archy believes that he hears two or three sleepers "turning over" below decks. Cabaco makes a joke of this notion, one reminiscent of Scrooge's rationalization of his visions, saying that it is no more than the supper biscuits "turning over" in Archy's stomach. The device of building a conversation about a single phrase is a familiar one in colloquial prose. But Melville complicates its use. A few moments later the original phrase has sunk into the mind of Cabaco. Then, teased, he answers, "Grin away; we'll see what turns up," and out comes the primary verb, *turns,* still close enough to consciousness to be used, though now below the threshold of Cabaco's awareness. Such a sequence has impressive psychological validity.

So does Melville's use of the word "bucket" as a linguistic frame for his scene. As we hear the rephrased demands for the bucket, we are aware of Cabaco's impatience and Archy's musing pauses: "Take the bucket, will ye, Archy?," "Pass along that return bucket," [53] "Look to the bucket!," and finally, rounding off the scene in comic exasperation, "Tish! the bucket!" Malcolm Cowley, in discussing the American vernacular style, identifies one of its characteristics as "the trick of repeating the same word in several sentences, so that it gives a keynote to the paragraph." [54] The trait clearly originates in speech (and not necessarily Midwestern American speech as Cowley suggests). But much more experimentation and development would have to take place before organization by repetition could be used deliberately and extensively in narrative prose.

Subtle as his use of repetition is, Melville's punctuation of the dialogue is puzzling. In the first half of the unit, pauses and interruptions are marked with dashes. In the second half the dashes are replaced by semicolons. It would appear that Melville stopped work one day halfway through the chapter, then picked up the next day with a new technical procedure. For example, although the method of punctuation changes there is more similarity than difference between the pauses established in: "It's the three soaked biscuits ye eat for supper turning over inside of ye — nothing else," and "Grin away; we'll see what turns up."

More important, this conversation remains too overtly expositional, too revelatory. We would discover implications by ourselves, delighting in our own perceptions and conclusions. As we discover shortly after this interlude in *Moby-Dick,* there are in fact several sleepers below-decks. But at this point it is impossible to imagine sounds penetrating up through a wooden deck that would suggest men turning over in their sleep. A cough, yes. A groan, yes. But the unnamed sound of sleepers stirring is unimaginable, and is mentioned only because Melville is straining to make a melodramatic point. So too Archy's concluding speech is far too explicit, too exact and shrewd a guess. As if embarrassed or suddenly aware of the improbability of these notions, Melville makes Archy explain that he had "heard Stubb tell Flask one morning watch that there was something of that sort in the wind." But with this sort of foreknowledge in his mind, Archy would surely have repeated Stubb's story near the beginning of the dialogue, and then would have gone on to elaborate the supporting evidence. When the revelation that Archy had heard a substantiating conversation comes *after* an unconvincing deduction, one can only assume this concluding explanation was Melville's attempt to mend the unmendable.

In spite of these cavils, this is the most spirited dialogue we have yet encountered and is altogether representative of Melville. Melville had an acute if not delicate ear, and when he erred it was on the side of excessive coloration of his dialogue. He also was guilty of the other general fault we are discovering everywhere we look closely — verbal carelessness. At the same time Melville was aware of the repetitive nature of colloquial speech, and was able to take advantage of the repetitions in order not only to achieve a measure of psychological fidelity, but also to give his scene a suggestion of formal unity. Slight but psychologically meaningful variations of repeated phrases growing into coherent linguistic structures have been important features of American prose style in the twentieth century, and here they are, incipient.

V

The middle class — it was omnipresent but invisible. It rarely fought Indians, went a-whaling, or acknowledged adultery. Its occupations were primarily sedentary ones, carried on in the decorum of the business office and the parlor. Its activities were temperate, its attitudes restrained, and its speech — ? No heavy concentration of vernacular particularity nor colloquial impetuosity helped identify it. Little wonder that some of the younger men like Stephen Crane turned to the vulgar classes for literary source material. But others continued to write about the environment they knew and understood best. Out of their struggle with the intractable surface placidity, not to say dullness, of middle-class life, they managed to work out new procedures for revealing inner truth. Middle-class speech, for the very reason that it lacked the distractions of excessive verbal color, began to uncover, to call attention to, the structural elements of colloquial prose.

William Dean Howells was one of the first major American writers to render this area of society successfully, to record the banalities of its social life in all their queer sobriety. Yet because he fundamentally respected the middle class and worried for its moral prosperity, Howells' picture of its features is less than incisive. It has something of the distortion of a portrait drawn by a talented member of the family. The face is there but lines have been smoothed out, the hair neatly parted, the carriage made more erect. When there is adverse criticism it is of that affectionate nature we can still observe in cheap contemporary fiction; the mouth may be "too generous," but never the nose, and the smile "a little crooked," but not the teeth. We appreciate the finesse of Howells' powers of observation — but at the same time we must arm ourselves against his predisposition to favor his subject. The following example taken from his first novel, *Their Wedding Journey* (1871), is typical in that Howells is at pains to soften yet brighten his characters' speech. The novelty of the dialogue lies in spending so much time in the reproduction of what is essentially trivia, yet that was the door to everyday speech:

"I knew you'd come back," she said.

"So did I," he answered. "I am much too good and noble to sacrifice my preference to my duty."

"I didn't particularly care for the two horses, Basil," she said, as they descended to the barouche. "It was your refusing them that hurt me."

"And I didn't want the one-horse carriage. It was your insisting so that provoked me."

"Do you think people *ever* quarreled before on a wedding journey?" asked Isabel as they drove gaily out of the city.

"Never! I can't conceive of it. I suppose if this were written down, nobody would believe it."

"No, nobody could," Isabel said musingly, and she added after a pause, "I wish you would tell me just what you thought of me, dearest. Did you feel as you did when our little affair was broken off, long ago? Did you hate me?"

"I did, most cordially; but not half so much as I despised myself the next moment. As to its being like a lover's quarrel, it wasn't. It was more bitter; so much more love than lovers ever give had to be taken back. Besides, it had no dignity, and a lover's quarrel always has. A lover's quarrel always springs from a more serious cause, and has an air of romantic tragedy. This has no grace of the kind. It was a poor shabby little squabble." [55]

This, to be sure, is early Howells. I choose it not to denigrate him, but to display a representative work of the decade following the Civil War, one which is neither fustian nor dependent upon local color. Howells was a real and successful pioneer in the exploration of middle-class speech, however hampered he was by his intimacy with that class.

In this frothy account of a honeymoon, Howells occasionally moves beyond the lines of fictional probability in his literary self-consciousness. Asked if he believes people ever quarreled before on a wedding journey, Basil replies with wry innocence, "Never! I can't conceive of it. I suppose if this were written down, nobody would believe it." With just this fictional demurrer Howells expects to gain the reader's confidence. He, Howells, is writing down an account of a *real* lover's spat, and unusual as it may be for fiction, such an event is doubtless commonplace for every actual honeymoon. At the same time he calls attention to the novelty of his approach.

This discussion between newlyweds is an attack upon preceding fiction, accomplished by means of extended redefinition. Here Isabel attempts to make the petty quarrel into a momentous one, whereupon Basil exposes its superficiality. Basil has an epigrammatic flair and makes the most of it in this conversation. He displays unusual powers of extemporaneous analysis and phrasing: "I am much too good and noble to sacrifice my preference to my duty." That is witty and entirely unexpected for an American. Upon investigation we may find Basil's dissection of the "poor shabby little squabble" a bit too prepared, too arranged for improvisation, but by and large the novelty of his attack allows this artificiality to pass unnoticed. Seeing a subject beloved by the sentimentalists under fire, the reader was sufficiently arrested not to notice the unreality (that is, the deliberate contrivance) of the attack upon unreality. Howells' stylistic technique for capturing middle-class speech without reproducing only a grey, flat surface was to break that surface into fairly small units. The process of deliberate fragmentation for rhythmic and emphatic purposes was finally under way. Then, the couple's vocabulary is reined in, so that the two adults discuss their quarrel, their present feelings, and their relationship with mannered equanimity. There is no vaulting from the norm, and even Basil's wit is only briefly displayed. The language is commonplace, relaxed, immediately apprehensible, unpoetic. It lacks metaphor, is commonsensical, businesslike. In its very dryness it embodies the values of the middle class with its ideal of social self-effacement. On the whole one can find this conversation interesting but far from vital.

Howells' use of brief, barebones phrases in dialogue foreshadows the next century's concentration upon the single word as a repository of multiple meaning. As I have indicated, American literature was embarking upon a long adventure in redefinition, an early example of which appears in this very passage, when Isabel asks Basil, "Did you hate me?" A variety of meanings adhere to the word "hate." Isabel hardly expects Basil to turn white and cry "YES!" Nor does she expect him to yawn in her face. What she really has in mind is a hatred not far from pique. In response to this expectation Basil provides a more urbane definition of hatred. He recognizes the triviality of the circumstances and refuses to inflate them. "I did [hate you], most cordially; but not half so much as I despised myself the next moment." By turning his admitted hatred against himself, verbally at any rate, he begins to sew up the rift, so that before he has finished he can move to another redefinition — that of the average lover's quarrel.

Such semantic exercises are not often carried on so openly. But in the post–Civil War period and after, writers are often implicitly testing the meanings of words, not only against changes in ethical fashions and scientific discoveries, but also against their privately experienced reality. In *Huckleberry Finn* when Mark Twain names the grounded and abandoned riverboat the *Walter Scott* he strips the title of nobility from that revered literary figure in an attempt to disperse the haze of reverence that enveloped Scott's work. Similarly, when Twain attacks Cooper he is implicitly stating his own view of what the real world is like.

Although Howells rendered an artful semblance of unexceptional speech, he still failed to locate the energies of the prosaic. If he was sensitive enough to know when words rang false in dialogue, he found it difficult to make his own ring true. His dialogue suffered from being prematurely polished, composed, arranged. The unique qualities of the American vernacular had not had time to fix themselves in his work, to grow to their full proportions. Howells usefully nurtured this normative American dialogue, but he vitiated his work by seeking to teach it manners.

Yet, dialogue in American literature had changed appreciably over a fifty-year period. It had become easy, and it discussed ordinary things in an ordinary way. It had largely escaped the dominance of formal narrative prose (Hawthorne), it had leveled out its disastrously uneven tone (Cooper), it had increased both its liveliness and its psychological acuteness (Melville), and now it had only to continue to draw out the emerging features of the vernacular without imposing social preconceptions upon them (Howells).

It was, in part, Howells' *arrangement* of dialogue that must have caused his friend Henry James to remark in print that Howells "believed, in particular, that he could not make people talk, and such have been the revenges of time that a cynical critic might almost say of him today that he cannot make them keep silent." [56] The comment is at once sympathetic and acid, and it suggests to us that James himself had a different standard for dialogue. That is true of James, and of Mark Twain too.

# THREE

# Henry James and Mark Twain

"We have organized an irregular commonplace and
we have made excess return to rambling."
*Portraits and Prayers*

I

STRESS, FRAGMENTATION, REPETITION first appeared as the result of mimetic preoccupations, and then slowly their formal implications and uses began to be understood. Almost simultaneously, Henry James and Mark Twain, two men with radically different interests as writers, confronted the necessity of ordering the jumble of colloquial elements. Their solutions were as dissimilar as the men themselves, but also complementary, so that with work, serious practitioners of the art of writing could fuse those solutions in a new and durable synthesis. To think of Henry James is to see a dignified figure at the social table, digesting random scraps of conversation for his later ruminative delight. Similarly, the essential Mark Twain crystallizes in a wry presence drawling anecdotes, delivering after-dinner speeches, and delighting the public from the lecture platform. It is not just coincidence that in the course of their careers each wrote plays (ill-advisedly) and that in his last years each turned eagerly to dictation.

To understand the significant parallels, though, we must be alert for distinctions. The most important concerns subject matter. Huck and the other characters in his book talk about things, whereas the Jamesian characters discuss states of being. The distinction is readily seen by comparing a line from *The Spoils of Poynton* with one from *Huckleberry Finn*.

"No, dear, you haven't a petty mind; you've a lovely imagination and you're the nicest creature in the world." [1]

"Ain't you a sweet-scented dandy, though? A bed; and bed-clothes; and a look'n glass; and a piece of carpet on the floor — and your own father got to sleep with the hogs in the tanyard." (ch. 5)

The difference in the two quotations is elementary but fundamental. Mark Twain uses concrete diction and moves his nouns with active verbs or enhances their brilliancy with neutral frames of conjunctions and copulas. James on the other hand deals primarily with abstractions, works around his subject without ever naming it (for it is unnameable), eventually defining its limits by the encirclement of his prose.

The fact that the two men approach the problem of rendering the vernacular in prose from such disparate starting points will have important consequences for American prose style. Mark Twain leads the reader to things again, things admired for themselves and their functions rather than for any investiture of symbolic or social portent. James, on the other hand, because the subjects of his art lack solid physical referents, emphasizes literary composition, word patterns, and placement. To look at a random piece of Mark Twain's prose is to see images rising from the words, whereas a James passage out of context draws as much attention to its own surface, to the words that compose it, as it does to its content. For example, compare the opening sentence of the twenty-seventh chapter of *Huckleberry Finn* with the opening of the twenty-seventh in *The Wings of the Dove:*

> I crept to their doors and listened; they was snoring, so I tip-toed along, and got down stairs all right.

> There was at last, with everything that made for it, an occasion when he got from Kate, on what she now spoke of as his eternal refrain, an answer of which he was to measure afterwards the precipitating effect.

Even if we are unfamiliar with the specific circumstances of Huck's movement, we shall still follow him from door to door, pause, listen, hear snores, then continue on tip-toe and descend the stairs. Our attention is absorbed by an imaginative playing-out of the action described by Huck. His language here is self-effacing. With as little fuss as possible it points to a series of concrete acts. But with James it is the language which demands both first and second attention. A door is a door unless otherwise indicated, but a "precipitating effect" is a verbal construct attractive in itself. We hopefully assume while reading that James's verbal construct has pertinence to some state of affairs in the book, and that if analyzed it will prove to be rationally apt. Still, the phrase initially catches our attention as a word formation. Inasmuch as a psychological state, unlike a door, has no visible existence and is attached to no image independent of words, it is anchored to the verbal phrases that make it up, which necessarily accentuates the words themselves. James's subject as well as his execution draws attention to the composition of his prose in a way that Mark Twain's normally does not.

For James all of this begins in dialogue. I suggested earlier that James had standards for dialogue other than those of the friend he shared with Mark Twain, William Dean Howells. James recognized the public's insatiable demand for that form of contrived dialogue he variously named "this easiest of lubrications," a "boneless dispersion," and "savourless dilution." He complained, however, that when speech was served "au naturel," readers of fiction rejected it outright. "Really constructive dialogue, dialogue organic and dramatic, speaking for itself, representing and embodying substance and form, is among us an uncanny and abhorrent thing," he commented in his preface to *The Awkward Age*.[2] It does not matter exactly when James worked out any given problem of dialogue, nor is an historical account of his successive refinements pertinent here. What we are interested to discover is his reproduction of those characteristic speech patterns that eventually helped to fix colloquial prose. James's goal was speech that could sustain itself without the props of melodrama, declamation, and forced wit, yet be an accurate verbal record of restless and contentious minds. This "organic and dramatic" dialogue helped James define his characters, or more properly, it allowed them to define themselves. And this turned out to be the stimulus that led to the use of repetition as a device operating beyond the limits of mere reportorial accuracy.

In his dialogue James often took a common phrase and repeated it again and again, passing it between his characters as an index of their agreement, or of their difference, or of a gradual redefinition of their positions. In the following exchange from *The Spoils of Poynton* Fleda Vetch and Mrs. Gereth are each concerned with the definition of terms. Fleda has just told Mrs. Gereth that her son Owen has "demanded" that she send all the household furnishings back at once. With an icily ironic question Mrs. Gereth now suggests to Fleda that she, Fleda, has failed to find the appropriate word to describe the situation.

> "Quite a 'demand,' dear, isn't it?" asked Mrs. Gereth, drawing in her cloak.
> "Oh, that's what I should call it!" Fleda laughed, to her own surprise.

Momentarily countered, Mrs. Gereth adds detail to support her implied criticism of Fleda's term.

> "I mean with the threat of enforcement and that sort of thing."
> "Distinctly with the threat of enforcement — what would be called, I suppose, coercion."

Their verbalization of the situation grows more precise. Accordingly, as the terms of Owen's demand come clearer, Mrs. Gereth seeks further precision.

> "What sort of coercion?" said Mrs. Gereth.
> "Why, legal, don't you know? — what he calls setting the lawyers at you."

Fleda has now contrasted the formal "coercion" with Owen's colloquially jaunty expression, "setting the lawyers at you." Mrs. Gereth responds to the contrast.

> "Is that what he calls it?" She seemed to speak with disinterested curiosity.

And Fleda rests at this point by holding to the phrase Mrs. Gereth has just introduced.

> "That's what he calls it," said Fleda.  (p. 132)

The dialogue continues in much the same manner. The scene is an intricate one, for not only are the two women attempting to locate a satisfactory definition of Owen's attitude, but they are also sparring with one another, each learning about the other by comparing definitions. The exercise is at once intellectual and emotional. The use of identical words and phrases underlines the difference in the two women's characters, not alone for themselves within the fictional matrix, but for the observant reader outside it.

In addition, the intense concentration upon *words* suggests a new awareness of the word as word, the word with a

particular appearance, sound, and relation to other words —
all of this aside from meaning. This is not, of course, a session
of the French Academy, and no word is thoroughly or even
adequately defined in lexicographic terms. But we are made
by James to feel the proportions of the words, to "size them
up" as it were, in relation to the weight of meaning they
are asked to carry. This is, so far as I know, a process unique
with James, although at the same time part and parcel of the
impulse that compelled Basil March to redefine the lover's
quarrel.

A second way in which James used colloquial repetition
was to establish certain phrases as points of departure, and
then to measure his characters by comparing their routes,
speed, and distance achieved from those common starting
points. I do not mean, certainly, that James himself worked
this out in anything like the yardstick method I am suggesting. The metaphor only works insofar as the characters identify themselves by their positions in relation to a single verbal
point of neutrality. In Chapter 41 of *The Portrait of a Lady*,
Gilbert Osmond and Isabel, now married, discuss Pansy's
frame of mind toward marriage. Osmond has been warned of
the danger of his daughter's being in love with Edward
Rosier. His conversation with Isabel revolves around two
verbs and a conjunctive phrase: "To please," variations of
"to speak," and "so that." Each provides a nucleus around
which the opposing views of Gilbert and Isabel can cluster.

> "Pansy would like to be a great lady," he re-
> marked in a moment, with a certain tenderness of
> tone. "She wishes, above all, to please," he added.
> "To please Mr. Rosier, perhaps."
> "No, to please me."
> "Me too a little, I think," said Isabel.
> "Yes, she has a great opinion of you. But she will
> do what I like."
> "If you are sure of that, it's very well," she said.

On that rather cool observation from Isabel the section centering on "to please" ends. As the subject changes to Lord
Warburton, the talk focuses on the verb "to speak."

> "Meantime," said Osmond, "I should like our dis
> tinguished visitor to speak."
> "He has spoken — to me. He has told me that it
> would be a great pleasure to him to believe she
> could care for him."
> Osmond turned his head quickly; but at first he
> said nothing. Then — "Why didn't you tell me
> that?" he asked quickly.
> "There was no opportunity. You know how we
> live. I have taken the first chance that has offered."
> "Did you speak to him of Rosier?"
> "Oh yes, a little."
> "That was hardly necessary."

Here the second verbal exchange finishes. A scheme similar
to that of the first unit has been observed. First the infinitive
form "to speak" was offered, then the verb was furnished
with different, successive objects, each emphasizing two wills
at odds. Now the dialogue moves to a tensely repetitive
conclusion.

> "I thought it best he should know, so that, so
> that — " And Isabel paused.
> "So that what?"
> "So that he should act accordingly."
> "So that he should back out, do you mean?"
> "No, so that he should advance while there is yet
> time."

Each "so that" introduces a new, or further qualified, explanation of why Isabel told Lord Warburton of the love
between Pansy and Rosier. The pressure of Osmond's rejoinders forces Isabel toward concision. Six times the phrase
"so that" is repeated in five lines. We are inevitably made

aware of the appearance of language by this, and are not so very far from experiments Gertrude Stein, an admirer of James, would make twenty-five years later. Whether this instance of patterning in what James once called a "medium intrinsically indocile" [3] stems from conscious arrangement or from chance, the reiteration of the phrase "so that" points the way to the use of words as counters on the page. Lacking a concrete referent, such a phrase as "so that" is even more unstable than conceptual language, and frees itself from context that much more easily. In itself only a syntactical guidepost for causal drift, the phrase "so that" need not be repeated often before it begins to assume a quasi-independent existence.

Mark Twain also approached his words with an appreciation of their visual and aural values, and he sometimes worked with them as units valuable in themselves. For a short time in *Huckleberry Finn* we are exposed to an exhibition of one kind of word-play. Then we are returned to the action. This virtuosity is not self-conscious, nor, in the bad sense, contrived. Mark Twain works his material naturally, developing its potentialities without strain. This unit of dialogue is framed by references at either end to the camp fire, even as Melville's sequence of talk between Archy and Cabaco opened and closed on the call for a bucket. Huck begins the conversation by suggesting that Jim build up the fire; then after a neat miniature duet played upon the central topics of what there has been to eat, how long each has been on Jackson's island, and what they should now do, Jim signals the end of the conversation by agreeing to build up the fire.

The whole is introduced by Huck's voice repeating "I warn't." Then Jim joins in to play variations against Huck's colloquial norm.

Well, I WARN'T long making him understand I WARN'T dead. I was ever so glad to see Jim. I WARN'T lonesome now. I told him I WARN'T afraid of *him* telling the people where I was. I talked along, but he only set there and looked at me; never said nothing. Then I says:

"It's good daylight. Let's get breakfast. MAKE UP YOUR CAMP FIRE GOOD."

"What's de use er MAKIN' UP DE CAMP FIRE to cook STRAWBRIES EN SICH TRUCK? BUT YOU GOT A GUN, HAIN'T YOU?"

"STRAWBERRIES AND SUCH TRUCK," I says. "Is that what you live on?"

"I couldn' git nuffn else," he says.

"WHY, HOW LONG YOU BEEN ON THE ISLAND, Jim?"

"I come heah de night arter you's killed."

"What, all that time?"

"Yes-indeedy."

"And ain't you had NOTHING but that kind of rubbage to eat?"

"No, sah — NUFFN else."

"Well, you must be most starved, AIN'T YOU?"

"I reck'n I could eat a hoss. I think I could. HOW LONG YOU BEN ON DE ISLAN'?"

"Since the night I got killed."

"No! w'Y, what has you lived on? BUT YOU GOT A GUN. Oh, yes, YOU GOT A GUN. Dat's good. Now you kill sumfn en I'LL MAKE UP DE FIRE." (ch. 8; capitals added)

Mark Twain has forewarned the readers of *Huckleberry Finn* of the presence of several dialects. In this instance a number of contrasted examples appear: ain't-hain't, island-islan', such-sich, of-er, and-en, been-ben, why-w'y, and strawberries-strawbries. These are especially accentuated when placed in almost identical phrases like "How long you been on the island," "make up the camp fire," and "strawberries and such truck." Huck provides the colloquial norm and Jim the variation; yet there is no insistence on correctness. The certainty that any given word has a fixed condition no longer exists. The necessity of fitting words to particular, unique characters calls into question the very possibility of objective definition. What is suitable, or better, what is real for one man is not necessarily so for another. What Owen calls "setting the lawyers" on his mother, Fleda calls a "demand," and Mrs. Gereth herself "a threat of enforcement." And what Huck knows as "nothing," Jim names "nuffn." Whether it be the appropriateness of the word for the situation under discussion, or its very constitution, its spelling and pronunciation, the realistic writer was beginning to ask his reader to devote more and more time to a conscious consideration of the individual word, rather than merely startling him with its incongruity as the earlier dialect humorists had done. In *Huckleberry Finn* Mark Twain did not simply assemble a mechanical system of misspellings in order to approximate dialect. Rather he sketched in just enough of the vagaries of human speech to sustain his illusion. As a rule though, care for words in one aspect promotes care for them in all. Whatever efforts Mark Twain made to distinguish his dialects and characters heightened awareness of all his diction.

It is not, of course, to be expected that the characters of *Huckleberry Finn* should indulge in extended Jamesian definitions. Nonetheless, Huck and Jim furnish instances of the elasticity of language that show how far meaning can be stretched and still retain comprehension. In the passage just quoted, for example, the word "good" is used to qualify three things: daylight, the making-up of a camp fire, and the fact that Huck has a gun. As it happens, "good daylight" is the extension of Huck's observation in the preceding paragraph that, "It was getting grey daylight now." And going further back in the text, we discover that "good" is the superlative of three observations: "Day was coming," "It was getting grey daylight now," "It's good daylight." Through these unobtrusive notations Mark Twain managed to indicate both the passage of time and Huck's uncomplicated appreciation of full morning light, all with the most commonplace of adjectives.

Just this has been the practice of some modern writers: the placement of the familiar word in an alien setting, or conversely, the placement of the unusual word among ordinary ones. In either case the word gains power. John O'Hara revived a phrase of prattle in this way:

> It was a beautiful, beautiful day and some of the hungry youngsters of teen age forgot about lunch and continued to swim and splash.[4]

The sudden intervention of this rhapsodic remark within the cool narrative prose gives the repetition of "beautiful" a freshness not otherwise possible, and which, were it caught between the confines of quotation marks, would be merely banal.

As an example of the unfamiliar word dropped into an everyday context, O'Hara provides another self-conscious example. He is writing about a young American priest serving his first Mass.

> His vestments didn't seem to fit him. The — what was it? — the amice almost looked like a scarf, and was no whiter than Okie's face. The chasuble *was* too big for him, and at the bottom step the alb got in his way and he half tripped.[5]

In this passage O'Hara has set the nomenclature of Catholic regalia against a colloquial background, giving the Latin terms the prominence of spots on a wall and forcing the reader to consider them as, first of all, words.

In examining such instances of verbal emphasis, we have temporarily advanced beyond dialogue before its potentialities as they bear on modern prose style have been fully explored. To return: It is out of the speaking voice that this uncommon emphasis upon words emerges, for the very reason that as people speak they can do only the most rudimentary planning of what they intend to say, and so must stress and repeat. Untrained speakers do not have the time to find the right word, but must trust to verbal luck and the forbearance of their listeners as they grope after accuracy. Nor do they have the opportunity to analyze, to pare away and subordinate, or to work out the various strategies of syntactical arrangement available to the writer in his study. For a contrast to modern conversational improvisation (or its literary representation) we again need only refer to the examples offered by Hawthorne and Howells to see prepared and guided, or "written," dialogue. James in his sympathetic monograph of 1879 commented of Hawthorne, "He has been almost culpably indifferent to his opportunities for commemorating the variations of colloquial English that may be observed in the New World." Significantly, James thought Hawthorne's characters spoke a language that was "apt to be too elegant, too delicate." [6]

Henry James and Mark Twain, to quote the latter now, desired that "talk shall sound like human talk, and be talk such as human beings would be likely to talk in the given circumstances." [7] When these two contemporaries tried to approximate such talk, they couched highly dissimilar content in remarkably similar forms. That is, to carry their disparate cargoes of human speech, each man independently evolved closely related vehicles. It is exactly these vehicles that we are anxious to observe.

To maintain coherence in their conversations, characters pause, stress, and repeat. By comparing two sequences of dialogue, one from Mark Twain and the other from Henry James, we can readily observe the formal relationships as well as the unusually strong emphasis put upon single words. The examples demonstrate that Jamesian characters repeat to define themselves, Twainians to keep a grip on reality.

In the very conclusion of *The Wings of the Dove*, we find the full arsenal of print being used to deepen the impression

each word makes. Initial phrases are repeated to establish
contrast (as was the case with "so that"); dashes separate
thoughts, allowing the mind either to prepare for the important observation to come, or to let one just past sink
further into the consciousness; single words or phrases are
isolated by full stops for emphasis; and the tension of italics
is fully exploited. Kate Croy begins:

> "I used to call her, in my stupidity — for want of
> anything better — a dove. Well she stretched out
> her wings, and it was to *that* they reached. They
> cover us."
>
> "They cover us," Densher said.
>
> "That's what I give you," Kate gravely wound up.
> "That's what I've done for you."
>
> His look at her had a slow strangeness that had
> dried, on the moment, his tears. "Do I understand
> then — ?"
>
> "That I do consent?" She gravely shook her head.
> "No — for I see. You'll marry me without the
> money; you won't marry me with it. If I don't con-
> sent, *you* don't."
>
> "You lose me?" He showed, though naming it
> frankly, a sort of awe of her high grasp. "Well, you
> lose nothing else. I make over to you every penny."
>
> Prompt was his own clearness, but she had no
> smile, this time, to spare. "Precisely — so that I
> must choose."
>
> "You must choose."
>
> Strange it was for him then that she stood in his
> own rooms doing it, while, with an intensity now
> beyond any that had ever made his breath come slow
> to him, he waited for her act. "There's but one
> thing that can save you from my choice."
>
> "From your choice of my surrender to you?"
>
> "Yes" — and she gave a nod at the long envelope
> on the table — "your surrender of that."
>
> "What is it then?"

"Your word of honour that you're not in love with her memory."

"Oh — her memory!"

"Ah" — she made a high gesture — "don't speak of it as if you couldn't be. *I* could, in your place; and you're one for whom it will do. Her memory's your love. You *want* no other."

He heard her out in stillness, watching her face, but not moving. Then he only said: "I'll marry you, mind you, in an hour."

"As we were?"

"As we were."

But she turned to the door, and her headshake was now the end. "We shall never be again as we were!"

So far as dialogue is concerned we need not quote James again, for this passage is model enough, containing as it does a high incidence of the verbal devices mentioned a moment ago. It is difficult to imagine a more highly formal conversation than this one, where meaning is altogether dependent upon the reverberations of simple words. This is its appearance with the repeated elements abstracted:

> They cover us.
> They cover us.
>
> That's what I give.
> That's what I've done.
>
> You'll marry me without.
> You won't marry me with.
>
> If I don't.
> You don't.
>
> You lose me.
> You lose nothing.
>
> I must choose.
> You must choose.

My choice.
Your choice of my surrender.
Your surrender.

Her memory.
Her memory.

As we were.
As we were.
We shall never be again as we were.

Words are repeated, modified, expanded, explored, drawn
in parallels and faced off as opposites. Densher and Kate are
engaged in a struggle at several levels, with the medium, to
an unusual degree, words. One sometimes feels the fool for
insisting that words are expressing a literary point, but here
the reason for the insistence must be clear.

Sometimes when specific things and physical acts are discussed, as is usually the case in *Huckleberry Finn,* repetition
draws the mind back from the referents to the prose surface,
but normally this will not happen, for we accept repetition as
a donnée of realism. In the dialogue of uninstructed characters, iteration is understood to result as a rule from their inability or superstitious unwillingness to substitute synonyms,
pronouns or verbal auxiliaries for the concrete terms of their
discussion. This steady, relentless hewing to a line of particulars suggests then that material reality is all that is trusted, all
that can be depended upon to convey meaning. Sometimes, it
is true, verbal phrases are repeated to emphasize the slow
irritating passage of time: Huck says of an auction, "it strung
along, and strung along," and of an investigation, "they kept
it up, and kept it up" (chs. 28, 29). But usually the repetition comes from an unspoken agreement between the
talkers to limit their discussion to a few reliable and specific
terms.

In the following example, the innate patterning of the dialogue gains undue prominence, perhaps, for the modern
reader because "nigger" is a noun about which the twentieth-
century American is abnormally sensitive.

The next minute he whirls on me and says:

"DO YOU RECKON THAT NIGGER WOULD BLOW ON US? We'd skin him if he done that!"

"HOW CAN HE BLOW? Hain't he run off?"

"No! THAT OLD FOOL SOLD HIM, and never divided with me, and the money's gone."

"SOLD HIM?" I says, and begun to cry: "why, HE WAS MY NIGGER, and that was my money. Where is he? — I WANT MY NIGGER."

"Well, YOU CAN'T GET YOUR NIGGER, that's all — so dry up your blubbering. Looky here — DO YOU THINK YOU'D VENTURE TO BLOW ON US? Blamed if I think I'd trust you. WHY IF YOU WAS TO BLOW ON US — "

He stopped, but I never see the duke look so ugly out of his eyes before. I went on a-whimpering, and says:

"I DON'T WANT TO BLOW ON NOBODY; and I AIN'T GOT TIME TO BLOW, NOHOW. I got to turn out and find my nigger."

He looked kinder bothered, and stood there with his bills fluttering on his arm, thinking, and wrinkling up his forehead. At last he says:

"I'll tell you something. We got to be here three days. IF YOU'LL PROMISE YOU WON'T BLOW, AND WON'T LET THE NIGGER BLOW, I'll tell you where to find him." (ch. 31, capitals added)

In this passage changes are rung on a very limited subject. A formal structure remarkably similar to that in the James example is embedded in Mark Twain's dialogue, even though the fictional motives for the repetition are radically different. Here one of Mark Twain's characters suddenly has an idea, puts it into words and then holds firmly to it. The duke fears someone may "blow" — that is, inform on him. First he sees the danger in Jim, then in Huck. Huck picks up the accusation, but fails to modify it, adjust it, qualify it, or substitute anything new for it. Denials, threats, assertions, and promises follow, all as expressions shooting off the main verbal spine. The problem emerges swiftly at the outset, then must be solved by action rather than by any verbal extension or manipulation.

These examples aid us, I should suppose, to see the close relationship between the work of Mark Twain and Henry James in dialogue. Both cinch their lines with an uncommon degree of repetition. Uncommon because, although any previous literary conversation necessarily involved some repetition, it had never been exhibited to such an insistent degree as it is here, and would be henceforth. Further, both men have simplified their diction and syntax. Fewer and fewer synonyms are used, less elaboration of thought occurs, and phrases of only a few components, or even single words, begin to assume more and more of the burden of meaning. This is signalled not only by repetition but also by the increasing use of italics. In the example from *Huckleberry Finn* a bare handful of concepts are put into words: then within and among the variations played upon them, central words are emphasized by italics (shown here by underlining). The appearance of italicized words indicates points of emotional pressure. Formally italics play, even as they did in the concluding lines of *The Wings of the Dove,* a counter-melody of emphasis to the repetition, being different from it in kind, but similar in the way they accentuate the word upon the page. This very pulsation of emphasis enriches the translation of speech rhythms into print, and in the twentieth century its use would be consciously extended.

II

Quotation marks erect an arbitrary barrier between dialogue and the other prose portions of a work of fiction. No more than a convention, they have been circumvented and demolished many times in this century of the spoken word. The paragraphing of dialogue lines has been dispensed with. The European dash has been substituted for quotation marks to allow the end of the quotation to blend into the narrative. Sometimes all the printer's signals of dialogue have been eliminated. And occasionally first-person narrative will swallow up dialogue to restore it as indirect discourse. The impingement of dialogue upon the narrative prose surrounding it has necessarily affected that prose over the years. At times the incongruity has been exploited for satiric effect, as in Damon Runyon where formal phrasing is imposed upon raffish diction: "Slats, I must confess I do not see Beatrice lately, but I never dream she does not provide the stone long before this as per her promise." [8] But generally the new and serious changes realism worked in dialogue necessitated an adjustment of the prose that accompanied it. In James the renovation was partial, in Mark Twain, total.

If dialogue be thought of then as a stream walled in by narrative, here and there in James we find the rhythm of the spoken word appearing in the narrative portions, emerging, for a moment, then disappearing. At other times James's dialogue flows into and through his narrative prose, so that except for the conventional marks of punctuation, it is indistinguishable from the mental monologue of his characters. At times too, one moves swiftly and without warning through various levels of narrative, passing from direct expression of speech to authorial condensation of speech, to indirect discourse and, from there further, to mental reflection (inner talk) and to authorial distillation of mental reflection. My generalizations can be illustrated by reference to a specific passage, one which appears early — 1881 — in *The Portrait of a Lady*.

Pansy has just told Isabel that her one desire in life is to marry Edward Rosier. Because of Osmond's refusal to consider the proposal, Isabel attempts to divert Pansy's feelings. After a page of dialogue, Pansy remarks:

> "No one can think of me as Mr. Rosier does; no
> one has the right."
> "Ah, but I don't admit Mr. Rosier's right." Isabel
> cried, hypocritically.

Here the direct rendition of the dialogue ceases and the narrative takes up the story.

> Pansy only gazed at her; she was evidently deeply
> puzzled; and Isabel, taking advantage of it, began
> to represent to her the miserable consequences of
> disobeying her father.

James is now summarizing Isabel's comments. It is clear that
in trying to "represent" the folly of Pansy's disobeying Osmond, Isabel is citing concrete instances, which James steps
in and condenses.

> At this Pansy stopped her, with the assurance that
> she would never disobey him, would never marry
> without his consent. And she announced, in the
> serenest, simplest tone, that though she might never
> marry Mr. Rosier, she would never cease to think
> of him.

Now James has moved to indirect discourse; we understand
Pansy to have said, approximately: "I'd never disobey Papa,
nor would I marry without his consent, but, although I may
never marry Mr. Rosier, I shall never cease to think of him."
From the authorial synthesis just preceding this segment,
James has now drawn closer to the immediacy of dialogue.

> She appeared to have accepted the idea of eternal
> singleness; but Isabel of course was free to reflect
> that she had no conception of its meaning.

When we reach the word "reflect" in the sentence, we enter
Isabel's mind. She thinks something like this: "Spinster-
hood — the child has no conception of what it means." James
has chosen to render this mental talk indirectly. The result

of this choice is formally indistinguishable from indirect verbal discourse. If we took "free to reflect" to mean that Isabel was "free to state thoughtfully," then her oral statement would still be phrased identically to her thought.

The passage continues in Isabel's mind, but then swerves, without warning, from indirect mental discourse into direct mental monologue. Still referring to Pansy:

> She was perfectly sincere; she was prepared to give up her lover.

This sentence has the familiar repeated platforms for launching successive thoughts — "she was . . . she was . . ." that we previously noted in James's dialogue. The newly developing realistic dialogue had suggested to James a way to render the mind at work. The spilling over of the colloquial manner into the narrative prose was not, of course, in itself an innovation, but the particular kind of speech characteristics accentuated in order to reform prose style were peculiar to this period. Soon enough writers recognized the disparity between the silent movements of thought and its ultimate verbalization, and (particularly in a Freudian world) fragmentary sentences and symbol-laden words have served to express the mind's erratic operation.

In this last sentence, then, James tried to reproduce Isabel's mind working. How novel his colloquial simplicity is can be felt at once by comparing this sentence with those quoted below, which complete the paragraph. James's language complicates and his phrasing becomes synthetic: "sweetness of fidelity," and "strange, exquisite intimation." There is evidence aplenty of analysis and rhetorical composition: notice the contrast set up between the lack of bitterness and the sweetness of fidelity, or the paradoxical conclusion that faithfulness is proved by refusing to marry.

> This might seem an important step toward taking another, but for Pansy, evidently, it did not lead in

that direction. She felt no bitterness towards her father; there was no bitterness in her heart; there was
only the sweetness of fidelity to Edward Rosier, and
a strange, exquisite intimation that she could prove
it better by remaining single than even by marrying
him. (ch. 45)

The very balance and organization of the conclusion demonstrate that James has summarized mental discourse — has
used his own words to state Pansy's ideas.

In the course, then, of a fairly short passage a number of
shifts in narrative manner have taken place, unsignalled and
barely perceptible. To recapitulate briefly, James began
with verbal speech and treated it (1) directly, (2) in summary, and (3) indirectly. He then entered Isabel's mind
and at the level of mental speech moved from (1) the indirect, to (2) the direct and hence colloquial, to (3) a
summary of thoughts, that is, of mental speech.[9]

This kind of detailed scrutiny is needed to show how James
began to adjust his narrative prose to harmonize with his dialogue. His prose flowed over bounds, now recording talk, now
summarizing it, now recording thought, now summarizing it;
and as I have said before, were it not for the punctuation and
some slight syntactical clues, one could not distinguish the
tongue's utterance from the mind's flow. This is more acutely
the case with James than with most of his contemporaries because in his work a single tone already informs the whole.
James is always present (even when he is most scrupulously
absent), animating his characters with his sensibility. Those
characters are not puppets by any means, any more than
Becky Sharp is, but they all are fragments of the parent or-
ganism. And because they are emanations of the experience
James absorbed and transformed, the prose with which they
are created necessarily reflects his controlling will. On the
bread-and-butter level of technique this means that almost
all of James's later prose would be a form of talk: his talk, his

characters' talk, his characters' inner talk: narrative, dialogue, rumination. James's late work is particularly marked by colloquial signs such as simple words, repeated words, parallel structures, emphasis by italics, emphasis by punctuation, and discursiveness. James never went the way Mark Twain did, but for a while his accomplishments paralleled Mark Twain's; and for Gertrude Stein his direction was to be crucial.

How close James came to extended colloquial narrative can be measured by considering a stretch of his interior monologue. None is better for the purpose than Isabel's famous nocturnal brooding by her fireside. Here one discovers a qualified version of the mind's talk. The words are not those of the author weaving his pattern carefully and at his leisure, nor, to speak of opposites, do the words partake of the staggered rhythms of extreme colloquial speech — its grasping for vocabulary, its pauses and rests, its unspoken phrases expressed by dashes and ellipses. James expresses Isabel's thoughts in a blend of formal and colloquial elements. A silent parley takes place within her mind, and however smooth the phrases may be made by the monitoring author, they are nonetheless set to a colloquial rhythm. The interlocking pattern of repetition is revealing here. Isabel ascends as on the rungs of a ladder from thought to thought on repeated phrases. Here then is a portion of that long meditation with capitals imposed to emphasize the repetition.

> SHE COULD LIVE it over again, the incredulous terror with which she had taken the measure of her dwelling. Between those four walls SHE HAD LIVED ever since; they were to surround her for the rest of her life. It was THE HOUSE OF darkness, THE HOUSE OF dumbness, THE HOUSE OF suffocation. OSMOND'S BEAUTIFUL MIND gave it neither light nor air; OSMOND'S BEAUTIFUL MIND, indeed seemed to peep down from a small high window and mock at her.

Of course it was not PHYSICAL SUFFERING; for PHYS-
ICAL SUFFERING there might have been a remedy. She
could come and go; she had her liberty; her husband was perfectly polite. HE TOOK HIMSELF SO SERI-
OUSLY; it was something appalling. UNDER ALL HIS
culture, HIS cleverness, HIS amenity, UNDER HIS good-
nature, HIS facility, HIS knowledge of life, HIS ego-
tism lay hidden like a serpent in a bank of flowers.
SHE HAD TAKEN HIM SERIOUSLY, but SHE HAD NOT
TAKEN HIM SO SERIOUSLY as that. How could she —
especially when she knew him better? SHE WAS TO
THINK OF HIM AS HE THOUGHT OF HIMSELF — as the
first gentleman of Europe. So it was that SHE HAD
THOUGHT OF HIM at first, and that indeed was the
reason she had married him. (ch. 42, capitals added)

It is a delicate question, probably unanswerable, as to how
much of the repetition occurring in this passage derives from
conventional rhetoric — as in the accumulated triplets — and
how much is a modification of the mind talking to itself.
There is no question, though, that a direct relation exists between this repetition and that which appears in James's dialogue. To this extent we shall be safe in agreeing with Ezra
Pound that "Of all exquisite writers James is the most colloquial," [10] and in claiming that James introduced important
elements of colloquial rhythm into American prose style.

To open any James novel after *The Portrait of a Lady* is to
find the surface of the narrative composed of a modified colloquialism not much different in kind from Isabel's medita-
tions. This surface in turn harks back to James's innovations
in dialogue. More important, this generalization holds true
even when the narrative is not concerned with a meditative
scene, such as Isabel by the fireside. James admitted elements
of the colloquial into his disciplined, urbane narrative style,
and then set about to complicate the received elements. In
other words James's prose gradually permitted itself to be
guided by the mind talking to itself. James stylized the mind's

verbal patterns, but not in the direction of slick, superficial clarity. His stylization centered around those repeated phrases that establish psychological distinctions, and those syntactically awkward additions that I have taken to be representative of the mind building its responses in time. For example, this description of Milly Theale from *The Wings of the Dove* helps to establish the continuity as well as the change in James's style over the twenty-year period that had intervened since the writing of *The Portrait of a Lady*.

> It was New York mourning, it was New York hair, it was a New York history, confused as yet, but multitudinous, of the loss of parents, brothers, sisters, almost every human appendage, all on a scale and with a sweep that had required the greater stage; it was a New York legend of affecting, of romantic isolation, and, beyond everything, it was by most accounts, in respect to the mass of money so piled on the girl's back, a set of New York possibilities. She was alone, she was stricken, she was rich, and, in particular, she was strange — a combination in itself of a nature to engage Mrs. Stringham's attention. (ch. 5)

The one important stylistic aspect of James's devoted, lifelong exercise yet to be discussed appears in the quotation just cited. Phrases are cut off with unusual regularity by the punctuation, so that the reader is forced to move in stages along the lines, to halt, absorb, and then move on. Instead of flowing through the reader's consciousness, this prose moves in bursts of energy. The mind is forced to accept the phrase in itself, barred off temporarily from the remainder of the sentence. Such a habit may be regarded as no more than a lamentable experiment, one effective but costly way of breaking up the monotony of a bland surface. But I am inclined to think that it derives from an attempt on James's part to reproduce an effect based upon the accents of the speaking voice. The speaker must formulate his ideas in discrete units and is obliged to correct and supplement his perceptions even as he speaks. We have already seen James using a modified version of colloquiality in representing Isabel's mind at work by the fire. When he tried to modify his narrative medium (through which as we have seen both mental and verbal discourse was already intimately threaded) he then developed the rougher side of speech. An extreme example of this appears in that thoroughly experimental book, *What Maisie Knew* (1897). The stuttering punctuation can be seen clearly.

> Mama's roof,    however,    had its turn,    this time,   for the child,   of appearing but remotely contingent,    so that,   to reassure her,    there was scarcely a need of her companion's secret,    solemnly confided —    the probability there would be no going back to mama at all.[11]

The mind, I suppose, does not think exactly this way, which is why I say that James stylized his assumptions of how the mind does work. Moving from a modified interior monologue, he worked out this spurting style. It is to his credit that eventually he discarded such oddness, or rather that he combined it with repetition in order to achieve a complexly rhythmic prose. But once he had discovered this radical punctuation he never gave it up altogether. Its special importance for the present study is that it represents one more emphasis upon words — as themselves, or in intimate tandem. One cannot help but be struck by the clots of words, and interested in their relationships (only idly and faintly now perhaps, but Gertrude Stein is just over the horizon).

This example from *What Maisie Knew* appears directed primarily by stylistic considerations. While he was learning, though, James sometimes managed to let organic purpose shape his style. In the same book he worked out successful

instances of emphasis through isolation. He wrote, for example, that Maisie was intended by her parents to

> serve their anger and seal their revenge, for husband
> and wife had been alike crippled by the heavy hand
> of justice, which in the last resort met on neither
> side their indignant claim to get, as they called it,
> everything. (pp. 18–19)

James's technique focuses our attention on the commonplace
word "everything," so that our emotional response to the
overlay of irony in this ugly human situation fills that word
with meaning. Adherence to a consistent rule of punctuation in this book would have demanded that the long sequence of words preceding "as they called it" be thoroughly
punctuated (as in the earlier example from *What Maisie
Knew*) so that it would read something like this:

> . . . which, in the last resort, met, on neither side,
> **their indignant** claim to get, as they called it, every-
> thing.

So done, however, the sardonic pressure on "everything"
would have been dissipated in the pulsation of syntax preceding it. There is no doubt from an example like this that
James did consciously experiment with new ways to enliven
his narrative prose.

Just such experimentation helps to explain the curious
phrasing of the last line of *The Wings of the Dove*. No one
can have failed to notice the slightly awkward construction of
Kate's last words: "We shall never be again as we were." The
phrasing is a little off balance, and yet this happens in the
concluding line of a very long and complex novel written by
a novelist unusually sensitive in matters of style and at the
very height of his powers. Further, when the book was
revised several years after its original publication, the rhythmic bump stayed in. How could James have overlooked the
fault? The answer, of course, is that he did not overlook it,

but wrote the sentence deliberately. At least two reasons for it are discoverable. First, inasmuch as the thematic idea of the enduring mark of experience is embodied in the phrase "as we were," James naturally found it felicitous to conclude on that note. Assuming that it is most effectively placed at the end of the sentence and book, we can discover by a little experimentation what alternatives were available to James, still using the same set of words.

> We never shall again be as we were.

This is too clumsy to merit serious consideration. But here are two other possibilities.

> We shall never again be as we were.
> Never again shall we be as we were.

These two versions conform to more normal patterns of colloquial phrasing. But their fault is that they set a small, single-syllabled word next to the key phrase "as we were." Composed itself of three small words, the phrase is not sufficiently differentiated from the rest of the sentence. Precede it with "again" as James did — "We shall never be again as we were" — and the phrase achieves minimal but sufficient isolation to subsist by itself without being formally broken off by something so direct, and in this case melodramatic, as a dash. There are visual, aural, and conceptual reasons for this. Visually, four small units tend to be swept together by the reading eye, as in the version, "again be as we were." Aurally, the accent on "-gain" makes a natural, perceptible division before one encounters the crucial phrase. And conceptually, the mind will relate "be as we were" as an integral phrase much more readily than it can or will "again as we were."

The second motive for James to arrange his line with a slight jar in it was to make its meaning stick with the reader. Inversions, odd conjunctions of words, syntax set slightly awry, these were all devices James employed to bring his prose — composed as it was of ordinary diction — alive. A rich variety of these effects appears in that concluding passage from *The Wings of the Dove* quoted in full on pages 90–91. Adverbs and predicate adjectives precede their nouns and verbs: "Kate gravely wound up," "she gravely shook her head," "Prompt was his own clearness," "Strange it was for him," "Then he only said." Adjectives are repeated in different, unconventional ways: "Her high grasp," "She made a high gesture," "a slow strangeness," and "Strange it was for him." Finally, the components of the last clause before the final line of dialogue are very unusual: "and her headshake was now the end." The formation "headshake" is abrupt and queer, and the placement of "now" immediately after the verb "was" is unsettling, for it rattles the sense of time, combining a verb in the past tense with an adverb denoting the present. This was, after all, a condition easily muffled by adjusting the structure of the clause a little: "and now her headshake was the end."

But that would be to betray James's intention. As the evidence demonstrates, he was using all of the stylistic resources available to him in order to project more life into his abstract prose. By breaking up familiar constructions, interrupting lulling rhythms, placing words in odd contexts, repeating and isolating them, James indicated his refusal to carry the reader down a placid stream of words. At the same time, by emphasizing the individual word or phrase, James ran the risk of abusing his reader's attention, and often did so, either because his syntax was insufficiently dynamic to carry the reader through to the end of the thought; or because the reader fell into a stupefied contemplation of the phrase and neglected to continue. This is, I think, one of the reasons readers often abandon their initial attempts to read the later James. Yet using some of these same devices with concrete diction, Ernest Hemingway achieved popular recognition, because the reader is less likely to drift when anchored to matter.

If I am correct about James though, he reached a point of radical punctuation by first working out a careful literary approximation of the spoken word. He then transferred some of his techniques in dialogue to the expression of the thoughts of his characters. Finally, he abstracted some of these effects and incorporated them into his own narrative prose. By this time, James's motive appears to have been primarily aesthetic rather than realistic. He found the fragmentation, stress, and repetition he derived from colloquial rhythms useful to strengthen and variegate a prose of almost unrelieved abstraction and attenuation.

### III

Henry James imported instances of the colloquial into his style, then exaggerated, emphasized, and otherwise worked them until he arrived at his own distinctively idiomatic blend. When Mark Twain wrote *Huckleberry Finn,* he moved directly into colloquial country to build his prose from local materials. I have suggested that, rather than being varied to accommodate the peculiarities of his characters, James's dialogue is fairly uniform and that his subject matter is predominantly abstract states of mind rather than concrete things in action. So his prose more readily drew attention to its surface than did Mark Twain's. Nonetheless, both men produced significantly similar results in form, such as the already observed examples of repetition and variation in their prose, as well as their shared preoccupation with the individual word.

Mark Twain especially was sensitive to particulars since, joined one by one, they formed his world. He had no very strong sense of the grand design. As Edgar Branch put it, Twain's "genius was for the particular, not for the abstract or the organizational. Like Walt Whitman he was a caresser of discrete experience." [12] His care for the individual detail made him seek the right word for the specific occasion. If anything, Henry James gives one the impression that no word is right for the evocation of a unique situation, and in a relativistic world he was correct. In his struggle to bridge the gap between words and experience, James threw out many lines. He groped like a blind man, feeling the contours of experience, now from this angle, now from that. Unable to say "elephant" with any certainty, he located the pillar legs, the snaky trunk, the ropey tail, the houselike body, and the leafy ears, leaving the reader with an impression that cannot be summarized, however powerfully it is felt. Mark Twain, however, thought that the thing could be named and its parts as well. For him the imaginative pen had to remain the servant of the accurate eye. In his arraignment of Cooper, Mark Twain made the point succinctly.

> If Cooper had been an observer his inventive faculty would have worked better; not more interestingly, but more rationally, more plausibly. Cooper's proudest creations in the way of 'situations' suffer noticeably from the absence of the observer's protecting gift. Cooper's eye was splendidly inaccurate. Cooper seldom saw anything correctly. He saw nearly all things as through a glass eye, darkly. [13]

For Mark Twain the relationship between word and thing, symbol and referent, was unusually direct. He ignored metaphysical dispute and assumed a right word could be found, not mechanically, but artistically: almost musically. This side of his credo also appears in the critique of Cooper.

> Cooper's word-sense was singularly dull. When a person has a poor ear for music he will flat and sharp right along without knowing it. He keeps near the tune, but it is *not* the tune. When a person has

> a poor ear for words, the result is a literary flatting
> and sharping; you perceive what he is intending to
> say, but you also perceive that he doesn't say it. This
> is Cooper. He was not a word-musician. His ear was
> satisfied with the *approximate* word. (p. 593)

Mark Twain's literary integrity, displayed in such offhand
remarks, approximates in its way the aestheticism of Flaubert, for which Henry James was the American representative. On the other hand, Mark Twain established the *mot
juste* by somewhat different standards from those used by
Flaubert. Twain first sought harmony between words and
felt experience and let the surface relations in his prose follow naturally. That is, he judged the correctness of his writing by comparing it with what he saw (is this description
accurate?) and with what he heard (is this how it was said?),
rather than by concentrating on the verbal relationships
as they developed on the page before him. Such a rationale
explains his characteristic defense of a colloquial phrase:
" 'Pretty much' may not be elegant English, but it is high
time it was. There is no elegant word or phrase which means
just what it means." [14] And it equally illuminates his comment on repetition: "In English, when we have used a word
a couple of times in a paragraph, we imagine we are growing
tautological, and so we are weak enough to exchange it for
some other word which only approximates exactness to escape what we wrongly fancy is a greater blemish. Repetition
may be bad, but surely inexactness is worse." [15] Mark
Twain's modified literary sans-culottism says fidelity to experience comes first, beauty second.

Honesty in words was a lifelong obsession with Mark
Twain. In his last years he was convinced that he was dictat-
ing such shrivelling truths into his autobiography that it
could only be published posthumously. His ideal was say it
out without artifice, and we can trace a common line from
Mark Twain to Gertrude Stein and her preoccupation with

"things as they are," to Hemingway and his search to recreate "the way it was." Although he delivers it amiably enough, there is a sharp edge to Huck's observation in *Tom Sawyer Abroad* that "the finer a person talks the certainer it is to make you sleep." [16] He is referring to Tom, who is notably glib and fanciful, and given to putting on "style." More than once Huck incisively criticizes the quality of Tom's stories. "I judged that all that stuff was only just one of Tom Sawyer's lies" (ch. 3). Here Huck's voice is identical with Mark Twain's. He once contemptuously projected Tom into manhood as he discussed in a letter to William Dean Howells his thoughts upon the completion of *Tom Sawyer*. "I perhaps made a mistake in not writing it in the first person," Mark Twain reflected. "If I went on, now, and took him into manhood, he would just lie like all the one-horse men in literature. . . . By and by I shall take a boy of twelve and run him on through life (in the first person) but not Tom Sawyer — he would not be a good character for it." [17] At this point in his career Mark Twain was obviously not satisfied either with Tom Sawyer or with himself as narrator for a new book.

Mark Twain admitted that the literary experience was not essentially a constructive one for him, but re-constructive. "Words realize nothing, vivify nothing to you," he wrote in *Connecticut Yankee,* "unless you have suffered in your own person the thing which the words try to describe" (XIV, 278). In "That Day in Eden" he was even more emphatic about the experiential foundation of literary communication. "Things which are outside of our orbit — our own particular world — things which by our constitution and equipment we are unable to see, or feel, or otherwise experience — *cannot be made comprehensible to us in words.*" [18] To this extent then Mark Twain was identical with Huck, and when Mark Twain decided to express his experience in Huck's voice, the American vernacular that had long been lapping at the top of the restraining dike surged over the quotation marks to flood his narrative with new and muddy life. What Huck sees and does is relived experience for Mark Twain in a way that fiction rarely is for Henry James, who even shied away from hearing the end of an anecdote, lest it contradict his private elaboration of its terms.

Oddly and yet appropriately enough, one of James's own stretches of theorizing helps to explain the success of Mark Twain's decision to speak as Huck. In his preface to *The Princess Casamassima* — a book published in 1886, about a year after *Huckleberry Finn* — James noted that "clearness and concreteness constantly depend, for any pictorial whole, on some *concentrated* individual notation of them." Referring to his novel specifically, he added, "That notation goes forward here in the mind of little Hyacinth, immensely quickened by the fact of its so mattering to his very life what he does make of things." [19] That the perceptions of Huck and Hyacinth are different no one could fail to agree, but it is equally certain that James's analysis goes a long way to explain the revelatory powers of Huck's idiom.

For it is Huck's concentrated observation of the world around him that allows him to express himself so acutely. Both his youth and his lack of sophistication contribute to his concentration. His immaturity and the necessary limitations of his brief life make his perception of a material world vivid, unencumbered, immediate. Huck does not normally see through a haze of acquired social attitudes, for as yet he has barely acquired any. When he does, as in his contradictory responses toward Jim, the purity of his inner light is still sufficient to pierce the haze. Nor is Huck's vision blurred by preoccupation with professional matters. He is still a free agent and can see a horse, for example, as a horse, undistorted by the special interest of a farmer, a trader, a smith, or a tanner. In short, Huck is disengaged.

The second source of Huck's remarkable clarity lies in the

fact that his environment is his only business. In James's words, his vision is "immensely quickened by the fact of its so mattering to his very life what he does make of things." Abroad in a hostile world of adults, unprepared by experience for what might happen next, but already sufficiently marked to be cautious and pessimistic, Huck lives in an almost unrelieved state of alert. His accounts come to us with the laconic tautness of battlefield reports. He sees with the intensity of one threatened when the steamboat drives his raft under; of one horrified in the Boggs episode; of one enraptured when the lady bareback riders perform. And it is to the particulars of his world that Huck pays the most attention. He is a brooder, a worrier, and an occasional talker, but he is not notably a thinker. His powers of generalization are almost nil. If these characteristics seem to apply to Huck's creator almost as well as they do to Huck himself, then they suggest how closely Huck's mask fitted Mark Twain.

No less important than Huck's personality is the source of his diction and his syntactical rhythms, for both supplement and extend the clarity of his narrative. If Joseph Warren Beach can properly describe the diction of James's characters as being without "any tincture of solecism, dialect or localism unless it be those of London," and add, "They speak, almost without exception . . . the purest of London drawingroom slang," [20] then in contrast it can be said that Mark Twain's characters in *Huckleberry Finn* speak several variations of what we may take to be the purest of Missouri small-town slang, for which Huck provides the norm. In a sense, despite his insistence in the prefatory note that he had "painstakingly" worked out seven varieties of dialect, Mark Twain is open to the charge of having writ no language. After an examination of Mark Twain's revisions of *Huckleberry Finn,* Sydney Krause remarked, "In order that it might *count,* he had to use dialect judiciously, and the same was true of his colloquial diction at large and his illiterate grammar. Twain regularized his grammar almost as often as he changed from the standard to the illiterate forms." [21]

Mark Twain, of course, always mediated between whatever inner voice he could hear speaking as Huck and the written expression of it. Sometimes he faltered — on the side of formality in "We shot a water-fowl now and then," or of strain in the parody of Shakespeare (chs. 12, 21). By and large though, *Huckleberry Finn* maintains a consistent tone. The language is interesting in itself and at the same time capable of vividly evoking the life of the novel. Reading the book, one is constantly moving between absorption in the action itself and pleasurable examination of the words that convey the story.

Mark Twain's conscious importation of words new to the literary context, his invention of dialectical oddities, his placement of familiar words in unfamiliar situations, his isolation of words through strings of co-ordinating conjunctions, his high-spirited word-play, his repetitions of sounds, his choice (if it can be called that) of words through apparently unconscious association — all these stylistic activities inevitably stressed the individual verbal unit, whether a phrase, a single word, or a part of one.

The opening of the king's speech at Peter Wilks's house furnishes an example. The king's words are florid, full of spurious rhetoric in the beginning, and tinged with illiterate usage. As such they successfully represent the fraudulent confidenceman at work.

> "Friends all, my poor brother that lays yonder, has done generous by them that's left behind in the vale of sorrers. He has done generous by these-'yer poor little lambs that he loved and sheltered, and that's left fatherless and motherless." (ch. 25)

As the king grows absorbed in his task following these opening lines, he lapses into rich linguistic barbarities, but considering his first words alone, we find that only one important word has been spelled phonetically — sorrers, that is, sorrows. The malformation usefully suggests dialect, but there is more to it than that. In context "sorrers" appears among references to friends, brothers, fathers, and mothers. The inevitable connotation then is to "sister," or "soror." The situation fully supports this apparently gratuitous suggestion, for now only three mourning sisters are left in the Wilks house, Mary Jane, Susan, and Joanna. This house is indeed "a vale of sorrers." Corroborating evidence of Mark Twain's interest at this time in etymology occurs a few paragraphs later as the king develops an elaborate etymological explanation of his reference to funeral "orgies" rather than "obsequies." "Orgies is better, because it means the thing you're after, more exact. It's a word that's made up out'n the Greek *orgo*, outside, open, abroad; and the Hebrew *jeesum*, to plant, cover up; hence in*ter*. So, you see, funeral orgies is an open er public funeral." [22]

One cannot insist too much on the verbal quality of *Huckleberry Finn*. When Huck concludes his story by saying,

> But I reckon I got to light out for the Territory ahead of the rest, because Aunt Sally she's going to adopt me and sivilize me and I can't stand it. I been there before.[23]

Huck has of course been in that situation before: not only in deed, but in words as well. On the first page Huck had told us that

> The Widow Douglas, she took me for her son, and allowed she would sivilize me; but it was rough living in the house all the time, considering how dismal regular and decent the widow was in all her ways; and so when I couldn't stand it no longer, I lit out.

Three terms appear in both passages: "sivilize," "can't stand it," and "light out." Although some of the efforts to make *Huckleberry Finn* a unified book seem strained, here is evi-

dence of significant verbal repetition at the two extremes of
the book. Such verbal echoes sound repeatedly throughout,
crossing and reviving, so that one is always faintly aware of
the book's music.[24]

Mark Twain contrived his verbal resonance in a variety of
ways. One of the simplest has already been indicated: the use
of dialectical variations of familiar words, as in the duet between Huck and Jim. This needs little expansion, except to
point out instances where dialect enlarges a word's potential
for multiple meaning. For example, when Jim describes the
face of the dead man in the floating house as "gashly," there
is an addition to meaning in this dialectal version of "ghastly"
(ch. 9). A more extended, virtually surrealistic version of
this kind of thing occurs in Mrs. Hotchkiss's monologue in
chapter 41. It is based on the observation that the colloquial
voice moves by means of partial recapitulation. Repetitions,
like kennings, afford the mind time to work up verbal ex-
tensions and variations of the central idea. In this monologue Mark Twain produces a spasmodic speech which at
the same time moves the reader through a whirlwind of
changes played upon two words: "nigger" (again) and
"crazy," plus various aspects of the verbal notation, "I says."

> Well, Sister Phelps, I've ransacked that-air cabin
> over an' I b'lieve the NIGGER was CRAZY. I SAYS so to
> Sister Damrell — didn't I, Sister Damrell? — s'I,
> he's CRAZY, s'I — them's the very words I SAID. You
> all hearn me; he's CRAZY, s'I; everything shows it, s'I.
> Look at that-air grind-stone, s'I; want to tell *me*'t
> any cretur 'ts in his right mind's agoin' to scrabble
> all them CRAZY things onto a grindstone, s'I? Here
> sich 'n' sich a person busted his heart; 'n' here so-
> 'n'so pegged along for thirty-seven year, 'n' all that
> — natcherl son o' Louis somebody, 'n' sich ever-
> last'n rubbage. He's plumb CRAZY, s'I; it's what I
> SAYS in the fust place, it's what I SAYS in the middle,

'n' it's what I SAYS last 'n' all the time — the NIG-
GER'S CRAZY — CRAZY's Nebokoodneezer, s'I. (capitals added)

In this amazing verbal display Mrs. Hotchkiss, Huck, and
Mark Twain are all very much aware that it is a *said* piece, as
the weird repetitions of "s'I," the claim "them's the very
words I said," and near the end the tripartite insistence that
she, the speaker, has never ceased saying the same thing at any
time all indicate. Isolated by dashes, Mrs. Hotchkiss's
original judgment is triumphantly reasserted finally — "the
nigger's crazy" — and then comes a comic explosion of sound,
"Nebokoodneezer." This is verbal inventiveness of a very high
order, for it holds carefully to a realistic line while at the
same time it builds, shapes, and orders the words to draw
from them their strongest effect.

Orthographical distortion was not, as we have seen,
original with Mark Twain; he worked out of an established
American tradition. But as Bernard DeVoto remarked, "The
orthography of humor . . . must be distinguished from the
American language. In the misspellings of Artemus Ward and
Josh Billings, for instance, there is no attempt to render
speech, still less to record the habit or personality of thought,
but only to produce the laughter of incongruity." [25] Mark
Twain is more inventive than that. Nothing could be
more appropriate than that a lady of the Bible Belt should
call up Nebuchadnezzar, the Babylonian infidel, as a comparison for Jim. Even her mistaken pronunciation has realistic integrity, for "Nebo" was the mountain from which
Moses saw the Promised Land, and Mrs. Hotchkiss's confusion of the two Levantine names is altogether believable.

This passage also indicates yet another way in *Huckleberry
Finn* in which the reader's attention was brought to the individual word, its composition, and its relation to the words in
company. When one of the criteria for literary composition is
realistic accuracy, then each word is subject to scrutiny and

tested mentally. The good writer, however, tries not to abuse the reader's attention by forcing it into incessant surface activity, as in the Uncle Remus stories, whose orthography may be an excellent guide to oral reading, but which makes silent reading arduous. He chooses the moments when he will nudge the reader. As Mark Twain well knew, such selectivity generates more power than does an overwhelming reproduction of verbal effects.

Again and again we are struck by terms that have an imaginative life of their own off the page: "if I could tip her the wink," "now for the grand bulge," "I let go all holts then," "don't you deffersit *me* no more deffersits, long's *you* live," "I knowed better than to move another peg," "we had a long gabble," and "I found him roosting on the bitts, forward" (chs. 29, 39, 33, 30, 16, 30, 13). These figurative expressions are like streaks of brilliant color in the narrative stream and they call for our appreciation as well as interpretation.

If emphasis upon the individual word results when dialectically distorted words are placed in a familiar context, so does it when familiar words are used for unconventional purposes. Slang expressions sometimes work this way, as when Huck says that after the Royal Nonesuch performance he expects that the audience will give the king "a gaudy time of it" (ch. 23). More often it is Huck's stimulated imagination that produces unexpected and, from a purist's point of view, unwarranted combinations of words. Their high imaginative order, however, is warrant enough. Running from the graveyard in a thunderstorm, Huck says the lightning occurs in "now-and-then glares" (ch. 29). Or as he is being quizzed by the harelipped girl at the Wilks house, Huck is asked a particularly pointed question, and remarks, "I see I was up a stump. I had to let on to get choked with a chicken-bone, so as to get time to think how to get down again." After he has painfully worked his way "out of the woods again," he is trapped once more. Then a truncated metaphor emerges, which, although consonant with past remarks, makes an odd and very distinctive clause: "I see I was up a stump again, so I played another chicken-bone and got another think" (ch. 26). This fanciful verbal structure gives "think" substance and uses the chicken-bone as if it were a card in a poker game — aptly, since Huck is at this moment gambling.

Mark Twain is usually prepared to invest words with new meaning. Tom Sawyer's description of the coat-of-arms he proposes for Jim is exemplary. Mark Twain takes words from the terminology of heraldry that have only the thinnest patina of meaning for most readers and then lays irrelevant, yet pertinent connotations over them. His most successful improvisation is "Crest, a runaway nigger, *sable,* with his bundle over his shoulder on a bar sinister; and a couple of gules for supporters, which is you and me" (ch. 38). Even "gules" (mispronounced) has a phonetic accuracy for the kind of boys who introduce snakes, spiders, and rats into Jim's cabin-prison.

And only acknowledgment of Mark Twain's conscious verbal adroitness can explain the inventive delirium of Huck's description of where he is to stay while at the Wilks house. There is no strain to it, the diction is completely natural, and yet the combination achieved has a flourish of nonsense. "Up garret," says Huck in a curious initial abbreviation, "was a little cubby, with a pallet in it. The king said the cubby would do for his valley — meaning me" (ch. 26).

Mark Twain sets up such play when he can, but he always builds out of his characters' normal diction. The surface of his prose is littered with queer ore quarried from Huck's mine. A melodeum is "pretty skreeky," a watchman refuses to be bribed by "spondulicks," Huck "smouches" a spoon, he has "clayey" clothes, and he notices "shackly" houses; he speaks of an undertaker's "softy soothering ways," and to him a thunder clap is a "sockdolager"; Colonel Grangerford is said to have no "frivolishness" about him; and another man

has a "startlish" way; after the duke "hove a sigh," the king
inquired what he was "alassing about"; and when an imagi-
nary horse-ferry bumps a real steamboat wreck, Huck describes the action by saying it "saddlebaggsed" on the wreck;
he guts a catfish by "haggling" it open with a saw; and finally
he says that a certain surprise would make "most anybody
sqush," by which he means "squshed down like a bluff bank
that the river has cut under" (chs. 27, 13, 37, 2, 21, 27, 20,
18, 13, 19, 13, 8, 29).

The effect of these words — dialect, nonce, slang — is that
of poetry. Carrying expository meaning, they flash out with a
light unique for prose. They are employed less to build an
effect cumulatively, more to make an effect immediately.
And they contribute to the gradually accumulating feeling in
American literature for the importance of the single word,
for verbal independence.

Huck's grammatical mistakes also serve to re-enforce potentially flat statements. The melodious jar of incorrect grammar catches the reader in "I been there before," and "There
set pap — his own self!" (chs. 43, 4). Both are significantly
the last words of chapters. The formulation of the past tense
on a present base increases the sense of immediacy. "We
catched a little section of a lumber-raft," and "I'd got to de-
cide, forever, betwixt two things, and I knowed it" (chs. 9,
31). Mark Twain augmented the life that he derived from
fresh diction by means of syntactical manipulation not very
different in kind from James's. Mark Twain's initial desire
was, as always, to approximate the accents of the speaking
voice in prose. He then refined the conventions he had established, especially when they heightened a dramatic point.
While Huck's pap is sleeping off an attack of delirium tre-
mens, Huck sits down with a gun "to wait for him to stir."
With that tableau the chapter ends — the father (who has already tried to kill his son with a clasp-knife) resting so he can
finish the job; the boy watching, with a loaded gun pointed

at his father. Huck's comment finishes the chapter: "And how slow and still the time did drag along" (ch. 6). The ticking one-syllable units of this sentence, with its periphrastic verb maintaining the rhythm, mark the heavy pulse beat of Huck's shocked sensibility. At the same time the monotony of the iambic rhythm expresses Huck's growing fatigue, and when the next chapter begins — " 'Git up! What you 'bout!' " — Huck is discovered asleep.

Earlier I pointed out that by using radical punctuation Henry James divided his sentence into a series of spasmodic units. I suggested that this technique was derived from an attempt to reproduce the way a mind thinks. James's concern for psychological imitation determined the punctuation of this typical sentence: "With time, actually — for the impression but deepened — this sense of the contrast, to the advantage of Merton Densher, became a sense of relief, and that, in turn, a sense of escape" (ch. 30). A similar divisiveness or fragmenting tendency appears in Mark Twain. His prose attentively marks each block of perception rather than blending them all into a fluid, synthetic compound. Huck's vision, that is, is direct and linear. Unlike, say, Dos Passos' impressionistically flooded Camera Eye, Huck's moves deliberately from object to object and detail to detail and his report of what he sees is rarely impeded by reflective considerations. The objects are enumerated in lists, lists not punctuated solely by the discreet turn of a comma at the base of the line, but by a chain of co-ordinating conjunctions. Huck's images, like a series of slides thrown upon a screen, come into focus in a succession of isolated moments. He observes, for example, that the gardens of Arkansas appear to contain only

> jimpsom weeds, and sunflowers, and ash-piles, and old curled-up boots and shoes, and pieces of bottles, and rags, and played-out tin-ware. (ch. 21)

The peculiar vividness of these objects, these *words,* is due in part to what they are and in part to how they are presented. They follow one another, undisturbed by commentary, indignation, uplift, or disgust. Without the mediation of "and" such lists would create a more confused and jumbled impression:

> jimpsom weeds, sunflowers, ash-piles, old curled-up boots and shoes, pieces of bottles, rags, and played-out tin-ware.

That has the frenetic sound of a Dickens catalogue. With the "ands" in place, each object emerges clearly as if Huck were again contemplating them one at a time. True, Mark Twain the writer makes an implicit judgment of the Arkansas householders when he enumerates the contents of their gardens, but Huck only sees. He is one kind of a camera.

There is some point to considering more closely Mark Twain's devices for separating objects. He uses the conjunction "and" and the comma throughout the book, mostly for the sake of rhythm, but also to separate and concentrate each item more fully than commas alone could do. An index of Mark Twain's care in punctuating appears in the series of compound nouns in the last cited passage. "Jimpsom weeds" is made two words (as it is not in the later editions of the novel), "sunflowers" is a single word, and "ash-piles" and "tin-ware" are hyphenated. Since usage never has absolute rules for compounds, Mark Twain must have made at least some semi-conscious decision about the punctuation of each. One scholar who worked closely with Twain's vocabulary pointed out that "he was careful in matters of minor detail, spelling, and punctuation, and insisted on accuracy in his printed works." [26] Another reported that when Mark Twain was "correcting proof on *Pudd'nhead,* he discovered that his punctuation had been tampered with — 'my punctuation

which I had deeply thought out and laboriously perfected!'
— and he demanded its restoration." [27]

The same tools of punctuation and conjunction are used to
mark off units of time. The following list demonstrates the
subtle pulsations of emphasis and grouping Mark Twain
could manage. Especially is this the case in the spate of
things contained in the reticule, and in the lapse of time indicated by the semi-colon near the end of the sentence.

> We got an old tin lantern,
> and a butcher knife without any handle,
> and a bran-new Barlow knife worth two bits in any
>    store,
> and a lot of tallow candles,
> and a tin candlestick,
> and a gourd,
> and a tin cup,
> and a ratty old bed-quilt off the bed,
> and a reticule with needles and pins and beeswax
>    and buttons and thread and all such truck in it,
> and a hatchet and some nails,
> and a fish-line as thick as my little finger,
> with some monstrous hooks on it,
> and a roll of buckskin,
> and a leather dog-collar,
> and a horse-shoe,
> and some vials of medicine that didn't have no label
>    on them;
> and just as we was leaving I found a tolerable good
>    curry-comb,
> and Jim he found a ratty old fiddle-bow,
> and a wooden leg. (ch. 9)

Normally the objects Huck sees are minimally qualified.
This habit clears, as it were, the area surrounding each noun,
so that it can be viewed as a self-sufficient integer. Mark
Twain once wryly spoke of editing manuscripts for young au-

thors by "removing unnecessary flowers and digging up some acres of adjective-stumps." [28]

Rather than by adjectives the objects Huck sees are more often qualified by clauses and participial phrases whose expressions of direct action better suit his literal mind. The lady bareback riders strike Huck serially.

> Every lady with a lovely complexion, and perfectly beautiful, and looking just like a gang of real sure-enough queens, and dressed in clothes that cost millions of dollars, and just littered with diamonds. (ch. 17)

Huck's remembering mind lays in these details one after the other without any urge toward subordination. The ladies have lovely complexions which partially explains the observation that they are beautiful; this judgment is augmented then by their regal dress, which is in turn explained as being expensive and complemented with diamonds. The relationship of these details is generally clear, but it is not formally established. Loose sentences like this one both focus greater attention on the component details and accumulate a series of individual responses such as the periodic sentence cannot: as if Mark Twain had written

> Perfectly beautiful ladies with lovely complexions, who, dressed in their million-dollar clothes littered with diamonds, looked like a collection of queens.

Supplementing the illusion of substance given to nouns by their isolation and emphasis are two minor but important techniques. The first is the extensive use of directional prepositions. Huck always tells the reader where *he* is, and then locates the other important objects in the landscape in relation to that central point. This scrupulously accurate sense of place confers substantiality by limiting and thereby filling space.

> We went tiptoeing ALONG a path AMONGST the
> trees BACK TOWARDS the end of the widow's garden,
> stooping DOWN so as the branches wouldn't scrape
> our heads. When we was passing BY the kitchen I
> fell OVER a root and made a noise. We scrouched
> DOWN and laid still. (ch. 2, capitals added)

If its directional guidance is felt, at the same time the prepositional movement sets up a sensible rhythm in the prose.
Huck tells us,

> I went UP and set DOWN ON a log at the head of the
> island, and looked OUT ON the big river and the black
> driftwood and AWAY OVER to the town three mile
> away. . . . (ch. 7, capitals added)

Kinesthesia is encouraged by the frequent juxtoposition of
two prepositions, as "back towards," "out on," and "away
over."

Kinesthetic suggestion is similarly encouraged by the frequent use of present participles in Huck's prose. In their evocation of an action taking place and enduring, while the
speaker prepares his next unit of statement, the participial
endings "-ing" are much like the lines a cartoonist will draw
following an object to suggest movement, or like the reverberations of a musical note. Huck uses participial constructions especially when there is a violent or otherwise memo-
rable action. Then the sense of solid bodies moving in space
is heightened. The Boggs episode is to the point.

> They swarmed up the street towards Sherburn's
> house, A-WHOOPING and YELLING and RAGING like In-
> juns, and everything had to clear the way or get run
> over and tromped to mush, and it was awful to see.
> Children was HEELING it ahead of the mob, SCREAM-
> ING and TRYING to get out of the way; and every win-
> dow along the road was full of women's heads, and
> there was nigger boys in every tree, and bucks and

wenches LOOKING OVER every fence; and as soon as
the mob would get nearly to them they would break
and skaddle back out of reach. Lots of women and
girls was CRYING and TAKING ON, scared most to
death.[29]

The very identifying feature of a participle, its "-ing" ap-
pendage, provides, of course, a form of repetition. Certainly
in a long passage it confers a rudimentary aural organization,
one that may be felt only faintly, but which is still more than
mere random rhyming. The participle and the reiterated
conjunction of a long list — "and . . . and . . . and . . .
and . . . and . . ." — are two of the least evident yet most
pervasive forms of repetition to be found in Huck's version of
the vernacular. Repetition is the most frequently encountered device for structural coherence in *Huckleberry Finn*.
Although the two eventually used repetition for similar ends,
Mark Twain's occasions for repeating differ from those which
brought it on in James's dialogue and prose. In Mark Twain,
the occasions can be illustrated quickly. The simplest form
overt repetition takes is emphatic iteration: "further and further," "higher and higher," "brisker and brisker." Like the
notation "for days and days," these examples are virtually
idiomatic (chs. 19, 28, 29, 31). More colloquial still, Huck
indicates action that is tedious or in some way troubling by
repeating words: "she counted and counted"; "they kept it
up and kept it up"; "he drank, and drank"; "they dug and
dug." Sometimes the effect is doubled: "The people woke up
more and more, and sung louder and louder" (chs. 37, 29, 6,
29, 20).

Repetition reaches a more nearly genuine and conscious
structural function in extended passages where phrases are
repeated:

We got a LICKING every time one of our snakes come
in her way, and she allowed these LICKINGS warn't

NOTHING to what she would do if we ever loaded up
the place again with them. I DIDN'T MIND THE
LICKINGS because they didn't amount to NOTHING;
but I MINDED the trouble we had to LAY IN another
lot. But we got them LAID IN. (ch. 39, capitals added)

Or where the subject is felt to be so essential that it cannot be
replaced with a pronoun:

We said there warn't no home like a RAFT, after all.
Other places do seem so cramped up and smothery,
but a RAFT don't. You feel mighty free and easy
and comfortable on a RAFT. (ch. 18, capitals added)

Or, very interestingly, where common attributes are applied
to a series of distinct, though related, objects:

I found plenty strawberries, ripe and prime; and
GREEN summer-grapes, and GREEN razberries, and the
GREEN blackberries just beginning to show.[30]

Other more complicated instances of repetition raise the
question of artistic purposefulness in prose construction, for
some seem results of only partial consciousness, if of any.
Mark Twain's description of Colonel Grangerford, for example, is incompletely organized around thinness and its complementary qualities of longness, highness, straightness, blackness, and whiteness — in short, the qualities of an etching.

Col. Grangerford was VERY TALL and VERY SLIM,
and had a DARKISH-PALY COMPLEXION, not a sign of
red in it anywheres; he was CLEAN-SHAVED every
morning, all over his THIN FACE, and he had the
THINNEST KIND OF LIPS, and the THINNEST KIND OF
NOSTRILS, and a HIGH NOSE, and HEAVY EYEBROWS,
and the BLACKEST KIND OF EYES, sunk so deep back
that they seemed like they was looking out of
caverns at you, as you may say. His FOREHEAD WAS
HIGH, and his HAIR WAS BLACK AND STRAIGHT, and
hung to his shoulders. His HANDS WAS LONG AND

THIN, and every day of his life he put a clean shirt
and a full suit from head to foot made out of LINEN
SO WHITE IT HURT YOUR EYES to look at it; and on
Sundays he wore a blue tail-coat with brass buttons
on it.[31]

Mark Twain never quite pulls his repetition here into a coherent whole. As a matter of fact, as the paragraph goes on
this forbidding moralist is metamorphosized into a sunny
gentleman beloved by all, and never again used in the book
in spite of all this elaborate preparation. Such extended carelessness is not common in *Huckleberry Finn*, but this one example suggests that Mark Twain had not thought out the
possibilities of repetition as a structural device. Years later
he was full of opinions on repetition.

> I do not find that the repetition of an important
> word a few times — say three or four times — in a
> paragraph troubles my ear if clearness of meaning
> is best secured thereby. But tautological repetition
> which has no justifying object, but merely exposes
> the fact that the writer's balance at the vocabulary
> bank has run short and that he is too lazy to replen-
> ish it from the thesaurus — that is another mat-
> ter.[32]

The plentiful instances in *Huckleberry Finn* of unconscious associations of sound and of meaning are related to
semi-conscious repetition. It is impossible to tell how aware
of them Mark Twain was. He never mentioned the psychology of associations in his critical writings, yet when he writes

> Cold corn-pone, cold corn beef, butter and butter-
> milk  (ch. 17)

it seems unlikely that he did not notice what he had written.
If he did, he made no attempt to change it, surely because
such repetitions do occur in natural speech. I am not so sure,
however, that Mark Twain realized just why he used the
word "rattling" in the following sentence.

> And so we went for the snakes, and grabbed a
> couple of dozen garters and house-snakes, and put
> them in a bag, and put it in our room, and by that
> time it was supper-time, and a rattling good honest
> day's work. . . . (ch. 39)

Even as "snakes" drew out "rattling," again and again in
*Huckleberry Finn* one encounters instances of rhyme, alliteration, and assonance whose beginning we can trace. When
the Grangerfords run down old Baldy Shepherdson, Huck
reports that they

> stayed on their horses and capered around the old
> man and peppered away at him and he peppered
> away at them. (ch. 18)

Here the sound pattern moves from 'ayed to 'apered to
'eppered and 'eppered. So: "I slid out and slipped off"; "but
he never meddled at all; just slid the lid along as soft as
mush"; " 'So,' says I, 's'pose somebody has hogged that bag on
the sly?' "; "the wind swished and swushed"; "knickknacks
and jimcracks" (chs. 18, 27, 27, 30, 26).
Sometimes Mark Twain deliberately builds a striking
sound relationship. "My bed was a straw-tick — better than
Jim's which was a corn-shuck tick," says Huck. Then he continues, "There's always cobs around in a shuck tick" (ch.
20). Alliteration occurs in Huck's prose: the duke has been
selling a product "to take the tartar off the teeth" (ch. 20),
and there is this sentence dominated by hard "c's" and "t's."

> So we got a canoe and took out after them and
> crossed over, but couldn't find nothing of them; so
> we cruised along up-shore till we got kind of tired
> and beat out; and tied up the canoe. . . . (ch. 41)

Downright rhyme, such as extemporaneous speaking encour-
ages, appears too. Thunder for Huck goes "rumbling, grumbling, tumbling." [33] The duke and the king carry "big fat,
ratty-looking carpet bags," and when the two scoundrels flee
a mob, the rhymed words in Huck's excited account are ac-

cented by exclamation marks: ". . . here they come! — and just a laying to their oars and making their skiff hum!" (chs. 19, 29).

Pressure of rhyme upon narrative prose also means that if the duke, king, and Huck find a printer's shop that is only "a little bit of a concern," then it will be a "littered-up place" from which Huck will shortly have "lit out" (ch. 21). It is not surprising to discover that the same psychology of sound associations determined such curious sentences as these from Henry James's story, "The Jolly Corner":

> She listened to everything; she was a woman who answered intimately but who utterly didn't chatter. She scattered abroad . . .

and

> "Not to have followed my perverse young course — and almost in the teeth of my father's curse . . ." [34]

Association of sound, probably unconscious, also produces this remarkable descriptive passage from *Huckleberry Finn:*

> All the stores was along one street. They had white domestic Awnings in front, and the country-people hitched their horses to the Awning-posts. There was empty dry-goods boxes under the Awnings, and loafers roosting on them all day long, whittling with their Barlow knives; and chAwing tobacco, and gaping and yawning and stretching — a mighty ornery lot. They generly had on yellow strAw hats most as wide as an umbrella, but didn't wear no coats nor waistcoats; they called one another Bill, and Buck and Hank, and Joe, and Andy, and talked lazy and drAwly, and used considerable many cuss-words. (ch. 21, capitals added)

I have emphasized only the repetition of sound in identical spellings; to this one could justifiably add the same "aw" sound as found in *all, along, long, called, talked,* and perhaps *horses* and *ornery.*

Even though the loose spontaneity of colloquial speech carried with it primitive elements of organization such as the ones just discussed, it is not possible to say that Mark Twain made use of them to any consistent aesthetic end. Although he provided these potential organizational elements in abundance, he often seems to have been unaware of their existence. When he did notice them and build on what he had found, it was for the pleasure of the moment rather than for the sake of the whole structure. Because he was amused by words, Mark Twain was willing to leave instances of their mercuriality in the texture of his work. His reckless display of queer combinations of words can only indicate a basic interest in the particular word at the expense of larger formal effects. Mark Twain's verbal fooling, conscious and otherwise, is extremely important, however, for it suggested ways by which stylization could wrestle down the vernacular and make of it a general rather than an eccentric medium of prose. Sometimes Mark Twain's results were almost indistinguishable from those of his follower Ernest Hemingway.

> I took the sack of corn meal and took it to where the canoe was hid, and shoved the vines and branches apart and put it in; then I done the same with the side of bacon; then the whiskey-jug; I took all the coffee and sugar there was, and all the ammunition; I took the wadding; I took the bucket and gourd; I took a dipper and a tin cup, and my old saw and two blankets, and a skillet and the coffee-pot. I took fish-lines and matches and other things — everything that was worth a cent. I cleaned out the place. I wanted an ax, but there wasn't any, only the one out at the wood pile, and I knowed why I was going to leave that. I fetched out the gun, and now I was done. (ch. 7)

But Mark Twain's art flowed from him as part of his personality in a way that Hemingway's did not. One cannot, for example, be sure that Mark Twain knew he had rounded off his paragraph with an anapestic rhyme, *out the gun* and *I was done,* whereas Hemingway built his prose, fashioned it from received materials. It is far too simple to say that Mark Twain's style traveled directly from Hannibal to Oak Park. It was detoured, delayed, manhandled, and finally delivered as quite a different package from 27 rue de Fleurus, Paris.

Admittedly the bringing together of Henry James and Mark Twain makes a queer combination. As Bernard De-Voto once observed, Mark Twain "had no conscious aesthetic. He stood at the opposite pole from Henry James . . . he was not a fully conscious artist." [35] One cannot imagine that James could or ever would write the paragraph that describes Huck's preparations to leave Pap's cabin. He had, in fact, consciously rejected the use of the immature voice. "Small children have many more perceptions than they have terms to translate them," he mused in the preface to *What Maisie Knew.*[36] Because the child's vision is richer than his vocabulary, James was certain that the experiment of restricting oneself to the child's terms would fail.

Yet, despite such persistently opposing views, we can justifiably assert that in the formal characteristics of repetition, interrupted phrasing, isolation of the word, accentuated peculiarities, and patterns of sound Henry James and Mark Twain corroborated and re-enforced one another's efforts. Each arrived at his stylistic peak through the faithful management of dialogue, followed by partial or wholesale importation of colloquial features into the narrative prose. Each dramatically advanced the movement toward an American prose by his efforts to purify the language of the tribe.

# FOUR

# Copies and Misfires

"What was that funny thing you said.
I am learning to say a break.
I am learning to say a clutch.
I am learning to say it in french. A house or lions.
A young lion looks like a dog. We laugh. I am not
satisfied."

*Geography and Plays*

I

ALTHOUGH BERNARD DEVOTO asserted that "since *Huckleberry
Finn* the well of American undefiled has flowed confidently," [1] in fact it took at least a generation for the waters to
flow. Aside from the experiments in form carried on by
Henry James, nothing very clear or purposeful happened to
the vernacular in literature for a quarter of a century following the publication of *Huckleberry Finn*. Gertrude Stein's
*Three Lives* did not appear until 1909, and it was five years
later that Ring Lardner's first letters from his bush-league
pitcher appeared. What, we might ask curiously, delayed the
immediate triumph of the American vernacular?

Any radical discovery, of course, requires time to be recognized and assimilated. Not until a decade after Ernest Hemingway first published his work did such imitators as John
O'Hara, James Cain, and Horace McCoy begin to appear. It
may be that only the young and malleable can profit by innovation, and that any major breakthrough will make its effect
only on the group of aspirants then approaching first artistic
consciousness. This theory, however, will not account for the

extended hiatus after *Huckleberry Finn* with which we are confronted. The answer rather lies first with the general public view of Mark Twain as an author, and second with the special problems presented by his inadvertently pioneering book. Frequently Mark Twain was not taken seriously, and even when he was, the leading writers never looked to *Huckleberry Finn* for stylistic guidance. They preferred to use the vernacular sparingly rather than make a total commitment to it. As for the few, including Mark Twain himself, who were taken by the style of *Huckleberry Finn,* they were baffled by what the author had wrought. Some fell to imitating Huck's style, while others made serious attempts to advance the age of the narrator. And Alps on Alps arose.

There can be no doubt that *Huckleberry Finn* was extensively read and enjoyed from the day it was published. In his memoirs, Harold Stearns, self-styled leader of the expatriate contingent after the First World War, asked rhetorically, "Is there any American of my generation who was not, so to speak, brought up on *Huckleberry Finn* and *Tom Sawyer* and *Roughing It?*" [2] Confirmation of this has been offered by authors of overlapping generations and disparate artistic allegiances: for example, by Pearl Buck, Carl Van Vechten, Ben Hecht, Kenneth Roberts, Edna Ferber, and Henry Miller.[3] But although these American writers testified to having read Mark Twain as children, they were not prepared to take him seriously as adults or as artists. As Floyd Dell put it: "Mark Twain was only a boyhood memory." [4] In 1880 Mark Twain ironically acknowledged the difficulty he had in escaping the reputation of the Wild Humorist of the Pacific Slope. When his daughter observed, "You must know a wonderful deal, papa," Mark Twain replied, "I have that reputation — in Europe; but here the best minds think I am superficial." [5] On the surface he was joking. Still in 1907 William Lyon Phelps corroborated Mark Twain's ironic judgment of himself. His comment is of some moment for our consideration of the mysterious delay in the development of the vernacular. "During the last twenty years, a profound change has taken place in the attitude of the reading public toward Mark Twain. I can remember very well when he was regarded merely as a humorist, and one opened his books with an anticipatory grin." [6] The accuracy of this assessment of Mark Twain's changing reputation is in turn substantiated by Upton Sinclair's testimony. "When I was a boy we all read *Tom Sawyer* and *Huckleberry Finn* and 'laughed our heads off' over them; but if anybody had suggested to us that Mark Twain might be one of the world's great writers, we should have thought it a Mark Twain joke." [7]

The point then is that much as *Huckleberry Finn* was enjoyed, it was not generally recognized as the revolutionary stylistic document it was. It appeared to be a unique phenomenon, a delightful freak capable of being imitated, but seemingly offering no further possibility of development. Even in their approach to childhood, writers turned for a stylistic model to *Tom Sawyer* rather than to *Huckleberry Finn,* so that one finds such derivative works as Brander Matthews' *Tom Paulding,* Stephen Crane's *Whilomville Stories,* and Booth Tarkington's *Penrod* series. The choice of *Tom Sawyer* as a model is especially interesting from the point of view of style, because it reverses the technique used in *Huckleberry Finn. Huckleberry Finn* gains a good part of its power by using the language of a boy to describe the actions of adults. This establishes an ironic distance between the adult intention and its immature verbalization, an economical example of which is Huck's remark that *Pilgrim's Progress* is

> . . . about a man that left his family it didn't say why. I read considerable in it now and then. The statements was interesting but tough.[8]

To this kind of observation — and *Huckleberry Finn* is full of them — the adult reader makes two responses. First he objects that Bunyan's book is much more than that; then on second thought he agrees that Huck's candor sums up some rarely admitted feelings about *Pilgrim's Progress*. The *Tom Sawyer* approach gains its irony in just the opposite way. The adult linguistically appraises the child.

> The imitator of Hard-Head and Uncas was late for breakfast.

> The shooting of the cow was plainly heinous, and undoubtedly their dungeons would be knee-deep in water.

> Penrod had rather vaguely debated plans for a self-mutilation such as would make his appearance as the Child Sir Lancelot inexpedient on public grounds.[9]

*Tom Sawyer*'s way is stylistically important because it uses the vernacular only on occasion rather than following out the consequences of a full commitment to colloquial speech. At best we can say that this line, derived from Mark Twain, *tends* to introduce new colloquial words and rhythms into American prose, but that it is far from a critical extension of *Huckleberry Finn*. It uses the vernacular as salt rather than as the main fare.

In this light there is meaning to the fact that Stephen Crane's favorite among Mark Twain's books was *Life on the Mississippi,* and that George Ade, who wrote "one of the first fully developed native styles in pure American idiom," [10] and who was considered a successor to Mark Twain, shared Crane's taste.[11] Nor was Ring Lardner a whole-hearted admirer of either Mark Twain or *Huckleberry Finn*. He once commented, "I wouldn't consider Mark Twain our greatest humorist. I guess that George Ade is." Asked if he admired *Huckleberry Finn,* Lardner replied, "Yes, but I like Booth Tarkington's 'Penrod' stories better." [12] Despite their lack of enthusiasm for *Huckleberry Finn,* there was no question that most admired Mark Twain himself as a writer. "He was a kind of literary god to me," Ade commented when Mark Twain died.[13] Booth Tarkington thought "He seemed to me the greatest prose writer we had." [14] But even though as early as 1900 Tarkington had "called for American writers to inject vigor and reality into American literature through the use of their native idiom, as Mark Twain had done in *Huckleberry Finn,*" [15] except for Lardner, none of these writers tried to explore the American language or the meaning of the colloquial style. The vernacular was of interest to them, it did offer amusement, color — "vigor and reality" to use Tarkington's phrasing — but it never seemed to occur to them that in itself the vernacular might furnish a new mode of revelation.

George Ade illustrates a typical way in which writers at the turn of the century and down through the 'twenties used American speech. He consciously accented and exploited the incongruities available in levels of word usage. His "Fable of the Professor Who Wanted to Be Alone" (1899) begins:

> Now it happens that in America a man who goes up hanging to a Balloon is a Professor. One day a Professor, preparing to make a Grand Ascension, was sorely pestered by Spectators of the Yellow-Hammer Variety, who fell over the Stay-Ropes or crowded up close to the Balloon to ask Fool Questions. They wanted to know how far up he Calkilated to go and was he Afeerd and how often had he did it. The Professor answered them in the Surly Manner peculiar to Showmen accustomed to meet a Web-Foot Population.[16]

Reading this paragraph, the reader confronts a verbal zoo. Ade's wit depends upon the improbably shifting, imaginative surface of his prose. For example: in the first sentence, the word "Professor" is provided an ironic definition by the author; "Grand Ascension" is a term drawn from the vocabulary of handbills and posters; "Spectators of the Yellow-Hammer Variety" parodies ornithological nomenclature (a yellow-hammer is variously a finch, a bunting, and a flicker); "Stay-Ropes" is technical jargon; "Fool Questions" is a phrase used to describe the activity of the very people who coined it; "Calkilated" and "Afeerd" are dialectal distortions indirectly quoted from the spectators who asked the fool questions; "Surly Manner" is authorial; and finally "Web-Foot Population" is an ironic variation of "Yellow-Hammer Variety."

Ade's stylistic strong point was just this kind of light handling of all kinds of diction. Not prepared to locate a norm himself, he fired good-natured shots at aberrations in the world of style, from the "Book that runs into a snarl of Dialect on the Third Page and never gets out," to the Bohemian who is writing "A Little Thing of his Own about Wandering in the fields with Lesbia," to the preacher who gave up "flying low along the Intellectual Plane of the Aggregation that chipped in to pay his Salary" in favor of a "rhetorical Roman Candle in each Hand" and "long Boston words." [17] At a time when literature was in the roiled waters where two strong currents, Standard and American English, met, it was not surprising that men like Ade exploited the stylistic confusion.

The counterpart of the comically variegated style is the "mixed style," in which the writer deliberately combines diction from various levels of discourse, but without necessarily seeking to amuse. This was used most consistently by Mark Twain himself, but as Harold Martin has observed there has long been an "established tradition of mixed diction in American literature." [18] Aside from the fact that current speech habits are always subtly affecting the standard written prose — "The direction of change in language is from ditch to castle" [19] — the mixed style is best explained by the fact that Americans use a borrowed language. As new things and new conditions were encountered in a New World, their names and attributes clamored for entry into the select company of standard literary vocabulary. Entering, they began a slow process of changing the prose medium in America permanently. As we have seen, the most insistent — because most readily and easily sanctioned — change took place in dialogue. In 1899, the same year that Ade published his *Fables in Slang* with their incongruously mixed diction, Stephen Crane was observing in his short story "The Blue Hotel" that

> Scully's speech was always a combination of Irish brogue and idiom, Western twang and idiom, and scraps of curiously formal diction taken from the story-books and newspapers. He now hurled a strange mass of language at the head of his son. [20]

Crane's description of Scully's speech is in itself conventionally rendered, but he goes on to *illustrate* this "strange mass of language" and there demonstrates his virtuosity with the vernacular. His ability to write dialogue coupled with his cool handling of adventurous material seems to constitute Crane's attraction for Ernest Hemingway.

> "What do I keep? What do I keep? What do I keep?" he demanded, in a voice of thunder. He slapped his knee impressively, to indicate that he himself was going to make reply, and that all should heed. "I keep a hotel," he shouted. "A hotel, do you mind? A guest under my roof has sacred privileges. He is to be intimidated by none. Not one word shall he hear that would prejudice him in favour of goin' away. I'll not have it. There's no place in this

here town where they can say they iver took in a guest
of mine because he was afraid to stay here." He
wheeled suddenly upon the cowboy and the
Easterner. "Am I right?"

"Yes, Mr. Scully," said the cowboy, "I think you're
right."

"Yes, Mr. Scully," said the Easterner, "I think
you're right." [20]

Crane shared with Mark Twain a desire for directness, for
what Ade called "the stubby Old English words." [21] Ford
Madox Ford reported Crane's exclamation: "By God! When
[Robert Louis] Stevenson wrote: 'With interjected finger
he delayed the action of the time piece,' when he meant 'he
put the clock back,' Stevenson put back the clock of English
fiction 150 years." [22] Mark Twain agreed: "I never write
'metropolis' for seven cents, because I can get the same
money for 'city.' " [23] This insistence upon the power of directness frequently accounts for the presence of vernacular
terms in otherwise standard prose. In his third-person narrative, Mark Twain was quite ready to use vernacular terms for
color, for exactness, for clarity, and for humor, but even he
customarily built on a standard base. In *Pudd'nhead Wilson*
(1894), for example, this is part of the description of the
heroine, Roxana:

Her face was shapely, intelligent and comely — even
beautiful. She had an easy, independent carriage —
when she was among her own caste — and a high
and "sassy" way withal; but, of course, she was meek
and humble enough where white people were. [24]

The interruptions and interpolations are signs of the conversational. On the other hand, "comely," "withal," and "independent carriage" are not vernacular terms, and quotation
marks literally apologize for "sassy." Pertinently, in *A Connecticut Yankee in King Arthur's Court* (1889), a novel possessing an acknowledged narrator, one meets this passage:

In my experience boys are the same in all ages. They don't respect anything, they don't care for anything or anybody. They say "Go up, baldhead" to the prophet going his unoffending way in the gray of antiquity; they sass me in the holy gloom of the Middle Ages; and I have seen them act the same way in Buchanan's administration; I remember, because I was there and helped.[25]

Here the rhythms are looser than in the example from *Pudd'nhead Wilson,* and "sass," because it is considered part of the normal fabric of the narrator's speech, appears without quotation marks. On the other hand, "unoffending way," "gray of antiquity," and "holy gloom" are synthetic phrases not easily associated with the Yankee narrator. This means that for Mark Twain, certain colloquial elements will often appear in his third-person narrative, while in his first-person *adult* narrative, one will find standard constructions. The waters of the Atlantic and the Pacific meet in Gatun Lake at the center of the Panama Canal, and this is where American prose was around the turn of the century — in a stylistic Gatun Lake.

To attain irony, Stephen Crane consciously built a narrative style whose diction fluctuated. In "An Experiment in Misery" (1896), Crane refers to derelicts with words ranging from straight description to elevated diction to slang: "aimless men," "mendicants," "sorry figures," "seedy men," "outcasts," "wanderers," "wretches." At the beginning of the sketch Crane outflanks the problem of how to include familiar colloquial terms without undue ceremony:

By the time he had reached City Hall Park he was so completely plastered with yells of "bum" and "hobo" and with various unholy epithets that small boys had applied to him at intervals, that he was in a state of the most profound dejection.[26]

Diction largely determines rhythms as well. Compare the rhythm of "yells of 'bum' and 'hobo' " with "various unholy epithets," or with "a state of the most profound dejection." The change is from monosyllabic deliberateness to fluid intricacy. Crane rarely used colloquial quick shifts, repetitions, or interruptions in his narrative prose, although as we have seen he knew how to render speech. If ever, it was in the Whilomville stories, which significantly are concerned with the adventures of a young boy, that Crane came closest to a colloquial simplicity.

> "Hello, Jim!" said Henry, poising his sponge. Water
> was dripping from the buggy. Sometimes the horses
> in the stalls stamped thunderingly on the pine floor.
> There was an atmosphere of hay and harness.[27]

Because Crane's career was short and hectic, it is difficult to establish a direction in his style. But his prose, and the literary responses of other writers we have touched on — the imitations of *Tom Sawyer,* George Ade's ironic fables in slang, Mark Twain's third-person narrative in *Pudd'nhead Wilson* — all represent stages on the way toward full employment of the vernacular. They fill the period which at first seems devoid of stylistic change, and they unmistakably continue the process of "loosening up the language." As it happens, the mixed style is in some ways richer than pure colloquial, and many American writers of the mid-twentieth century have found it profitable to return to deliberately mixing the colloquial with standard prose. But such writers know the limitations as well as the potentialities of the colloquial style, because, insofar as such a thing is possible in a dynamic medium, they possess examples of it reduced to its essentials. Today stylistic complexity is built up from a colloquial base. In 1910 a mixed style represented a failure, or an inability, to take the American vernacular on its own terms.

II

One obvious way of sustaining the vernacular, which several
writers including Mark Twain himself adopted, was to imitate *Huckleberry Finn*. The adolescent narrator provides a
frame of reference by which the dictional level and rhythmical norm can be monitored — the very guide the mixed style
lacked. Mark Twain published two stories using Huck as narrator, "Tom Sawyer Abroad" in 1894 and "Tom Sawyer,
Detective" in 1896. As he was writing the first story — which
he once proposed to name "New Adventures of Huckleberry
Finn" — he described its content: "I have started Huck Finn
& Tom Sawyer (still 15 years old) & their friend the freed
slave Jim around the world in a stray *balloon,* with Huck as
narrator . . . & find that the humor flows as easily as the adventures and surprises." [28] Mark Twain's description suggests the limitations of the story. Although the style was occasionally as accomplished as it had been in *Huckleberry
Finn,* the fantastic situations reminiscent of Jules Verne and
the emphasis on surprises in the air and on the Egyptian
desert hobbled it. The greatness of *Huckleberry Finn* comes
from its direct, serious confrontation of the realities of
nineteenth-century Midwestern American life. Huck's words
reproduced beauties and horrors heretofore concealed by
styles incapable of revealing them. But in "Tom Sawyer
Abroad" the style is wasted on trivial material.

Mark Twain did continue to satirize high-flown language,
as when Tom, Jim, and Huck haggle over Tom's use of the
word "welkin." Asked its meaning, Tom replies,

> "I don't know, and nobody don't know. It's just
> a word, and it's a mighty good word, too. There ain't
> many that lays over it. I don't believe there's *any*
> that does."

"Shucks!" I says. "But what does it mean? — that's the p'int."

"I don't know what it means, I tell you. It's a word that people uses for — for — well, it's ornamental. They don't put ruffles on a shirt to keep a person warm, do they?"

"Course they don't."

"But they put them *on,* don't they?"

"Yes."

"All right, then; that letter I wrote is a shirt, and the welkin's the ruffle on it." [29]

Moral observations are made as well, but equally incidentally, equally by the way. There is never anything imperative in Huck's remarks; they remain at the level of the "Was Sollermun Wise" chapter in *Huckleberry Finn.* For example, it is a familiar but not really involved Huck who defines bird-lovers:

> . . . Jim knowed more about birds than both of us put together. You see, he had killed hundreds and hundreds of them, and that's the way to find out about birds. That's the way people does that writes books about birds, and loves them so that they'll go hungry and tired and take any amount of trouble to find a new bird and kill it. Their name is ornithologers. . . . (p. 37)

Lacking direction, such remarks come to no purpose. Style helps the incidental thought, but is given no opportunity to enlarge meaning. In "Tom Sawyer Abroad," Huck's idiom is rudderless and drifting.

Tom is the director of the action in "Tom Sawyer, Detective," a story involving a murder, impersonations, and a trial — Mark Twain's favorite adventure ingredients. Again the style is prepared to work, but is never seriously used. Because Tom stage-manages the plot, Huck is retained primarily as a commentator. He admires Tom's ingenuity:

> Think of that now. I never see such a head as that
> boy had. Why, *I* had eyes and I could see things, but
> they never meant nothing to me. But Tom Sawyer
> was different. When Tom Sawyer seen a thing it
> just got up on its hind legs and *talked* to him —
> told him everything it knowed. *I* never see such a
> head. (p. 144)

And Huck is permitted to set scenes:

> It was a most lovely day, now, and bright and sun-
> shiny; and the further and further we went over the
> hill towards the prairie the lovelier and lovelier the
> trees and flowers got to be and the more it seemed
> strange and somehow wrong that there had to be
> trouble in such a world as this. (p. 155)

But Huck is never centrally engaged, so neither is his style.
Dependent upon a mechanically ingenious plot, the effect of
"Tom Sawyer, Detective" is very much that of the last ten
chapters of *Huckleberry Finn*. The prose is well written, but
it fails to generate power.

Mark Twain made other attempts to re-enter the vernacular with Huck's voice, but the fragmentary manuscripts
testify to his bewilderment before the problem. Since Mark
Twain, other writers have taken up imitations of the great
model, with limited success. In 1912 Don Marquis began his
career with the novel *Danny's Own Story*. It is told in a vernacular similar to Huck's, which interestingly enough an
anonymous reviewer for *The New York Times* thought
"would read more easily and perhaps more satisfactorily" if it
were told "in a somewhat modified dialect." [30] Like many
colloquial writers Marquis incorporated observations on language into his story.

> Only the doctor says he "reckons" instead of he
> "guesses," which they all do down there. And they
> all had them easy-going, wait-a-bit kind of voices,

and didn't see no pertic'ler importance in their "r's."
It wasn't that you could spell it no different when
they talked, but it sounded different.[31]

Christopher Morley, who believed Marquis to be "our closest
spiritual descendant of Mark Twain," correctly diagnosed
*Danny's Own Story* as "much too obviously Mark Twain material. It is written with savor and charm, but the memory of
Huck Finn and Tom Sawyer keeps blurring the reader's focus." [32] In his newspaper column for the New York
*Evening Sun,* Marquis subsequently turned to other modifi-
cations of the colloquial voice such as the thoughts of
archy the cockroach and of the Old Soak. But whatever the
extent of his celebrity, like the accomplishments of George
Ade and Will Rogers, Marquis's were of minor importance
for the vernacular.

Although imitations of *Huckleberry Finn* have continued
to be popular in this century, they avoid the central dilemma
of the vernacular: how to escape the limitations a narrator
imposes of age, education, regional dialect, topical slang, and
occupational jargon, and still preserve something common to
all — the essence of the vernacular. Somewhere in all the various forms of American talk there should be some shared
characteristics, there ought to be a middle ground free of the
hampering peculiarities of speech, yet independent of standard English.

Mark Twain saw the problem early and tried to solve it by
selecting a typical American for his narrator. The title of his
next book after *Huckleberry Finn, A Connecticut Yankee in
King Arthur's Court* (1889), names the special voice Twain
contracted to imitate. But because the limits of the diction
and syntax of this Yankee's speech were not clear in Twain's
mind the contract was quickly broken. John C. Gerber, in-
vestigating "The Relation Between Point of View and Style
in the Works of Mark Twain," recently pointed out that
Twain "does not write four chapters before he bursts

through his persona and takes over the story himself. Hank Morgan remains as the narrator, but the point of view, the basic attitudes, and the language are Twain's." Gerber continues, "Like *Innocents Abroad,* such uniformity as the style of the *Connecticut Yankee* possesses it gains from its basic colloquialism, but it is a badly battered colloquialism before the book comes to an end." [33] The style was uncontrolled and liable at any moment to slip from sentimental floridness to colloquial expansiveness to aphoristic wit. We have already encountered the phrase, "They sass me in the holy gloom." Much of the book is written in a similarly mixed style.

> Straight off, we were in the country. It was most lovely and pleasant in those sylvan solitudes in the early cool morning in the first freshness of autumn. (p. 87)

This passage of artfully mixed diction is found amidst larger blocks of stylistically contradictory material. The book opens,

> I am an American. I was born and reared in Hartford, in the State of Connecticut — anyway, just over the river, in the country. So I am a Yankee of the Yankees — and practical; yes, and nearly barren of sentiment, I suppose — or poetry, in other words. (p. 5)

That person, however, could hardly have seen either the "sylvan solitudes" of the preceding quotation, or this:

> . . . a castle which stood on high ground; a huge, strong, venerable structure, whose gray towers and battlements were charmingly draped with ivy, and whose whole majestic mass was drenched with splendors flung from the sinking sun. (p. 119)

Gerber justifiably calls the writing in *A Connecticut Yankee* "patchwork." Lacking a firm control for his style,

Mark Twain simply wrote at any given moment as he was in-
spired to. Having an extensive stylistic repertoire at his command, he produced a hopelessly uneven book. *A Connecticut
Yankee* only returns us to the main problem of the practitioner of the colloquial. How to govern it?

Despite the obvious drift of American writers toward an
undistorted American prose, the fact is that such a prose did
not and could not exist among adults, unless it was consciously constructed, or in terms of this book, unless it was
stylized. But none of the writers we have considered so far in
this chapter was much concerned with the construction of a
vernacular prose style. Because so few were aware yet of the
value of a formally integral vernacular prose, stylistic ad-
vances were scattered and random. There were mixed styles
sprinkled with the vernacular, there were imitations of *Huckleberry Finn,* there were sporadic and uneven attempts to
raise the age limit of the narrator — all in all a large shape-
less movement was still under way toward the literary use of
American speech, but it lacked a rationale.


### III

Ring Lardner and Sherwood Anderson both developed styles
capable of sustained exploratory effort in the field of the vernacular. Lardner came first by a year or two, and he can represent a number of journalists who, in their daily stints for
the amusement of a vast, semi-literate, restless urban audience,
played and still do play with the vagaries of the American
language. Lardner possessed the sharpest ear and the most
formidable wit of his fellows. During his twenty-year examination of the peculiarities of lower-class speech in America,
his career was marked with such striking success combined
with such disillusioned bitterness that it sometimes seems a
minor reprise of Mark Twain's own experience.

To gain a consistent version of the vernacular above the level of a boy, Lardner depended on two givens: the conventions of letter-writing and of a semi-educated narrator. In his first and most popular efforts, that narrator was an ignorant, brash, young baseball pitcher, Jack Keefe. Eventually Lardner assumed other roles: the Midwestern businessman in *The Big Town,* the young cynic in *A Caddy's Diary,* and as a columnist, he even created a public figure called Ring Lardner. He did not, however, fashion a style out of whole cloth. His sports reporting allowed him to slip gradually into the garrulous role of Jack Keefe. Donald Elder, Lardner's biographer, has pointed out that, "It was on the [Chicago] *Tribune* from 1908 to 1910 that Ring developed a unique style in reporting baseball games." His predecessors had encouraged experimentation. "Two generations of Chicago sports writers before him had won for themselves a greater freedom than other journalists of the time enjoyed." The freedom they won was in language, but although Elder says that when Lardner was eighteen his favorite books were *Huckleberry Finn* and *Tom Sawyer,* he discounts any direct influence from Twain. "The writers who influenced him most immediately were those who were currently popular and those he had known personally. . . . They all wrote about the contemporary scene and used to some extent language as it was actually spoken. . . . They were all sports writers or popular magazine writers; their medium allowed them considerable freedom to develop a personal manner." [34]

Lardner never seems to have struggled consciously with the problem of extending Twain's discoveries in language. Rather, as Elder shows in detail, the conception of Jack Keefe grew in the fillers Lardner composed for his *Tribune* column, as well as in his own private correspondence where he assumed various dictional guises to amuse his friends. The step was a short one to "A Busher's Letters Home," the first of which was published in March 1914 in the *Saturday Evening Post.*

By using an ill-educated narrator supposedly writing letters, Lardner was able to impose a distinctive style upon his prose. The long, monotonous, virtually unpunctuated sentences, and the misspellings emphasize rhythm, sound, and surface. Prose harmonics was beside the point. At the cost of eccentricity Lardner bought homogeneity. Using the rambling sentence and the strategically placed misspelling, he was able to approach a norm of colloquial prose more closely than anyone since Twain.

*You Know Me Al,* the collection of Jack Keefe letters published in 1916, is accordingly based on run-on sentences varied with sprawling compounds. The infrequently paragraphed prose flows on and on, rarely broken into short units. Rather than on punctuation, its sense depends upon syntactically forced hesitations and unsignalled shifts of subject. Lardner's prose observed a high degree of superficial specification, but its effect is pertinently akin to Gertrude Stein's monotonously revolving, slowly advancing style. Here is a single Lardner sentence:

> Well Al I guess you know by this time that I have worked against them 2 times since I wrote to you last time and I beat them both times and Mcgraw knows now what kind of a pitcher I am and I will tell you how I know because after the game yesterday he road down to the place we dressed at a long with me and all the way in the automobile he was after me to say I would go all the way a round the world and finely it come out that he wants I should go a long and pitch for his club and not pitch for the White Sox.[35]

Like Gertrude Stein, Lardner eliminated most of the punctuation inside his sentences, thereby shifting the responsibility for rhetorical organization from the printer to the reader.

> I says Well if we dont get there until febuery we
> wont have no time to train for the next season and
> he says You wont need to do no training because this
> trip will take all the weight off of you and every thing
> else you got. (p. 240)

Because the mind is obliged to establish sense pauses independently, it is attentive to every detail. Lardner quietly forces delicate adjustments along each line. One must, for example, account for the space between "every" and "thing" in the quotation above, just as one must compensate for the loss of an "a" in "You just stick round town" (p. 126). Even as Gertrude Stein wrote in *Tender Buttons,* "look a bout," [36] so Lardner in *You Know Me Al:* "I would rather throw $45.00 a way then go on a trip a round the world" (p. 238). The variety of these subtle foilings of expectation is endless. If carefully attended, their cumulative effect forces new rhythms upon the prose. When Gertrude Stein obliged the reader to establish Sam not as the object of the verb but as the person addressed in " 'You know Sam,' Rose said very often to him," [37] she was anticipating Lardner's commaless title, *You Know Me Al,* as well as technically doing what he did when he wrote, "because you are hog fat" (p. 141). The insistence that just to apprehend words and sentences the mind must work harder than it customarily did in reading standard prose has always been one of the stubborn positions of the colloquial style. (That it requires unusual attention is substantiated by a specialist in children's literature who observed that most children prefer *Tom Sawyer* (mixed style) to *Huckleberry Finn* (pure), because the latter "is written in the first person, and the vernacular is harder to read." [38])

That there should be significant local as well as general similarities between Gertrude Stein and Ring Lardner is only superficially odd. Both worked out highly stylized versions of colloquial speech, and although the directions they

took were totally different, each was amused by the quirki-
ness of the individual word or phrase, each sought release
from such restrictive bonds of standard prose as paragraphing
and punctuation, and each was interested in the changes of
meaning available in subtle variations of repeated material.

With the exception of the third-person barbarisms "he
don't," "she don't," "it don't," Lardner habitually used periphrastic verb forms in the Keefe letters. Periphrasis demands
that the reader make his way word by word through the verbal construct rather than sweeping it up as a phrasal unit.
This too is related to the early practice of Gertrude Stein.
For example, compare:

> You certainly had ought to be very good to poor
> Melanctha.[39]

and

> You should ought to remember he has only got a
> little stumach.  (p. 182)

Within his serpentine sentences Lardner often played
repetitions, especially the name "Al," against unmarked
pauses. As Gertrude Stein often punctuated long stretches of
her prose with the name "Melanctha," so "Al" reappears like
a tack in a tire, fixing the rhythm, the tick, of the prose.

> Old Pal: It is pretty near midnight Al but I been
> to bed a couple of times and I can't get no sleep. I am
> worried to death Al and I don't know where I am
> going to head in at. Maybe I will go out and buy a
> gun Al and end it all and I guess it would be better
> for everybody. But I cannot do that Al because I
> have not got the money to buy a gun with.  (p. 112)

Lardner, it has been said, possessed an "uninhibited
flair for free association."[40] Late in his career he wrote
Dadaish nonsense plays for his friends to perform, and
even earlier, the vernacular provided Lardner frequent op-

portunity to transcend mere phunny phellowness. Although
he was not above having Jack Keefe remark that he hated
spending four nights in a Pullman because "I am not built
right for a sleeping car birth" (p. 15), he generally used misspelling for irrational purposes quite beyond punning, spot-
ting a word strategically and allowing it to develop a life of
its own, even as when Mark Twain's "valley" was shown to
his "cubby." Keefe reminds Al,

> I will want a hack at the deepo. . . .  (p. 209)

During spring training he observes complacently,

> They is no fat on me and if I am a little bit bigger
> than last year it is because my mussels is bigger. (p.
> 134)

And in a showdown argument, Keefe reports,

> I says You can't because Detroit won't give no wavers
> on me. He says Detroit will give wavers on you
> quick enough if I ask them. (p. 131)

These simple constructs, *deepo, mussels,* and *wavers,* all
threaten a surrealistic overturn of reason. But in a larger
sense Lardner remained inhibited. He lacked the audacity,
the mania, let alone the encouragement, to extend his talent
into what might have been a field worth examining.

Dozens of writers in this century have been identified as
Mark Twain reincarnated, but none more so than Lardner.
Or rather, his potentiality to succeed Mark Twain was insisted upon while his failure to live up to that potentiality
was lamented. Sherwood Anderson believed, "He is covering
up, sticking to the gang, keeping out of sight. And that is all
right too, if in secret he is being another Mark Twain and
working in secret on his own *Huckleberry Finn*." [41] Edmund Wilson inquired in 1924, "Will Ring Lardner, then,
go on to his *Huckleberry Finn* or has he already told all he
knows? . . . If Ring Lardner has anything more to give us,

the time has now come to deliver it. . . . What bell might not Lardner ring if he set out to give us the works." [42]

In spite of this urging that he be a literary immortal, Lardner persisted in remaining trapped by the very conventions he had established to manage the vernacular. Quite aside from the fact that in order to use colloquial speech Lardner had to make the crippling concession of writing almost exclusively about people whom he regarded with contempt — the ignorant, shallow, arrogant American boobs and mongrels — he had imposed a stylistic handicap upon himself. His makeshift answer to the basic problem of the vernacular ultimately betrayed him. His personal friend and admirer, F. Scott Fitzgerald, saw this: "However deeply Ring might cut it," he wrote after Lardner's death in 1933, "his cake had exactly the diameter of Frank Chance's diamond. Here was his artistic problem. So long as he wrote within that enclosure the result was magnificient: within it he heard and recorded the voice of a continent. But when, inevitably, he outgrew his interest in it, what was Ring left with?" [43]

Lardner was left with the dead weight of an acknowledged narrator. Although he honed the vernacular, sustained and even advanced colloquial rhythms, he could not escape that albatross of a fool narrator. The monologue might take the reader satisfactorily through breakfast in the newspaper, but in any quantity it became a tedious drone. The only way to escape this dilemma was to take the vernacular on its own terms. Gertrude Stein had done it, and peculiar as her results were, both Sherwood Anderson and Ernest Hemingway were able to profit by them.

## I V

Unlike Lardner, who viewed Mark Twain as an opponent to be bested,[44] Anderson wholeheartedly admired Mark Twain, placing him "among the two or three really great American artists" [45] and referring to *Huckleberry Finn* as "that amazingly beautiful book." [46] When Van Wyck Brooks was writing *The Ordeal of Mark Twain* (1920), Anderson carried on a worried, eloquent correspondence with him, for he was both anxious lest the New Englander Brooks should misunderstand his fellow Midwesterner, and hopeful that the terrible artistic mutilation he believed Mark Twain had suffered would be properly explained to the American public.[47] In Anderson's work critics have since discerned plentiful evidence of his indebtedness to Mark Twain.

Stylistically, though, Anderson's results were at times so seriously flawed as to put his artistic reputation in permanent jeopardy. This led Frederick Hoffman to remark that "Anderson could have had only a damning consequence for American letters, through his having provided a constant justification for crudity and made a virtue of it." [48] Yet it was by justifying the simple style that Sherwood Anderson took the next considerable step toward the establishment of an independent American prose medium. On occasion he managed to dispense with the narrator and still retain a balanced style — but at costs we will later assess. Anderson was a shrewd and complicated man. As his biographers have pointed out — indeed, as he himself recognized — there was something of the poser about him. Still, he took his critical statements seriously and tried to mold himself and his work to fit them. Although they were never carefully formulated, their general tenor was that America remained a young, simple nation which as yet could truly express itself only in simple words. Anderson was always suspicious of the intellectual writer, preferring the supposed spontaneity of "word slingers" and "story tellers." He characteristically thought that the trouble with James Joyce was that "The man is scientific, an experimenter. When he tries to tell a story he is a poor story teller, God knows." [49] This bias for artlessness led him to observe "If, just now, American writing is on the

whole better than English writing, and I think it is, it is because it is more amateurish, more free, less professional"
(p. 293). Similarly, he was once led to the extreme comment
that "the future of writing in America lies with the newspaper boys who do not know they are writing" (p. 138).

Anderson made these last statements in the late 'twenties
when, as owner of two small newspapers in Marion, Virginia,
he was a "newspaper boy" himself; but he had always
felt — with some justification in his own case — that truth lay
among "farmers, working men, business men, painters," and
could best be expressed in their language, in their way. As
early as 1916 he offered his "Apology for Crudity" in which
he admitted that "For a long time I have believed that crudity is an inevitable quality in the production of a really significant present-day American literature. How indeed is one
to escape the obvious fact that there is as yet no native subtlety of thought or living among us? And if we are a crude
and childlike people how can our literature escape the influence of that fact? Why indeed should we want it to escape?" [50]

This is an admirable exhibition of making a virtue of necessity, but it is also appallingly close to sentimentalizing the
relation of life and letters. Holding this position, Anderson
romanticized Mark Twain, choosing to believe that when he
wrote *Huckleberry Finn* Mark Twain "forgot Howells, and
the good wife and everyone. Again he was the half-savage,
tender, god-worshipping, believing boy. He had proud, conscious innocence. I believe he wrote that book in a little hut
on a hill on his farm. It poured out of him." [51] Thinking of
Mark Twain, Anderson again revealed his basic suspicion of
the professional writer. "He belonged out here in the Middle
West and was only incidentally a writer. I've a notion that
after Twain passed under the influence of Howells and others
of the East he began to think of himself as a writer and lost
something of his innocence." [52] Anderson thoroughly identi-

fied himself with all the traits he ascribed to Mark Twain, those mysterious powers accruing to a rural Midwestern American, or even better, a *childish* rural Midwestern American, if in Anderson's mind that was not tautological. "I am immature," he wrote Brooks, "will live and die immature. A quite terrible confession that would be if I did not represent so much." [53]

Anderson's vaguely and incompletely stated series of relationships between environment, language, and self gave him all the justification he needed for using the vernacular. At the same time his mystic belief in the powers of spontaneous sincerity in writing left the door open to unchecked aberrations. For style the advantages of his credo are clear. He was the first writer since Mark Twain to take the vernacular as a serious way of presenting reality. He did not regard it as mere seasoning, nor was he tempted to investigate its comic possibilities. To him the vernacular was an innately honest medium, worthy of respect.

The history of Anderson's style is complicated, beginning in the third-person in *Windy McPherson's Son* (1916), where he attempted to hold experience at a distance, and ending with that total commitment to the speaking self, the posthumous publication in 1942 of *Sherwood Anderson's Memoirs*. In the first ten years of his career Anderson tried as many entrances to the vernacular as he could find, without ever quite settling on any one. *Winesburg, Ohio* (1919) and *Poor White* (1920) represent his finest work in the third-person. Both are related to the vernacular, but in different ways. *Winesburg* is deliberately primitivistic, stated with a sober, humorless intensity that moves at a slow pace from word to word, object to object. Long series of hardly varied declarative sentences are set down, key nouns are repeated, qualification is pared, and subordination minimized. The main resources of the vernacular are used by Anderson dead seriously. The result is at once impressive and irritating. The central symbolic statement of the book, a passage from the story "Paper Pills," illustrates the best and the worst of Anderson's dogged allegiance to simplicity.

> The story of Doctor Reefy and his courtship of the tall dark girl who became his wife and left her money to him is a very curious story. It is delicious, like the twisted little apples that grow in the orchards of Winesburg. In the fall one walks in the orchards and the ground is hard with frost underfoot. The apples have been taken from the trees by the pickers. They have been put in barrels and shipped to the cities where they will be eaten in apartments that are filled with books, magazines, furniture, and people. On the trees are only a few gnarled apples that the pickers have rejected. They look like the knuckles of Doctor Reefy's hands. One nibbles at them and they are delicious. Into a little round place at the side of the apple has been gathered all of its sweetness. One runs from tree to tree over the frosted ground picking the gnarled twisted apples and filling his pockets with them. Only the few know the sweetness of the twisted apples.[54]

The pace here is monotonous, but its one tone comes from careful stlyization. The components of Anderson's argument have been reduced to a few verbal elements whose repetition chimes delicately throughout the thin, direct syntax, chimes to bind the paragraph together. Implicitly, the paragraph insists upon the ability of a selective vocabulary to generate emotion. Anderson builds a mood of rural nostalgia to the center of the paragraph — delicious, apples, orchards, ground, frost, apples, trees — then drops in the sterile urban words — barrels, cities, apartments, books, magazines, furniture, people — then returns to restate the main theme in contrast to urban deadness — apples, delicious, sweetness, tree, frosted ground, apples, sweetness, apples.

The symbolism of this example is cloudy, however, and not

fully coherent. Not only is there something silly about the catalogue of things contained in the city apartments, but in the midst of the paragraph, knuckles and nibbling are unfortunately joined. "They look like the knuckles of Doctor Reefy's hands. One nibbles at them and they are delicious." This is worse when one recalls that three paragraphs earlier Anderson had made the strained point that the doctor's knuckles "looked like clusters of unpainted wooden balls as large as walnuts fastened together by steel rods" (p. 18).

Anderson evidently learned to accentuate the repetition of words and phrases from Gertrude Stein. Although, according to Irving Howe, he initially mocked her,[55] he soon became interested in her work. In 1922 he wrote his brother Karl, "As a matter of fact, you did introduce me to Gertrude Stein's work and I afterwards got a good deal out of it." [56] In his introduction to her *Geography and Plays* (1922), Anderson said, "For me the work of Gertrude Stein consists in a rebuilding, an entire new recasting of life, in the city of words." [57] Certain obvious influences from Gertrude Stein are permanently fixed in Anderson's style, especially the bare syntax and repetition. "I do try constantly," he said, "for a kind of simplification." [58] This can be seen in the introduction to *Winesburg* in 1919:

> Man made the truths himself and each truth was a composite of a great many vague thoughts. All about in the world were the truths and they were all beautiful. The old man had listed hundreds of the truths in his book. There was the truth of virginity and the truth of passion, the truth of wealth and of poverty, of thrift and of profligacy, of carelessness and abandon. Hundreds and hundreds were the truths and they were all beautiful. (p. 4)

In 1940, the year before he died, although the subject was different and the prose further simplified, the same basic structure sustained his prose.

It had begun between them and it went on. It was in the moonlight, when they were in the corn field at night. It was in the barn. It was upstairs, in the house, at night. He went up to her. He went up in his bare feet. Her father snored and her mother snored. He waited until he heard it, and then he went up to her.[59]

In the quarter of a century separating these two quotations Anderson experimented with several mutations of the vernacular. Before going on to the mixed style of *Poor White,* he pushed the pseudo-poetic implications of his *Winesburg* style to and beyond their limits in a series of *Mid-American Chants* (1918). Here he sought to wring the last drop of energy from a kind of Biblical spareness. The results were disastrous; the only advantage of the experiment was to show the dangers of certain aspects of the vernacular. Anderson spoke for "Chicago":

I am mature, a man child, in America, in the West, in the great valley of the Mississippi. My head arises above the corn fields. I stand up among the new corn.
I am a child, a confused child in a confused world. There are no clothes made that fit me. The minds of men cannot clothe me. Great projects arise within me. I have a brain and it is cunning and shrewd.[60]

And he sang, apparently for Dreiser, a "Song of Theodore":

I am alone in my room at night and in me is the spirit of the old priests. What cunning fingers I have. They make intricate designs on the white paper. See, the designs are words and sentences. . . .
I would make love always, to all people — men and women — here — in Chicago — in America — everywhere — always — forever — while  my  life lasts.[61]

It is to Anderson's credit that he abandoned this "prose-poetry" which parodied the very basis of the colloquial. The distance is impressive between such an ejaculative style and the fluent mixed-style Anderson used in *Poor White:*

> Hugh McVey was born in a little hole of a town stuck on a mud bank on the western shore of the Mississippi River in the state of Missouri. It was a miserable place in which to be born. With the exception of a narrow strip of black mud along the river, the land for ten miles back from the town — called in derision by river men "Mudcat Landing" — was almost entirely worthless and unproductive. The soil, yellow, shallow and stony, was tilled, in Hugh's time, by a race of long gaunt men who seemed as exhausted and no-account as the land on which they lived.[62]

"A little hole of a town stuck on a mud bank," "a miserable place," "no-account" are all vernacular born, but in effect are countered by "derision," "unproductive," and "gaunt." The relatively elaborate syntax represents a departure from the extreme simplification Anderson had tried in his chants. At the same time, by reversing the direction the vernacular was taking in literature, this book renewed the stylistic compromises of the past. Anderson seems to have recognized this, for he then abandoned the mixed style for first-person narrative.

He worked through several different narrators: the boy speaking in the manner of Huck; the man speaking of his boyhood, as Theodor Fischer does in Twain's *The Mysterious Stranger;* the man speaking of his own adult experience; the man observing and reporting the experience of others; and finally, the narrator discreetly withdrawn but with some traces of his speech still in the prose. Anderson, like his predecessors, was attempting to work out the main problem of the vernacular — how to drop the speaker yet retain the

speaking style. He began where Twain had found the vernacular at its purest — with Huck — and then progressively
raised the level of maturity. After he had raised it, he tried to
eliminate the narrator, but his prose had imperceptibly
grown more and more complicated, so that at last Anderson
found himself back in a mixed style only a little more colloquial than that of *Poor White*. Although he did not proceed
in so deliberate a fashion as my summary has suggested, the
fact that his 1923 short-story collection, *Horses and Men*, contains examples of each approach is sufficient proof that Anderson possessed some awareness of the stylistic problems
involved.

The narrator of "I'm a Fool" in *Horses and Men* says he is
"a big lumbering fellow of nineteen," yet he repeatedly uses
the adolescent interjections, "Gee Whizz, craps amighty,"
and "Gosh darn his eyes." Irving Howe thought "the monologue comes from Anderson's own mouth, Sherwood mas-
querading as an adolescent." [63] The impersonation, however,
allowed Anderson to separate and emphasize single details
in a conversational tone.

> Here's how it was. The place we were setting in
> was dark, like I said, and there was the roots from
> that old stump sticking up like arms, and there was
> a watery smell, and the night was like — as if you
> could put your hand out and feel it — so warm and
> soft and dark and sweet like an orange.
> I most cried and I most swore and most jumped up
> and danced, I was so mad and happy and sad.[64]

This has none of the strained pretentiousness of the twisted
apple sequence from *Winesburg*, and the scene is finely
evoked, culminating in the night sweet as an orange. But in
the next single-sentence paragraph Anderson insists on extending the sequence of "ands," and this exaggeration of the
polysyndeton typical of colloquial speech dissipates his effect.
Quite as extraneous as the extra "z" in "Gee Whizz," this

over-insistence is entirely typical of Anderson, whose greatest stylistic fault was a lack of tact.

"The Man Who Became a Woman" [65] is told through the perspective of an adult looking back upon an adolescent experience. Here Anderson is still able to retain a colloquial tone. Things and acts are still evoked one by one with minimal qualification. The narrator says he must tell this experience; the need is like Catholic confession, or better, like cleaning a room.

> The room gets pretty mussy and the bed not made some days and clothes and things thrown on the closet floor and maybe under the bed. And then you clean all up and put on new sheets, and then you take off all your clothes and get down on your hands and knees, and scrub the floor so clean you could eat bread off it, and then take a walk and come home after a while and your room smells sweet and you feel sweetened-up and better inside yourself too. (pp. 189–90)

By means of a kind of hypnotic reminiscence Anderson here managed to retain a childlike clarity. But with the next move, using an adult narrator dealing with an adult experience, synthetic constructions and qualifications began to attach themselves like limpets to the basic components of the prose. "The Triumph of a Modern" begins,

> Inasmuch as I have put to myself the task of trying to tell you a curious story in which I am myself concerned — in a strictly secondary way you must of course understand — I will begin by giving you some notion of myself.
> Very well then, I am a man of thirty-two, rather small in size, with sandy hair. I wear glasses. Until two years ago I lived in Chicago, where I had a position as a clerk in an office that afforded me a good enough living. (p. 21)

In "A Chicago Hamlet" the narrator has backed still further away from the immediate experiences told in the story. He tells a story told to him. Because the original experience is doubly filtered, through two minds, by this convention, the tone becomes more subjective and brooding. The narrator is disappearing, but so too is the crisp directness associated with Huck. Anderson tried to meet the problem head-on.

> . . . In telling this tale I have an advantage you who read cannot have. I heard the tale told, brokenly, by the man — who had the experience I am trying to describe. Story-tellers of old times, who went from place to place telling their wonder tales, had an advantage we, who have come in the age of the printed word, do not have. They were both story tellers and actors. As they talked they modulated their voices, made gestures with their hands. Often they carried conviction simply by the power of their own conviction. All of our modern fussing with style in writing is an attempt to do the same thing. (p. 177)

In "The Man's Story" Anderson admits that not only is the medium for telling the story imperfect, but so is his understanding of the story. "I have to bring up to you just what I can find, after diving down into this sea of motives and impulses — I admit I don't rightly understand." (pp. 300–301)

With "An Ohio Pagan" the narrator had withdrawn altogether. But so had the colloquial tone.

> That was a life! Round and round the track they went, young colthood and young manhood together, not thinking but carrying life very keenly within themselves and feeling tremendously. The colts' legs were to be hardened and their wind made sound, and for the boy long hours were to be spent in a kind of dream world, and life lived in the company of

something fine, courageous, filled with a terrible,
waiting surge of life. (p. 322)

By this point Anderson could only suggest colloquial speech
by exclamations ("How different the life of the city streets in
the springtime!"), by dashes ("On the evening of the day
when Tom Edwards — for the first and last time in his
life — went into a church, there was a light shower . . ."),
and by questions ("What went on in such a town? What happened at night in the houses of the towns?") (pp. 323, 330,
342).

Anderson tried to work out an objective colloquial prose
by repeating the experiments of past writers, but as he gradually eliminated his narrator, his prose became increasingly
fuzzy and flat, and his stories often lapsed into what Edmund Wilson called "those dreamlike and humorless fables
in which people almost never talk like the kind of provin-
cial Americans among whom the author had spent most of
his life." [66] Alfred Kazin accurately located the source of
Anderson's stylistic trouble. "Where Miss Stein and Hemingway both had resolved their break with the 'rules' into a conscious principle of design, Anderson had no sense of design at
all save as life afforded him one." [67] This was where his belief in American crudity betrayed him. In the central years of
his artistic life Anderson repeatedly confronted the problem
of the vernacular and left a legacy of distorted and flawed results. As John Peale Bishop remarked, "The trouble with
Anderson was there was never any telling just how long he
could keep up his pace. He had a bad way of stumbling. And
when he stumbled he fell flat." [68] Anderson tried to avoid
this, or thought he tried. In 1934 he wrote "You must know
it is extremely possible to be, for example, a fine novelist but
a bad writer. I have never wanted that. To me manner is all
important." [69] Yet he often seemed deaf and blind to what he
was writing, a condition particularly dangerous for a writer

of bare-bones prose. If on one page Anderson says a doctor drove a "jaded white horse," shortly it turns into "the jaded grey horse." [70] If he develops an extended description of a "drizzly wet October rain," in the midst of the paragraph he will suddenly refer to "dry shrivelled potato vines." [71] "He was clumsy and sentimental," Kazin thought. "He could even write at times as if he were finger-painting." [72] He seemed unaware of the contradictions in his style, and when he did recognize them, he tried to make them graces, to make bewilderment, inconsistency, and confusion indices of honesty. And yet for all of this, by insisting upon the dignity of the vernacular, by offering fresh demonstrations of its communicative powers, and by making the mistakes his younger, brighter, harder contemporaries would learn to avoid, Anderson contributed to the making of an American prose.

Anderson's experience, like Mark Twain's, and George Ade's, and Don Marquis's, and Ring Lardner's, shows how very hard it was to discover the underlying structure of the vernacular. Forced to operate through the convention of a narrator, and lacking the theoretical knowledge by which one might control his linguistic resources, these writers repeatedly failed, or achieved only seriously qualified successes, in their quest for style. The knowledge they lacked was being furnished, however, by Miss Gertrude Stein, a former medical student, who in the opening years of the century was methodically dissecting colloquial prose and lecturing upon its anatomy.

# FIVE

# Gertrude Stein

"I like anything that a word can do."
*Everybody's Autobiography*

## I

WE GAVE ARTIFICIAL PROMINENCE to the examples of word play, of semantic exploration, of punctuational emphasis, and of patterns of repetition in the work of Henry James and Mark Twain through capitalization, italics, and extraction from the surrounding text. While reading their books, one is often likely to pass over such innovations altogether, or to give them no more than that interested but necessarily perfunctory attention a driver gives to a curious smear on the highway ahead. To see, one must stop the car, get out, and look. So in order to focus on significant verbal and phrasal mutations, one is often obliged virtually to ignore the subject matter.[1] From the first years of her career Gertrude Stein did precisely that, increasingly detaching her prose from subject matter as conventionally understood and making it increasingly abstract. The bareness of her prose accentuated the colloquial characteristics of fragmentation, stress, and repetition we have been discussing and furnished invaluable examples of stylistic technique to those few willing to look attentively at her work.

Gertrude Stein's various critics have been inclined to accept her as a self-made revolutionary, somehow born into a garden of innocence from which she subsequently departed, alone and maddeningly unaware that she had sinned. Her sternest denigrator, Ben Reid, asserts that "the question of literary 'influence' upon Miss Stein's writing has little significance. Gertrude Stein is free of literary influences to a degree that has scarcely been true of any other writer since Homer. With the exception of *Three Lives,* her writing seems entirely *sui generis.*" [2] Her old personal friend, Louis Bromfield, shared this opinion. Gertrude Stein had not, he thought, "a cultivated mind but a naturally brilliant one. It is not like the minds of most of us, a derivative mind, formed by tradition, by culture, by the reading of books and daily papers and magazines. The thoughts which come from it are purely original, like the thoughts of a brilliant child." [3] Perry Miller left the issue up in the air; it was not clear to him whether she had arrived at her perceptions with help, or through "unassisted mother-wit." [4] Occasionally critics have acknowledged that her first work, *Quod Erat Demonstrandum* — published posthumously under the title of *Things As They Are* — was Jamesian, yet even her most subtle critic, Donald Sutherland, was led to muse, "It is very strange that when she could have started so well from Henry James she did not." [5]

On the other hand Perry Miller suggested an oblique relationship between Gertrude Stein and Mark Twain. He saw her as "the apparently artless child of instinct" who was in fact "a deliberate workman, securing her effects by careful plotting and getting out of them a poker-faced satisfaction that aligns her with nothing so much as with the tall-tale humorist of the American frontier." [6] Little external evidence exists, however, to link the two. Her brother Leo with whom she lived and traveled as a young adult admired *Huckleberry Finn,* calling it "that inestimable classic." [7] Alice B. Toklas, Miss Stein's life-long companion, once indicated privately that Mark Twain was Gertrude Stein's "favorite American writer — whom she was continuously reading," [8] but inasmuch as this appeared in a letter to a Mark Twain

biographer, it may have been courteous hyperbole. Gertrude
Stein herself tells us that she read *Huckleberry Finn* when
she was "very young," [9] and in *The Autobiography of Alice
B. Toklas* she not only describes a man as looking "exactly
like the pictures of Huckleberry Finn's father," [10] but also
indicates that she thought Hemingway was "yellow . . . just
like the flat-boat men on the Mississippi River as described
by Mark Twain" (p. 265).

In spite of her awareness of Mark Twain as a writer and in
spite of her being frequently placed in his camp by critics, it
was in Henry James that Gertrude Stein found her original
stylistic impetus. In her lecture, "What Is English Literature," she made a significant comment about what she saw in
James. "The thing to notice," she said, was that "his whole
paragraph was detached what it said from what it did, what it
was from what it held, and over it all something floated not
floated away but just floated, floated up there." [11] All of Gertrude Stein's experiments with language are no more than
explorations of what floated up there and how it was sustained.

When Adele, the character in *Things As They Are* with
the closest resemblance to Gertrude Stein herself, was asked,
"Haven't you ever stopped thinking long enough to feel,"
her answer was

> "Why I suppose if one can't think at the same time
> I will never accomplish the feat of feeling. I always
> think. I don't see how one can stop it." [12]

This perceptive self-analysis goes a long way to explain Gertrude Stein's stylistic course. Her active interest in the mind
and its workings had begun at least as early as 1894 when
with a fellow student, Leon Solomons, she had carried on a
series of experiments with automatic writing in the Harvard
laboratory of Hugo Munsterberg. In September 1896 they
published an article describing their results, "Normal Motor

Automatism," in the *Psychological Review*. Gertrude Stein retained this experimental and objective point of view throughout most of her writing career. Even when she was recounting what were apparently severe personal emotional traumas in both *Things As They Are* and "Melanctha," the emotion was filtered and stylized in its passage through her mind. It is ironic that a writer often accused of permitting the pen to follow free associations should be one who placed so much importance on intellectual control.[13]

To return to the exchange from *Things As They Are* quoted above: As important as the admission that Adele can not stop thinking was the way in which the thought was expressed. The question mark has vanished because it was superfluous. (As Gertrude Stein commented years later, "A question is a question, anybody can know that a question is a question and so why add to it the question mark when it is already there when the question is already there in the writing." [14]) The anticipated comma following "why" has disappeared too, as has the possible one separating the two clauses between "time" and "I." Dropping punctuation is the opposite of James's normal practice, but curiously this technique, which Gertrude Stein later pushed toward its limit, produces much the same result as does excessive punctuation. Both methods isolate thoughts in a series of units, although by different means.

Here usage is made to conform to the evidence supplied by a sensitive ear coupled with the demands of a logical mind. If there is no good semantic reason for a question mark, neither is there one for separating "why" from "I suppose." That phrase can be delivered in two ways: either with a deliberate, thoughtful pause after "why," in which case the comma is obligatory; or by running the words together, with "why" becoming no more than a mannerism, an automatic verbal addition used for the sake of delay. With the sanction of psychological accuracy behind it, Gertrude Stein could then (only occasionally and cautiously here) deny the reader's expectations, give him a slight shake by changing the direction of her prose. By gradually increasing the incidence of novelty, she worked out her unique and often opaque style.

Gertrude Stein was quite willing to locate herself in the Jamesian fold. She once referred to her Radcliffe period saying, "It is rather strange that she was not then at all interested in the work of Henry James for whom she now has a very great admiration and whom she considers quite definitely as her forerunner, he being the only nineteenth-century writer who being an American felt the method of the twentieth century." [15] She went on, "Oddly enough in all of her formative period she did not read him and was not interested in him. But as she often says one is always naturally antagonistic to one's parent and sympathetic to one's grandparents." In support of this Robert McAlmon reported in 1925 that Gertrude Stein had said to him, "Nobody has done anything to develop the English language since Shakespeare, except myself, and Henry James perhaps a little." [16]

The phrase "perhaps a little" can be glossed usefully by an examination of Gertrude Stein's first work, *Things As They Are*. Only eighty-eight pages long, the book describes a triangular relationship among three women. Each one is intended to represent a "civilization" and an ethical attitude. The whole is methodically divided into three sections, and it ends with no issue: " 'I am afraid it comes very near being a deadlock,' she groaned dropping her head on her arms" (p. 88). An overt reference is made to *The Wings of the Dove* when Adele says to herself, "I know there is no use in asking for an explanation. Like Kate Croy she would tell me 'I shall sacrifice nothing and nobody' " (p. 75).

John Malcolm Brinnin thought the book "naïvely colored by touches of Henry James," [17] and Donald Sutherland believed that "in its way it is a Jamesian study or demonstration." [18] Both critics deduce the influence of James upon

Gertrude Stein from the two writers' shared interest in "the endless resources of the mind when it is moved to make interpretations of events or to register the climates of emotional situations." [19] But the enduring significance of Gertrude Stein's apprenticeship to James lies in her assumption of his stylistic mannerisms. It was her elaboration of them that showed Ernest Hemingway how similarities in the styles of Twain and Ring Lardner could be utilized in order to organize colloquial language.

Both the dialogue and the narrative of *Things As They Are* make use of the rhetorical patterns of repetition that we have seen in James. The mannerism happened to be especially useful for the "mathematical proof" Gertrude Stein proposed to make. As soon as the trio of women are introduced, conscious rhetoric and unconscious alliteration emerge in the prose.

> All three of them were college bred American women of the wealthier class but with that all resemblance between them ended. Their appearance, their attitudes and their talk both as to manner and to matter showed the influence of different localities, different forebears and different family ideals. They were distinctly American but each one at the same time bore definitely the stamp of one of the older civilizations, incomplete and frustrated in this American version but still always insistent. (p. 4)

The women share a single aspect (they are of the wealthy educated class) but they are differentiated in three ways (appearance, attitudes, and talk). These three ways are in turn divided into two more (manner and matter). This division is determined, Gertrude Stein says, by three more distinctions (locale, ancestors, and family ideals). The urge here is clearly toward charting, toward the establishment of fixed relationships, in short, toward extreme formalization.

Adele sets up a similarly rigorous rhetorical pattern in a letter whose essential structure is this:

My dear Sophie . . .
  Either . . .     or . . .
  If the first . . .    then . . .
  If the second . . .   then . . .
  If you don't . . .    then . . .
  If you do . . .     then . . .[20]

Such structural repetition provides an appropriate support for the carefully objectified account Gertrude Stein had undertaken. However, when phrasal repetition occurs in the dialogue, then an important link is being established between James and Hemingway. These examples suggest the continuity.

> "Dear WE ARE NEITHER OF US SORRY that we know enough to find it out, are we?" "No," Helen answered "WE ARE NEITHER OF US SORRY." (p. 43, capitals added)

> "I CERTAINLY NEVER EXPECTED TO FIND YOU one of the most gentle and considerate of human kind," she commented quietly and then Helen made it clearer. "I CERTAINLY DID NOT EXPECT THAT YOU WOULD FIND ME SO," she answered. (p. 11, capitals added)

> "SHE IS QUEER AND WILL INTEREST YOU and YOU ARE QUEER AND WILL INTEREST HER. Oh! I don't want to listen to your protests, YOU ARE QUEER AND INTERESTING even if you don't know it and YOU LIKE QUEER AND INTERESTING PEOPLE even if you think you don't and you are not a bit bashful in spite of your convictions to the contrary, so come along." (p. 28, capitals added)

Gertrude Stein also employed repetition as thematic reinforcement. For example, accused of selfishness and a lack of restraint, of indulgent egocentricity, Adele launches into a defense of herself that, in the reiteration of "I," reveals the accuracy of the criticism.

"(I) do not admit," she said, "that (I) was wrong
in wanting to know. (I) suppose one might in a spirit
of Quixotic generosity deny oneself such a right
but as a reasonable being, (I) feel that (I) had a
right to know. (I) realize perfectly that it was hopelessly wrong to learn it from Sophie instead of from
you. (I) admit (I) was a coward, (I) was simply afraid
to ask you." Helen laughed harshly. "You need not
have been," she said. "I would have told you nothing." "(I) think you are wrong, (I) am quite sure
that you would have told me and (I) wanted to
spare myself that pain, perhaps spare you it too,
(I) don't know. (I) repeat (I) cannot believe that (I)
was wrong in wanting to know." (p. 42, paren-
theses added)

Sometimes the repetition of a word is joined with associative rhyme, as in " 'I honor you for being honest.' 'Oh honest,' returned Adele lightly. 'Honesty is a selfish virtue. Yes I
am honest enough' " (p. 15). Sometimes sounds are uncon-
sciously counter-posed one against the other. "Her ACCUS-
tomed DEFinite resignation and the tremendous DIFFiculty of
ACCOmplishment" (p. 40, capitals added). And sometimes a
word unexpectedly crosses the boundary between narrative
and dialogue in order to be repeated. "SUDDENLY she stopped
and dropped heavily on a bench. 'Why' she said in a tone of
intense interest, 'it's like a bit of mathematics. SUDDENLY it
does itself and you begin to see,' and then she laughed" (p.
16, capitals added). I can hardly explain the source of these
examples, but they need pointing out, for they are not normally found in nineteenth-century prose. Although I doubt
that they are consciously composed, they do seem to be deliberately retained. I then take them to be an important part of
the colloquial tradition which retains evidences of extempo-
raneity that had been formerly eliminated in revision as
blemishes.

On several occasions in *Things As They Are* Gertrude

Stein openly indicates her understanding of how the mind operates. Thought gathers to a verbalization.

> ADELE CONTINUED A LONG TIME TO LOOK OUT ON THE WATER. "I wonder" SHE SAID TO HERSELF AGAIN. FINALLY IT CAME MORE DEFINITELY. "Yes I wonder. There isn't much use in wondering about Helen. I know no more now than I did last night and I am not likely to be much wiser. . . ." AND SHE RELAPSED ONCE MORE INTO SILENCE. HER MEDITATIONS AGAIN TOOK FORM. "As for me is it another little indulgence of my superficial emotions or is there any possibility of my really learning to realise stronger feelings. If it's the first I will call a halt promptly and at once. If it's the second I won't back out, no not for any amount of moral sense," and she smiled to herself. (p. 13, capitals added)

On another occasion the same idea is even more clearly expressed. " 'Was I brutal this afternoon?' SHE THOUGHT IT IN DEFINITE WORDS 'and does she really care?' " (p. 14, capitals added)

If one thinks in words, then one hypothesis will hold that the original, the primal statement represents pure truth. This belief was to influence Gertrude Stein's stylistic progress. Evidence of the mind operating by associations of sound already can be found in the narrative prose of her first novel. Even as Henry James fell into fits of alliteration — the more so when he began to dictate his work as an expression of confidence in controlled spontaneity — so Gertrude Stein this early displays similar signs of associational workings in the mind. Such moments are still infrequent and obscured by the narrative movement, but the seeds are planted. As here:

> The two were left settled down again quietly but somehow the silence now subtly suggested the significance of their being alone together. (p. 7)

There would be no need of recognizing their existence, but these two people who would be equally
familiar if they were equally little known would as
the acquaintance progressed, undoubtedly expose
large tracts of unexplored and unknown quantities,
filled with new and strange excitements. (p. 3)

Finally there are phrases determined as "the feat of feeling"
was; they present an equally odd sound and appearance, as
"and so she lay there quite quiet, quite dulled" (p. 10).

## II

Gertrude Stein made one more attempt to deal with love.
This time she further increased the distance between herself
and her material. In "Melanctha," the second of her *Three
Lives*, she outlined the history of a heterosexual love affair.
Using personal experience acquired when she was a medical
student at Johns Hopkins, she transferred the action from the
white upper-middle class to the Baltimore negro. She also reduced the affair from a triangle to a psychological tug-of-war
between Jeff Campbell and Melanctha Herbert. Essentially,
however, much of the emotional climate and motivation of
"Melanctha" are identical with those of the earlier story. The
Adele of *Things As They Are,* whose resemblance to Gertrude Stein herself has been noted by B. Reid,[21] becomes Jeff
Campbell, while Helen is changed into Melanctha.[22] Other
figures are added to or erased from the cast, but the main
contest between the two intelligent members of the triangle
in *Things As They Are,* between the mind-heart and the
mind-conscience, is retained.

Just how and when Gertrude Stein decided to transform
the material of *Things As They Are* into "Melanctha" is not
clear, for we possess differing accounts of the genesis of the
later work. At least a superficial connection with Flaubert's
*Trois Contes* is obvious.[23] Since Henry James had been a

qualified admirer of Flaubert, having called him in his preface to *Madame Bovary* in 1902 "the novelist's novelist," [24] Gertrude Stein's interest in him is understandable. Flaubert stressed those aspects of writing congenial to her, objectivity and accuracy in content, rhythm and harmony in treatment. But whatever his effect upon her writing, the important consideration here is the link between *Three Lives* and *Things As They Are*. Was the shift sudden, abrupt, and absolute, or a gradual, clear extension of learned principles?

The most accomplished of the three histories, "Melanctha" contains an abundance of materials related to *Things As They Are*. Two sentences in particular are useful guides to the stylistic reorganization Gertrude Stein imposed on her old material. Each sentence appears first in *Things As They Are,* and is then amplified in "Melanctha."

> "Tell me how much do you care for me." "Care for you my dear," Helen answered, "more than you know and less than you think." (p. 15)

> "I certainly do care for you Jeff Campbell less than you are always thinking and much more than you are ever knowing." [25]

> "You have no right to constantly use your pain as a weapon" Adele flashed out angrily. (p. 60)

> "You ain't got no right Melanctha Herbert," flashed out Jeff through his dark, frowning anger, "you certainly ain't got no right always to be using your being hurt and being sick, and having pain, like a weapon. . . ." (p. 172)

The epigrammatic concision of the original sentences is sacrificed to a programmatic conception of style. The elements emphasized by Gertrude Stein are familiar by now: repetition, punctuation and its lack, and numerous present participles, all of which are intended to produce local emphasis, immediacy, and a noticeable rhythmic effect.

"Melanctha" is a conglomeration of such eccentric and apparently uncontrolled effects. Although a close reading can demonstrate the relevance of many of the author's experiments to the story's thematic development, quite as many instances seem to be no more than inexplicable fussing, distortion for the sake of distortion. A simple example of this is Gertrude Stein's random hyphenation, reminiscent of Mark Twain's fondness for varying his punctuation of compound words. If on page ninety-one of the Modern Library edition Melanctha is said to have "break neck courage," then on page ninety-five it becomes "breakneck," and shifts back again on page ninety-seven to "break neck." [26] Inconsistent as the technique may be it still makes a distinct impression of innovation.

The diction of "Melanctha" is considerably simplified.[27] By using a carefully restricted vocabulary Gertrude Stein was able to point up patterns of language, rhythms, and verbal combinations. Her ironic juxtaposition of words, her shifting meanings, and her dislocation of syntax depended on simplicity of diction in order to be noticed. In the following passage the fact that few words are used emphasizes the distinctions gradually established between being "bitter" and "a little bitter," and between "beauty" and "real beauty." [28]

> Now Jeff had come to where he could understand Melanctha Herbert. Jeff was not bitter to her because she could not really love him, he was bitter only that he had let himself have a real illusion in him. He was a little bitter too, that he had lost now, what he had always felt real in the world, that had made it for him always full of beauty, and now he had not got this new religion really, and he had lost what he before had to know what was good and had real beauty. (p. 190)

"Melanctha" still contains a few instances of word play:
the desire of two lonely people to "talk low some" (p. 115),
"real religion" (p. 191), "your kind of kindness" (p. 176),
"patient doctor" (p. 170). But their frequency is low, as is
that of rhyme, alliteration, assonance, and other instances of
aural association. Gertrude Stein steadily drew away from
puns and portmanteau words; although evidence of the vola-
tility of language as well as accidents of syntax were often left
in her early work, neither were of much interest to her. She
weeded them out and made her prose answer to that mon-
strous, often comic, internal logic that was her specialty.

Gertrude Stein generally arranged and punctuated her
narrative in three ways. Rarely employing subordinate conjunctions or the semi-colon, she often relied upon a series of
short declarative sentences, in the manner of Henry James,
begun on a repeated or slightly varied phrase. Or she used
commas to do the work of the stronger signals of pause, which
gave her prose something of a run-on effect. Or she used polysyndeton, that is, the frequent repetition of the co-ordinating
conjunction. No matter which method she used, her narrative moved methodically through a sequence of experiences,
or if it sought to render a complex state in time, then each
part of that state was laid on separately without any attempt
at synthesis. The difference is, roughly, that existing between,

Although she was smiling, her feet hurt.

and:

She smiled. Her feet hurt.

She smiled, her feet hurt.

She smiled and her feet hurt.

The first example is synthesized, while the other three represent typical Steinian procedures.

Within this restricted set of structural patterns, Gertrude

Stein executed endless verbal variations. Some were semantic (as in the distinction between "bitter" and "a little bitter"), some syntactic (as in the placement of the adverb in this example: "She didn't know how well now I know you," p. 151), and some rhythmic.

When her narrative was punctuated by commas, Gertrude Stein made it sound very much like an off-key product of Henry James.

> Then it came that Jeff knew he could not say out any more, what it was he wanted, he could not say out any more, what it was, he wanted to know about, what Melanctha wanted. (p. 161)

Such choppy rhythms are sometimes useful, as here in organically rendering Jeff's uncertainty, but they are derivative and annoying. Gertrude Stein soon dropped them, preferring plain, run-on sentences. In *Lectures in America,* composed and delivered in the 'thirties, she called the comma "servile," announcing cheerfully that "a comma by helping you along holding your coat for you and putting on your shoes keeps you from living your life as actively as you should lead it" (pp. 219–20). The accumulation of a series of brief declarative sentences is more characteristic of Gertrude Stein's achieved style. "Jeff Campbell never asked Melanctha any more if she loved him," begins a typical sequence. "Now things were always getting worse between them. Now Jeff was always very silent with Melanctha. Now Jeff never wanted to be honest to her, and now Jeff never had much to say to her" (p. 188).

When on the other hand Gertrude Stein connected her narrative with a series of "ands," she departed from Mark Twain's example in *Huckleberry Finn.* He normally provided colloquial ease and untroubled clarity, but Gertrude Stein stirs the reader with bumps, blocks, and slight detours. Laid out in units the following sentence demonstrates how, on a monosyllabic base of the simple acts (and even of the clichés) of a distraught lover, a harmonic structure is built.

> All that long day,
> with the warm moist young spring stirring in him,
> Jeff Campbell worked,
> and thought,
> and beat his breast,
> and wandered,
> and spoke aloud,
> and was silent,
> and was certain,
> and then in doubt and then keen to surely feel,
> and then all sodden in him;
>
> and he walked
> and he sometimes ran fast to lose himself in his rush-
>     ing,
> and he bit his nails to pain and bleeding,
> and he tore his hair so that he could be sure he was
>     really feeling,
> and he never could know what it was right,
> he now should be doing. (pp. 195–6)

Phrases such as "he bit his nails to pain and bleeding" and "wanted to be honest to her" are precisely what Donald Sutherland must have meant when he said that Gertrude Stein works out of "a version of the most popular phrasing." [29] It is this "version" too that helps to explain John Peale Bishop's description of the style of *Three Lives* as "a curious formalization of the common speech." [30]

As a complement to this kind of phrasal organization Gertrude Stein continued to expand her use of repetition.[31] Near the end of "Melanctha" an instance occurs in which variations are played upon exactly the same kind of repetition Isabel Archer employed, "Osmond's beautiful mind, Osmond's beautiful mind." Here Melanctha, having broken almost altogether with Jeff Campbell, wants to move in with her old friend Rose Johnson. But Rose will not invite her

> IT COULD NEVER COME TO MELANCTHA to ask Rose to let her. IT NEVER COULD COME TO MELANCTHA to think that Rose would ask her. IT WOULD NEVER EVER COME TO MELANCTHA to want it, if Rose should ask her, but Melanctha would have done it for the safety she always felt when she was near her. Melanctha Herbert wanted badly to be safe now, but this living with her, that, Rose would never give her. ROSE HAD STRONG THE SENSE for proper conduct, ROSE HAD STRONG THE SENSE to get straight always what she wanted, and she always knew what was the best thing she needed and always Rose got what she wanted. (p. 215, capitals added)

Such repetition fulfills an organic purpose. It graphically expresses the difference between the "subtle, intelligent, complex" Melanctha and the "shrewd, simple, selfish" Rose. Melanctha's phrases shift slightly each time they are repeated, and periods isolate her thoughts in separate sentences. But Rose's mind goes straight to the point, three times saying exactly the same thing. As the paragraph ends it is abundantly clear why Rose always got what she wanted.

Sometimes, however, the repetition becomes playful. In the following instance, the seriousness is eased by the pattern of words.

> Dr. Campbell BEGAN TO FEEL A LITTLE about how she responded to him. Dr. Campbell BEGAN TO SEE A LITTLE that perhaps Melanctha had a good mind. Dr. Campbell was not sure yet that she had a good mind, but he BEGAN TO THINK A LITTLE that perhaps she might have one. (p. 116, capitals added)

This repetition guides us to a recognition that Dr. Campbell's feelings, senses, and mind are all beginning to respond to the warmth of a woman. Yet the chilly shell of his caution is symbolized by the repeated professional title, "Dr. Campbell."

Other words are repeated not only locally but throughout the work. They often bear a symbolic meaning that only becomes partially clear through repeated use in separate contexts. "Wandering," for example, is an ambiguous term usually associated with Melanctha to suggest activity of a sexual nature. And if Jeff Campbell's steady verbal signal for sexual activity is "getting excited," then for him its opposite is "living regular." His ultimate accusation of Melanctha is that she cannot "remember right" — that is, she rearranges reality to fit her emotional needs (p. 181). Melanctha in turn is proud that she never "hollers," that she can stoically bear both physical and psychical pain. These are all major terms in the central patterns of the story. Other words used less frequently but often enough to develop an aura of meaning that wavers and changes as each is placed in relation to the others are "summer," "tender," and "sunshine." Others like "sweetness," "patient," "decent," "good," "happy," "simple," and "suffer," although repeated frequently, do not become symbols but carry only the weight they accumulate through usage.

Two words, however, drone steadily throughout "Melanctha." "Always" and "certainly" recur in every possible combination to lend support to the epigraph of the book, which says that there is misery in the world, but neither human nor cosmic responsibility for it: "Donc je suis un malheureux et ce n'est ni ma faute ni celle de la vie." The characters in "Melanctha" move to an inexorable rhythm determined by the pulse of an apparently indifferent universe. With the repetition of these two words we are given ironic insight as we hear the characters qualify their words with absolutes just when they are losing control.

I certainly do know . . .
I certainly do understand . . .

I certainly do see . . .
I certainly do believe . . . (pp. 122–4)

*We* know that Jeff and Melanctha are engaged in still another mathematical proof, in a "struggle that was as sure
always to be going on between them as their minds and
hearts always were to have different ways of working" (p.
153). But in the full light of our knowledge, even as we are
slowly impressed by the menacing beat of inevitability we
also pity these people in their blind certainty.


### III

In her next book, *The Making of Americans* (written
1906–8, published 1925), Gertrude Stein turned repetition
to another purpose. She used it to establish what she called
"the continuous present." This was the next stage beyond
that "prolonged present" she felt she had achieved in "Melanctha." That is, in "Melanctha" there were clots of extended, revolving, repeated conversations strung upon a simple, short narrative line. But in *The Making of Americans*
the prose was all of a piece, like the later prose of Henry
James. In that it had no story, she thought her mammoth
book was like *Remembrance of Things Past* and *Ulysses,* the
other two of "the three novels written in this generation that
are the important things written in this generation." [32] Story
obviously depended upon memory, and as she explained in
"Composition as Explanation," the lecture she delivered at
Oxford University in 1926, she believed that the immediate
moment had to be embodied in literature. "The composition
is the thing seen by every one living in the living they are
doing." [33] Composition is an explanation of the world as understood, and people, she felt, understand reality as a "continuous present." Memory and past associations are not, in
the deepest sense, important. Immediacy simply is. The importance then for prose style is that conventional rhetoric

isn't. "Composition is not there, it is going to be there and we are here" (p. 456). It was this desire for immediacy that explained why, as Donald Sutherland pointed out, she was eventually obliged to give up science. "Science is description and prediction in terms of the already familiar." [34] The idea of presentness is also helpful in clarifying her abuse and distortion of syntax. When she discusses grammar in *How To Write* (1931), many of her remarks are witty denials of memory and the synthesizing mind.

> Grammar makes dates.
> Grammar may be reconstituted.
> Grammar includes excuse felicity.
> Grammar has been called a list of what is to be done with it.
> Grammar is in our power.
> Grammar means that it has to be prepared and cooked.
> Grammar is not grown.
> Grammar is resemblance.
> Grammar who hesitates. [35]

The immediate stylistic consequence of her desire for a continuous present had two aspects: it brought on a new spate of participles and gerunds, and it multiplied the instances of repetition a hundredfold. Both stylistic quirks had appeared in "Melanctha," but these were only part of a kaleidoscope of experiment. Now they were to be reinforced by theory.

When participles and gerunds come in "Melanctha," they come in bunches. Jeff Campbell tries to explain to Melanctha why he objects to colored people seeking only sensual experience.

> Instead of just working hard and caring about their working and living regular with their families and saving up all their money, so they will have some to bring up their children better, instead of living

> regular and doing like that and getting all their new
> ways from just decent living, the colored people just
> keep running around and perhaps drinking and
> doing everything bad they can ever think of. . . .
> (p. 121)

Gerunds keep reverberating here after they have been passed
by, and their tones blend into one another, while, like a gyro-
scope, the whirring repetition of the word "just" helps to
steady the passage. Yet there is no strong sense of purpose
here, for Gertrude Stein is still groping for a style. A similar
instance occurs in this sequence excerpted from a much
longer letter Jeff writes to Melanctha.

> I find it very hard, and I never said it any different,
> it is hard to me to be understanding, and to know
> really what it is you wanted, and what it is you are
> meaning by what you are always saying to me. I
> don't say ever, it ain't very hard for you to be stand-
> ing that I ain't very quick to be following whichever
> way that you are always leading. (p. 147)

In that last sentence, "standing . . . following . . . leading" form a related series, but because it depends on a second
meaning of the word "standing" (which here denotes "toler-
ating" or "bearing") this relationship possesses a semantic
tension that can only be resolved in amusement or irritation.
Again the construction has more play to it than purpose.

The very uncertainty of intention evident in "Melanctha"
helps to explain why Gertrude Stein usually chose to discuss
her career as dating from *The Making of Americans.* In her
later lectures and autobiographical work she never, so far as I
know, mentions the other two stories in *Three Lives,* and in
spite of its very considerable reputation, only rarely does she
refer to "Melanctha." But by the time she wrote *The Making
of Americans* — which she explicated in a lecture characteristically entitled "The Gradual Making of the Making of

Americans" — Gertrude Stein had begun to work out a com-
prehensive theory by which she could direct her stylistic pro-
pensities. No longer was she obviously derivative. Now she
possessed a rationale for her reorganization of prose.

Whether, in fact, as that rationale proposed, participles do
create an impression of presentness or not is of little importance here. Gertrude Stein felt they did. Insofar as participles
suggest continuity of action, there is at least a general relationship between participles and that moving continuum
that Gertrude Stein understood to be the present. As we have
seen, Mark Twain had already used participles extensively in
*Huckleberry Finn.* Especially when Huck was excited by an
incident, as he was when he observed the Sherburne lynch
mob, he fell into a series of participles and imperfect constructions which re-created movement and kept the action
continuous. Mark Twain told a dramatic story that involved
a world so substantial and variegated that the color of his
story obscured his mechanisms. But as Gertrude Stein worked
more and more through the mind and expressed her abstractions with an emphasis on manner, expression virtually over-
whelmed meaning. Still, the two impulses toward immediacy,
Huck's and Gertrude Stein's, are virtually the same, the
difference being in the subject — on the one hand, matter,
and, on the other, mind. With such similarities and distinctions in mind, it is instructive to compare Huck's account of
the steamboat smashing through his raft with a typical ruminative passage from *The Making of Americans.*

> Well, here she comes, and we said she was *going to*
> try to shave us; but she didn't seem to be *sheering*
> off a bit. She was a big one, and she was *coming* in
> a hurry, too, *looking* like a black cloud with rows
> of glow-worms around it; but all of a sudden she
> bulged out, big and scary, with a long row of wide-
> open furnace doors *shining* like red-hot teeth, and
> her monstrous bows and guards *hanging* right over

us. There was a yell at us, and a *jingling* of bells to
stop the engines, a pow-wow of *cussing,* and *whistling* of steam — and as Jim went overboard on one
side and I on the other, she come *smashing* straight
through the raft. (ch. 16, italics added)

Huck calls upon the direct present in this account and laces it
heavily with the imperfect tense and present participles and
gerunds, so that the action swirls around our ears. Gertrude
Stein, on the other hand, by means of participles and gerunds
makes herself felt as a presence meditating meaning.

There is then as I am *saying* complete disillusion
in *living,* the *realising,* completely *realising* that not
any one, not one *fighting* for the same *thinking* and
*believing* as the other, not any one has the same *believing* in her or in him that any other one has in
them and it comes then sometime to most every
one to be *realising* with *feeling* this thing and then
they often stop having friendly *feeling* and then
often they begin again but it is then a different thing
between them, they are old then and not young then
in their *feeling.*[36]

Gertrude Stein understood repetition to have a psychological function as well as an aesthetic one. She had been led in
her work in psychology, she said, to realize that "everybody
said the same thing over and over again . . . until finally if
you listened with great intensity you could hear it rise and
fall and tell all that that there was inside of them, not so
much by the actual words they said or the thoughts they had
but the movement of their thoughts and words endlessly the
same and endlessly different." [37]

Stimulated by this realization, Gertrude Stein began to
spin out her long ribbons of words, confident that she had a
defensible theory behind the practice. That theory derived in
part from William James's understanding of the nature of

experience. Cited by his student Gertrude Stein as "one of
the strongest scientific influences that I had," [38] he believed
that in our experiences "changes are not complete annihila-
tions followed by complete creations of something absolutely
novel. There is partial decay and partial growth, and all the
while a nucleus of relative constancy from which what decays
drops off, and which takes into itself whatever is grafted
on, until at length something wholly different has taken
place." [39] In the lecture, "The Gradual Making of the Making of Americans," Gertrude Stein defended her approach
and at the same time embodied the defense in her style. William James's "nucleus of relative constancy" I take to be equivalent to the identity which people, according to Gertrude
Stein, slowly but inevitably display.

> A history of any one must be a long one, slowly it
> comes out from them from their beginning to their
> ending, slowly you can see it in them the nature
> and the mixtures in them, slowly everything comes
> out from each one in the kind of repeating each one
> does in the different parts and kinds of living
> they have in them, slowly then any one who looks
> well at any one will have the history of the whole
> of that one.[40]

In brief stretches this is readable and clear. Over a long period it begins to fit the description Marcel Proust once applied to Flaubert's prose: "Ce grand Trottoir Roulant . . .
au défilement continu, monotone, morne, indéfini." [41] As
for Gertrude Stein, she simply denied that she repeated at all,
arguing that "if anything is alive there is no such thing as
repetition." [42] "It is," she wrote by way of illustration, "very
like a frog hopping he cannot ever hop exactly the same distance or the same way of hopping at every hop" (p. 167). All
the technique in *The Making of Americans* was put to work
to make a series of subtle psychological distinctions, to sug-

gest delicate shifts in meaning, to push nuance to its furthest limits. The placement of words became of the utmost importance.

James, Gertrude Stein, and Hemingway then all share an uncommon interest in so arranging words as to produce a series of close but not identical meanings. A shared aesthetic and psychological interest unites James's characters as they carefully test, compare, and criticize their definitions of words; Gertrude Stein's meditative mind slowly makes distinctions by means of the very slightest verbal adjustments; and in Hemingway's world laconic repetitions conceal a variety of emotions.

I V

With *Tender Buttons,* Gertrude Stein moved in the direction of what Henry James called in another connection "divinations of private congruity." [43] She reached the idea for this queer book through a series of apparently logical steps. In *The Making of Americans* she had tried to record the composition of an American family. Dissatisfied because she was still bound to historical memory, she then turned to "portraits" of her contemporaries. These she found more satisfactory, for "the making of a portrait of any one is as they are existing and as they are existing has nothing to do with remembering any one or anything." [44] But after working with portraits for a time, Gertrude Stein perceived that she was still harassed by memory. "The trouble . . . was that in regard to human beings looking inevitably carried in its train realizing movements and expressions and as such forced me into recognizing resemblances, and so forced remembering and in forcing remembering caused confusion of present with past and future time" (p. 188). It was to avoid this that she turned at last to making "portraits of rooms and food and everything because there I could avoid this difficulty of suggesting remembering more easily . . . than if I were to describe human beings" (p. 188).

In *Tender Buttons* then Gertrude Stein contemplated the object and wrote as she concentrated on it. Her technique is very much like an artistic implementation of a remark made by Henri Bergson, whose lectures Gertrude Stein had attended in 1908. "Either there is no philosophy possible, and all knowledge of things is a practical knowledge aimed at the profit to be drawn from them, or else philosophy consists in placing oneself within the object itself by an effort of intuition." [45] As with Henry James often and Hemingway sometimes, Gertrude Stein described her subject without naming it: "If you feel what is inside that thing you do not call it by the name by which it is known." [46] By working around the object, by packing the clay of words around it, she built a subjectively accurate form.

For all intents and purposes though, this meant that conventional meaning had dropped from her prose. She later acknowledged that "At the end of all this I had come to know I had a melody and to be certain of my melody that melody carried me . . ." (pp. 200–201). But she knew very well that "melody should always be a by-product it should never be an end in itself . . . and so as I say I very exactly began again" (p. 201). In *Tender Buttons,* however, she continued to work with words as counters, as seemingly empty, although interestingly shaped, containers that gained significance only by means of their relationships with other words on the page. All remembered action was eliminated. Attention centered on the page, the paragraph, the phrase, the single word. This "discontextuated activity" focused the reader's attention on the surface of the prose by emphasizing the appearance of the word, syntactical relationships, prose rhythms, and harmony of sounds. Although she did not intend her work for this purpose, Gertrude Stein did colloquial prose a very considerable service by emphasizing its submerged patterns. Without her experiments it appears likely — as the last chapter suggested — that writers working the colloquial vein might soon have had to abandon their work, for men like Damon Runyon were already marketing fool's gold.

For those seriously interested in the art of writing, *Tender Buttons* became a hectic primer of possibilities. If *The Making of Americans* was dynamic, moving constantly on a participial and gerundive base, then *Tender Buttons* was static, nounal, concentrated on objects. Its very method presupposed stability. To be contemplated, the object must be poised, to be entered it must rest. This accounts, I think, for the excessive use of the verb "to be" in the book. The copula connects the subject with its qualities without requiring activity. "A white hunter is nearly crazy," and "A blind agitation is manly and uttermost." [47] It especially mediates between a series of assertions about a single object.

> A purse was not green, it was not straw color, it was hardly seen and it had a use, a long use and the chain, the chain was never missing, it was not misplaced, it showed that it was open, that is all that it showed. (p. 414)

The commonest relationship in *Tender Buttons* is that of plain contiguity.

> A light white, a disgrace, an ink spot, a rosy charm. (p. 416)

The items in such an enumeration may be separated by conjunctions:

> A seal and matches and a swan and ivy and a suit. (p. 408)

Or the series may be provided with a conclusion:

> The lamp and the cake and the cover are not the only necessity altogether. (p. 412)

Or its elements may be qualified:

> A cool red rose and a pink cut pink, a collapse and
> a sold hole, a little less hot. (p. 417)

Nothing here is simple, nothing mechanically pure. *Tender Buttons* is a scrambled text in which play and colors, particulars and abstractions are all mixed together. Whatever rational meaning these phrases may be intended to have is not very important. It is the rhythms they carry, the "melody" that demands attention. Each word must be read carefully if one is to read the text at all. The search for meaning forces the attention to probe each word in turn, never certain whether it will join the word it precedes or the one that follows, or both. Throughout all this the various forms of the verb "to be" provide a percussive beat for the verbal melody. Twain did something like this at times, but without sacrificing what we conventionally understand to be meaning. He implicitly asserts the importance and value of accurate details when he expresses them, whereas Gertrude Stein asserts the importance of *words,* especially as they have been heretofore made subservient to plot. But as Huck enumerates things for themselves, the copulative base sometimes emerges.

> There WAS some books too, piled up perfectly exact, on each corner of the table. One WAS a big family Bible, full of pictures. One WAS "Pilgrim's Progress," about a man that left his family it didn't say why. I read considerable in it now and then. The statements WAS interesting, but tough. Another WAS "Friendship's Offering," full of beautiful stuff and poetry; but I didn't read the poetry. Another WAS Henry Clay's Speeches, and another WAS Dr. Gunn's Family Medicine. . . . (ch. 17, capitals added)

Gertrude Stein brings her words forward freed of any obligation to be anything but themselves, so that they may make a real, if elusive, mark.

Dining is west.

Chain-boats are merry, are merry blew, blew west, carpet.

Roast potatoes for.[48]

Sometimes her words are divided:

Eggs ear nuts, look a bout.

Eat ting, eating a grand old man said roof. . . .[49]

Occasionally there is still — surprisingly — word play:

This made some sum.

Sam in. [Followed by the boldface title: SALMON]

Pea cooler. [Set close to "chicken is a peculiar bird."] [50]

The sound, appearance, and placement of words: upon these *Tender Buttons* centers, with meaning left largely private. This was necessary in order to show the power of the simplest word. Mina Loy testified to the success of this attempt in the *transatlantic review,* calling Gertrude Stein

> Curie
> of the laboratory
> of vocabulary
>     she crushed
> the tonnage
> of consciousness
> congealed to phrases
>     to extract
> a radium of the word.[51]

The vitality of the word relieved of its burden of conventional literary meaning suggested the possibility of greater use of understatement, of simplicity, and of the rhythmical counterpoint of poise and movement. The distance is considerable, to be sure, between *Tender Buttons* and a piece of

Hemingway's prose, but Hemingway was able to make good use of the examples Gertrude Stein provided him.

Although repetition remained a mainstay of coherence for Gertrude Stein in *Tender Buttons,* punctuation was joggled, or eliminated. Except for the period, most terminal and emotional marks of punctuation were omitted. The value of this diminished punctuation is that more attention must be invested in the words themselves. They then prove whether they are well enough placed to make themselves understood without additional help. What was lost and what was gained appear in as simple a sequence as the following:

Is it so, is it so, is it so, is it so is it so is it so.[52]

Although Gertrude Stein pursued still other tacks before Ernest Hemingway met her early in 1922, her important technical contributions were made by 1914 when *Tender Buttons* was written. To retrace her development briefly, after having studied psychology under William James, she began writing as a literary student of his brother Henry. When she wrote *Things As They Are* she adopted Henry James's way of rendering the cultivated mind at work. Thought was expressed by means of talk, and so was often organized on a rhetorical structure of repetition. Gertrude Stein then conserved some of the verbal and punctuational innovations she found in the colloquial voice. In "Melanctha" she simplified her diction in order to stress the developing patterns of repeated words. There too she began to stretch given moments in time to abnormal length. With *The Making of Americans,* she eliminated action, yet by using extended repetition broken by slight changes in phrasing that allowed slow conceptual accretion, she managed to conserve a dynamic subject matter. Finally in *Tender Buttons,* conventional subject matter disappeared except insofar as some single thing stimulated Gertrude Stein's mind into action. Words were arranged as objects sufficient in themselves upon the page; and both alone and in series they made their effects by the associations roused through their composition. The stylistic process was one of gradual loss of story (movement) and of subject (thing) until, at her most obscure, Gertrude Stein offered arrangements quite as abstract as those painted by her friends, Braque, Picasso, Gris, and Picabia. In so doing she emphasized the underlying structures of colloquial speech, even as the Cubists isolated and stylized the geometrical components of the human figure. To accomplish this she worked out of a tradition congenial to her, the European aesthetic tradition, particularly as it was represented in the prose of Gustave Flaubert and Henry James.

It is because Mark Twain also imported colloquial devices into literature that he has sometimes seemed a source for Gertrude Stein's art. But although her discoveries and refinements helped some of those who followed her to locate Mark Twain's submerged stylistic patterns, it is a mistake to place her in a direct line between Mark Twain and Hemingway. Sympathetic as she obviously was to Mark Twain's work, and useful as her theories and practice were for understanding the stylistic potentialities of *Huckleberry Finn,* Gertrude Stein was still unmistakably apprenticed to Henry James. With the help of his examples she finally brought the structural lines of colloquial language into sharp focus.

# SIX

# Ernest Hemingway

"If you begin one place you always end at another."
*Everybody's Autobiography*

I

AROUND 1916, when Ernest Hemingway first addressed himself to the art of writing, the American vernacular still had
not found a secure place in prose fiction. Ring Lardner was
mechanically exploiting it for satirical purposes, Sherwood
Anderson was trying to use its supposititious honesty with
indifferent success, and it looked as if the reserves of power
Mark Twain had discovered in the vernacular were lost
again. The job of shaping the vernacular for general service,
of giving substance to Gertrude Stein's lessons in abstraction,
or conversely, of imposing aesthetic form on eccentric colloquial material remained undone. To Hemingway fell the
task of joining the two lines leading from Henry James and
Mark Twain.

Hemingway opened his career in the Oak Park high school
newspaper, writing clever imitations of Ring Lardner, who
was himself then writing for another local paper, the Chicago
*Tribune*. As late as 1918 when he was serving in Italy, Hemingway still indulged in Lardnerian pastiche. "Well Al we
are here in this old Italy and now that I am here I am not
going to leave it. Not at all if any. And that is not no New
Years revolution Al but the truth." [1] But after Hemingway
was wounded, he dropped the hampering cynicism inherent
in Lardner's style. Hemingway wrote Maxwell Perkins that

he had "not been at all hardboiled since July 8, 1918 — on the night on which I discovered that that also was vanity." [2]

Charles Fenton has shown us how Hemingway's early work as a newspaperman and foreign correspondent helped to prune his style. Whether it was the style sheet of the Kansas City *Star* demanding "Avoid the use of adjectives, especially such extravagant ones as *splendid, gorgeous, grand, magnificent*" ("The best rules I ever learned for the business of writing"), or the economy demanded in transmitting one's stories by transatlantic cables ("Isn't it a great language?"),[3] the demand for concision bore steadily down upon Hemingway throughout his apprentice years. This, coupled with his intense desire to render "what really happened in action" [4] and to exorcise the commercial smugness and sentimentality which he felt deliberately sought to obscure life as he had known it, naturally led Hemingway to admire *Huckleberry Finn*.

Aside from Hemingway's own tribute to that book then, it should come as no surprise to hear Philip Young propose that "throughout [*Huckleberry Finn*] there is the same simplicity of rhythm, vocabulary and sentence structure that we associate with Hemingway. Hemingway's effects of crispness, clarity and a wonderful freshness are there." [5] At the same time we must be prepared to qualify radically the kind of simplicity we are willing to acknowledge is present. Both Gertrude Stein and Sherwood Anderson are proof enough that limitation of vocabulary and simplification of syntax are not in themselves sufficient to earn clarity and directness. In fact, short of servile imitation, it is hard to see how the construction and management of these qualities *could* be learned directly from Mark Twain. Carlos Baker, after noting similarities between Hemingway and Mark Twain, commented, "No influence is alleged. What Hemingway found effective in Twain was whatever corroborated his own point of view about the writer's obligation to truth" (op. cit., p. 181).

Much of my own view of Hemingway's stylistic relationship to his predecessors is an elaboration of Baker's. We know that Hemingway came to Paris with a predilection for the Midwestern vernacular and that this was already linked in his style with extensive journalistic experience. But as we shall see, he needed the schooling he received from Gertrude Stein and Ezra Pound, not to speak of the secondary influences and examples of Conrad, Crane, Ford, Joyce, and others then living in Europe, before he could draw much profit from Mark Twain's example. Once Hemingway's mind was fixed upon the discipline of form, once his attention was brought to the surface and structure of his prose, once, in short, he was equipped with technical theory, he could then understand his enthusiasm for *Huckleberry Finn* and make something of it.

Hemingway's first published book, *Three Stories and Ten Poems* (Summer 1923), lays down the significant lines of his stylistic progress. The loss of a suitcase containing a year's work accounts in part for the symbolic aptness of the three stories.[6] But, in addition, the evidence provided in both *in our time* (Spring 1924) and *In Our Time* (Fall 1925) shows that Hemingway was consciously testing various approaches and stylistic techniques. He rarely repeated an experiment that failed to advance him stylistically. Even if a particular tack succeeded — as "My Old Man" did — Hemingway abandoned it unless it contributed to the construction of a satisfactory stylistic conveyance for his meaning. "My Old Man," if not directly derived from Sherwood Anderson, is close enough to be "fairly described as Andersonian." [7] It is the account of the career and death of a dishonest jockey seen through the eyes of his son, and it seems to be the only story Hemingway ever told in the voice of a child, although some of the Nick Adams stories concern boyhood experiences. The second of the three stories, "Up in Michigan," uses Gertrude Stein's insistent repetition and dictional simplification to de-

scribe an act of seduction among the closest American equivalent to peasants. "Up in Michigan" is Hemingway's sole
venture into a past preceding his birth and therefore unknown to him. The third story, "Out of Season," represents
vintage Hemingway in the 'twenties, for it combines a European background, fishing, and a strained American marital
relationship. Its one jarring stylistic note is the sardonically
reiterated designation of the male principal — "the young
gentleman." When Hemingway was assured of his footing on
the slippery ground of style he became better able to control
his satirical impulse. But however familiar the stance of "Out
of Season" may seem through the perspective of hindsight,
Hemingway could not be certain in 1923 that it was the one
he needed, and so he continued to experiment.

Sherwood Anderson can be dismissed quickly as a stylistic
guide for the young journalist. He was a friend to Hemingway, a counselor, a correspondent, a model of seriousness, an
admirer — "a young fellow of extraordinary talent" [8] — and
he suggested possible sources for thematic material, especially
those of sexual frustration and childhood misery. But as John
Peale Bishop observed, what neither Mark Twain nor Sherwood Anderson "could supply was a training in discipline." [9]
Anderson had identified an area of sensual life worth exploration and to express it he had adopted a potentially useful
version of the vernacular. What he could not manage, however, was a scrupulous concentration either upon that area or
upon his language. Knowing where the material lay but not
how to express it, Anderson was at once a valuable and an irritating master. Hemingway eventually made a spirited if
slipshod attack on Anderson in *The Torrents of Spring*
(Spring 1926), wherein he parodied Anderson's fuzziest
mannerisms. The elder man's partially synthetic pose of naïveté, his imprecision, his sentimental expansiveness, his la-
ment for dumbness were all intolerable to Hemingway, who
unlike Anderson was sure he knew very well why, could he

only learn to express it. The young Hemingway "was thoroughly hostile, inevitably, to Anderson's concept of unconscious art." [10]

Gertrude Stein was another matter. In time Hemingway emancipated himself from her too, beginning with a vulgar, adolescent parody that opened, "In the rain in the rain in the rain in the rain in Spain / / Does it rain in Spain / / Oh yes my dear on the contrary and there are no bullfights." [11] Hemingway struck out at her again in *The Torrents of Spring,* entitling its fourth part "The Passing of a Great Race and the Making and Marring of Americans." "Miss Stein," he told an interviewer after her death, "wrote at some length and with considerable inaccuracy about her influence on my work. It was necessary for her to do this after she had learned to write dialogue from a book called *The Sun Also Rises.*" He then added more kindly, "Here it is simpler and better to thank Gertrude for everything I learned from her about the abstract relationship of words." [12]

In that final phrase lies, I think, the main clue to Gertrude Stein's usefulness to Hemingway. She taught him to see "the abstract relationship of words." For a time he very much admired her writing, believing it to be "invaluable for analyzing anything or making notes on a person or place." [13] Even his posthumously published memoirs, *A Moveable Feast,* which contain a last supremely vicious thrust at Gertrude Stein's private life, acknowledge: "She had also discovered many truths about rhythms and the uses of words in repetition that were valid and valuable and she talked well about them." [14] He personally arranged to have a portion of *The Making of Americans* published in the *transatlantic review.* Feeling that Anderson had misunderstood and misused Gertrude Stein's theories, in *The Torrents of Spring* Hemingway made the Andersonian Yogi Johnson reflect: "There was a street in Paris named after Huysmans. Right around the corner from where Gertrude Stein lived. Ah, there was a

woman! Where were her experiments in words leading her?
What was at the bottom of it? All that in Paris." [15] Hemingway himself for a time found it difficult to control the more
obvious influence of Gertrude Stein. In "Up in Michigan"
this derivative paragraph appears:

> Liz LIKED Jim very much. She LIKED it the way he
> walked over from the shop and often went to the
> kitchen door to watch for him to start down the
> road. She LIKED it about his mustache. She LIKED it
> about how white his teeth were when he smiled. She
> LIKED it very much that he didn't look like a black-
> smith. She LIKED it how much D. J. Smith and Mrs.
> Smith LIKED Jim. One day she found that she LIKED
> it the way the hair was black on his arms and how
> white they were above the tanned line when he
> washed up in the washbasin outside the house. LIK-
> ING that made her feel funny. [16]

Hemingway only freed himself slowly from the reiterated
"liked." In two other stories in the *In Our Time* collection
he aped himself, writing in "Cat in the Rain":

> The wife LIKED him. She LIKED the deadly serious
> way he received any complaints. She LIKED his dig-
> nity. She LIKED the way he wanted to serve her. She
> LIKED the way he felt about being a hotel-keeper.
> She LIKED his old, heavy face and big hands. [17]

And in "Soldier's Home":

> He LIKED to look at them from the front porch as
> they walked on the other side of the street. He LIKED
> to watch them walking under the shade of the trees.
> He LIKED the round Dutch collars above their sweat-
> ers. He LIKED their silk stockings and flat shoes. He
> LIKED their bobbed hair and the way they walked. [18]

Equally symbolic of Hemingway's stylistic education was
the inclusion of ten poems in addition to the three stories in
his first book. They serve to remind us of Hemingway's early

uncertainty as to whether he was more properly a poet than a prose writer. They point too to his friendship with Ezra Pound, who, in exchange for boxing lessons, helped Hemingway to see his object more clearly. John Peale Bishop reported the now familiar Hemingway remark: "Ezra was right half the time, and when he was wrong, he was so wrong you were never in any doubt about it. Gertrude was always right." [19] Fiercely dedicated to aesthetic values and a vigorous proponent of both Flaubert and James, Pound spoke and corresponded in an exaggeratedly crude version of the American vernacular. Although he has never referred to Mark Twain in his published writing, Pound's anomalous character was recently summed up by Sylvia Beach: "There was a touch of Whistler about him; his language, on the other hand, was Huckleberry Finn's." [20]

As a letter-writer Pound delivered an unequivocal series of lessons on style, which we may suppose he matched orally. Pound embodied a host of attitudes then current in Paris and his crystallization of these theories helped Hemingway master the vernacular. Initially enrolled under the banner of Imagism, Pound wrote Amy Lowell in 1914 that he "should like [Imagism] to stand for hard light, clear edges." [21] In other elaborations of his meaning one can see at once the usefulness of his theories for Ernest Hemingway's prose. [22] Writing Harriet Monroe in 1916, after making his famous assertion "Poetry must be as well written as prose," Pound summarized what he felt he had learned from such prose masters as De Maupassant, Flaubert, and Stendhal. "No book words, no periphrases, no inversions . . . no interjections. No words flying off to nothing . . . no clichés, set phrases, stereotyped journalese. The only escape from such is by precision, a result of concentrated attention to what is writing. The test of a writer is his ability for such concentration AND for his power to stay concentrated till he gets to the end" (*Letters*, pp. 48–9).

These were the very ideas needed to dissipate Anderson's

murkiness. What is more, Pound also insisted upon particularity, a virtue that neither Stein nor Lardner could offer
Hemingway. "Language is made out of concrete things. General expressions in non-concrete terms are a laziness" (ibid.).
The whole art of writing, Pound felt, was "concision, or style,
or saying what you mean in the fewest and clearest words." [23]

Exactly that became Hemingway's goal in prose. The vernacular offered new words and new rhythms whose expressive
beauty had been revealed by Mark Twain. Gertrude Stein,
working out of the style of Henry James, had analyzed and set
forth some underlying patterns of the vernacular, and had
indicated the residuum of energy remaining in a word detached from its conceptual meaning. If Hemingway desired
both the word cleanly placed and the object directly evoked,
then the two original masters of the American colloquial tradition, Mark Twain and Henry James, offered — either directly or through at least two practicing theorists, Pound and
Stein — ways of achieving both ends, ways which often coin-
cided. Something larger than mere eccentric theory is afoot
when three writers as apparently distant as Mark Twain,
Pound, and Gertrude Stein share a basic stylistic tenet. "As to
the Adjective: when in doubt, leave it out." "The only adjective that is worth using is the adjective that is essential to the
sense of the passage." "The first thing that anybody takes out
of anybody's writing are the adjectives." [24]

The vernacular impulse we have been following is an in-
tensifying one, and whether the intensification centered primarily on linguistic qualities as in James and Stein, or primarily on physical evocation as in Mark Twain and sometimes
Anderson, the stylistic techniques for achieving intensity frequently overlapped. It only required a writer willing to sub-
mit himself to the disciplines then current in Paris for a style
to emerge holding compressed within it a focused world of
experience *and* a series of verbal elements formally arranged.
I have not forgotten that style and literary achievement are

composed of other elements, willed and fortuitous, but one is repeatedly brought to recognize that in Hemingway's case, models, tutelage, and conscious experimentation were all three pre-eminently involved in the development of his style. Its concinnity was no fluke.

II

If, as I have suggested, *Tender Buttons* is a primer of stylistic possibilities, then Hemingway's *in our time* is a deliberately composed book of stylistic exercises. It was published in Paris in 1924 at the Three Mountains Press; later it was revised, conservatively, and most of its "chapters" renumbered and inserted between the short stories in the 1925 New York collection, *In Our Time*. The original version is rich with technical demonstrations of style, and some of its chapters can stand as brilliant, independent miniatures. Only thirty pages in length, the book contains eighteen consecutively numbered chapters, hereafter designated by number. We have no specific name to give these chapters; they do not tell a consecutive story, nor do they in any way develop what we conventionally understand to be a plot, although they are both thematically and formally related. They have been called vignettes, sketches, and miniatures. Unprecedented in English prose and subsequently unimitated, these pieces served Hemingway eminently well, primarily as tests of the narrative voice. Because they so well illuminate his devoted effort to locate the pitch and tone of voice suited to his understanding of life, they deserve close attention.

Half of the chapters are told in the first person (1, 2, 4, 5, 11, 13, 14, 15, 18), and half in the third person (3, 6, 7, 8, 9, 10, 12, 16, 17). To begin with the extremes of the first-person group, chapters 2 and 5 are distinctly marked with dialect. Chapter 5 is told by a British officer whose dialectal intensifiers — "frightfully," "absolutely," and "topping" — establish

an ironic distance between the reader and the event that occasions the officer's schoolboy enthusiasm: the successful
placement of a barricade across a bridge. The whole chapter
reads:

> It was a frightfully hot day. We'd jammed an abso-
> lutely perfect barricade across the bridge. It was
> simply priceless. A big old wrought iron grating
> from the front of a house. Too heavy to lift and you
> could shoot through it and they would have to
> climb over it. It was absolutely topping. They tried
> to get over it, and we potted them from forty yards.
> They rushed it, and officers came out alone and
> worked on it. It was an absolutely perfect obstacle.
> Their officers were very fine. We were frightfully
> put out when we heard the flank had gone and we
> had to fall back.[25]

The British voice was useful to Hemingway beyond mimicry
because of the opportunity it gave him to hold his material
far enough off to see and exhibit it without emotional distortion. But he could hardly base his career on a British dialect;
consequently, he abandoned it.

Chapter 2 is American colloquial speech, pocked with
slang expressions, grammatical mistakes, and syntactical expansiveness. In part it reads:

> The kid came out and had to kill five bulls because
> you can't have more than three matadors, and the
> last bull he was so tired he couldn't get the sword
> in. He couldn't hardly lift his arm.

Other idiomatic terms in 2 such as "crazy drunk," "slug,"
"puked," and "hollered" not only create the style but also
provide the excuse for it. And so long as the expedient of an
assumed character was needed to justify the vernacular, then
we know that Hemingway had not yet liberated himself from

the need to appeal to realism for sanction to use the vernacular.

Charles Fenton has said that Chapter 4, like 5, was taken by Hemingway "directly from post-war conversations with his friend Dorman-Smith, a professional English soldier. The clipped upper-class diction of Sandhurst was unmistakable and deliberate" (p. 238). Chapter 4, the briefest of the vignettes, is considerably less radical in its dialect than Chapter 5, with fewer eccentricities of speech, and is the more interesting as a consequence.

> We were in a garden at Mons. Young Buckley came in with his patrol from across the river. The first German I saw climbed up over the garden wall. We waited till he got one leg over and then potted him. He had so much equipment on and looked awfully surprised and fell down into the garden. Then three more came over further down the wall. We shot them. They all came just like that.

Just three words are used in a British manner: "young" as applied to a name, "potted," and "awfully." Yet an American could use each of them in this way without strain or affectation. In other words, Hemingway had begun to work back toward one of the voices we have since come to associate with the young Ernest Hemingway.

In Chapter 1 (quoted in full on page 215), the other first-person chapter with a particular linguistic identity, the bulk of the paragraph is a discursive, repetitive reminiscence ending on the observation, "That was when I was a kitchen corporal." The tone of this chapter is anecdotal, the product of an uncomplicated American mind. It is no instance of a man compressing an account in order to keep his sanity, such as we sometimes associate with Hemingway's prose, but rather the bemused reminiscence of a simple soul. The repetition then points first to character — even though this is at best shadowy — rather than to formal structure. But a reversal of this emphasis could be quickly effected. In the meantime, neither Chapter 1, 2, or 5 is free of eccentricity in diction. Chapter 4 (which may be British) is still unsteady but closing in on the needed neutral voice.

Three of the other five first-person chapters of *in our time* (11, 13, 18) are the words of a quiet, cool observer, who impassively reports the details of an incident. Each exposes a character to a low-keyed and rather sympathetic irony. Chapter 11, long enough to be retitled "The Revolutionist" and offered as a short story in *In Our Time,* recounts the meeting of the speaker with a pleasant, devoted agent of world revolution. The narrator speaks but once. Asked how the movement is going in Italy — " 'Very badly,' I said." He does, however, make aloof, somewhat condescending judgments of the revolutionist: "a very nice boy and very shy," "I took him with me," "He thanked me very much." These I take to be the sentiments of Hemingway the foreign correspondent, wise in the ways of world politics, friendly but unwilling to engage himself. Altogether, the voice forms a familiar part of the Hemingway literary personality.

It was used again in 13 where a bullfighter disgraces himself in the ring and later admits in a matter-of-fact tone, "I am not really a good bull fighter." The change in voice between an American dialect and this one is clearly demonstrated by comparing the last line of Chapter 2 with the first line of 13.

> He sat down in the sand and puked and they held a cape over him while the crowd hollered and threw things down into the bull ring.

> The crowd shouted all the time and threw pieces of bread down into the ring, then cushions and leather wine bottles, keeping up whistling and yelling.

The latter version eliminates the slang "hollered" and replaces it with "shouted." It builds up the vagueness of "things" into the particularity of "pieces of bread," "cushions," and "leather wine bottles." Hemingway also executes a technical trill in the Stein manner with the participle-gerund phrase, "keeping up whistling and yelling." Such a phrase indicates that here he is working to perfect the powers of style rather than seeking realism. He does this by filling in, strengthening, and emphasizing some elements, while underplaying the obtrusive signs of the vernacular. He is moving away from extremes toward Malcolm Cowley's "middle American style." [26]

Chapter 18 is the wry account of a chat with the king of Greece. The narrator devotes most of the paragraph to what the king said. At the same time, the first-person permits Hemingway to modulate the observations at the end.

> The king was working in the garden. He seemed very glad to see me. We walked through the garden. This is the queen, he said. She was clipping a rose bush. Oh how do you do, she said. We sat down at a table under a big tree and the king ordered whiskey and soda. We have good whiskey anyway, he said. The revolutionary committee, he told me, would not allow him to go outside the palace grounds. Plastiras is a very good man I believe, he said, but frightfully difficult. I think he did right though shooting those chaps. If Kerensky had shot a few men things might have been altogether different. Of course the great thing in this sort of an affair is not to be shot oneself!
>
> It was very jolly. We talked for a long time. Like all Greeks he wanted to go to America.

The success here is not primarily technical — although the dialogue is experimentally rendered. Rather it lies in the calm, worldly view provided of the king. Neither thrilled nor cynical nor denunciatory, the narrator is dispassionately agreeable. "It was very jolly."

The third-person narratives of *in our time* undertake to solve the problem of stabilizing colloquial prose from the opposite direction: instead of throttling down the obtrusive colloquiality of the first-person, they try to loosen up the lines of standard prose. Three of Hemingway's experiments, however, must be counted as failures. Chapter 8 is the cynical account of a soldier under fire praying and promising Christ, "I'll tell everyone in the world that you are the only thing that matters." Delivered from danger, "he never told anybody." Such cheap purchase of irony remained one of Hemingway's enduring weaknesses. Chapter 9, which tells of the shooting of two Hungarian thieves by a detective whose sole justification for the murders is his certainty that they were "wops" is also mechanically ironic. Finally, Chapter 10 (since reprinted as "A Very Short Story") mixed the lyric and satiric modes in a sketch of hospital lovers separated at the last by woman's fatal inconstancy. Hemingway later lopped off the sardonic Flaubertian echo in his ending: "A short time after he contracted gonorrhea from a sales girl in a loop department store while riding in a taxicab through Lincoln Park." Then he expanded the story into *A Farewell to Arms*. It is significant that Hemingway rarely used dialect or the satiric mode again in his fiction.[27] Of the ten new stories introduced in *In Our Time* (counting "The Big Two-Hearted River" as a single story) none is in dialect and only one — "Mr. and Mrs. Elliot" — can be regarded as satiric in intent.

Three of the third-person vignettes, like three of the first-person ones, are distinguished by the factual journalistic flavor of their prose. Chapter 3 describes the evacuation of refugees through Thrace; Chapter 6, the execution of six cabinet ministers; and Chapter 17, the hanging of a man in an American county jail. No narrator explicitly appears and no emotion is expressed, although the very baldness of the style generates it by implication.

The first paragraph of Chapter 17 reads:

> They hanged Sam Cardinella at six o'clock in the morning in the corridor of the county jail. The corridor was high and narrow with tiers of cells on either side. All the cells were occupied. The men had been brought in for the hanging. Five men sentenced to be hanged were in the five top cells. Three of the men to be hanged were negroes. They were very frightened. One of the white men sat on his cot with his head in his hands. The other lay flat on his cot with a blanket wrapped around his head.

Eccentricities of diction have been eliminated from this account, as well as names and dates, the irrelevant particularities of journalism. Objective reportage of this sort remained one of Hemingway's favorite tools for rendering otherwise intolerable scenes. Moreover, it contributed to his determination to control the vernacular. The reader cannot really distinguish the journalistic chapters written in the third person from those written in the first. One is not often aware of a particular speaker in these sketches free of dialect and illiteracies, which means that the speaker can now be manipulated for special emphasis. He can enter and withdraw silently, commenting and reacting at need. When Hemingway tried to explain to Edmund Wilson why he had inserted the chapters of *in our time* between the stories of more conventional length included in *In Our Time,* he described an impulse similar to this subtle tonal mobility. The alternating effect would be, he wrote, "Like looking with your eyes at something, say a passing coast line, and then looking at it with 15X binoculars. Or rather, maybe, looking at it and then going in and living in it — and then coming out and looking it again." [28]

While he was learning to write a prose that could employ a

form of colloquial speech remaining at a fairly constant level, with or without an announced narrator, Hemingway also had to learn how to construct a prose with sufficient internal coherence to resist the corrosion of time and how to develop sufficient internal complexity to redeem that prose from the curse of over-simplification. Answers to these problems were available but had to be recognized as answers. As we have come to see, similar stylistic conditions are visible in both branches of the vernacular. These are, first, fragmentation of syntax causing concentration on the individual word, and second, many kinds of insistent repetition. In the first case, new sources of diction, odd conjunctions of words, isolation of single words and phrases by means of syntactic adjustments and of punctuation, and even repetition itself all helped to bring new, unusual pressure to bear upon the single word. As for repetition, although it was originally used in conversations for ease of speaking and for emphasis, writers imitating those conversations soon found its aesthetic uses to be manifold.

These practices were hardly visible, however, until Gertrude Stein highlighted them. The help she gave Ernest Hemingway was comparable to that a confirmed abstractionist might give a young "realistic" painter by teaching him to recognize the formal elements underlying the compositions of his favorites. Once Hemingway knew what to look for, he could find examples aplenty, even in his own early prose. As far back as November 1916 in a high-school short story, he had written this passage of dialogue:

> "Yes. He was a bad Indian. Up on the upper peninsula he couldn't get drunk. He used to drink all day — everything. But he couldn't get drunk. Then he would go crazy; but he wasn't drunk. He was crazy because he couldn't get drunk." [29]

This dialogue bears a remarkable resemblance to Hemingway's later work, but close as it is, it has still to meet the problem of transferring the characteristics of this talk over into narrative prose without bringing the talker with it. Once the older writers had brought Hemingway's attention to this problem, he began to experiment. The balance of his laboratory work involved isolating, refining, and harmoniously joining those elements native to the American vernacular. To do this he drew extensively on examples afforded by the past.

I I I

Hemingway's experience as a journalist and his colloquial facility assisted him as he moved toward his finished style. So extensively was he trained and exercised on the Kansas City *Star* and Toronto *Star* that Charles Fenton confidently maintained, "The principal instrument of his literary apprenticeship was journalism" (p. ix). It is a reporter's distance that dominates the treatment of the Greek evacuation and the two execution scenes of *in our time*. The Greek refugee sketch was in fact originally a cabled story for the Toronto newspaper.[30] On the other hand Hemingway also came at his spare prose by means of colloquial imitation, as in his early pastiches of Lardner, and his reproductions of British and American slang in *in our time*. He sought to retain the best of both approaches, to maintain what was most distinctive and least eccentric about each, and to work out a more highly charged synthesis of the vernacular than current practice offered.

Hemingway recognized that journalistic prose lacked durability. "In writing for a newspaper you told what happened and, with one trick and another, you communicated the emotion aided by the element of timeliness which gives a certain emotion to any account of something that happened on that day; but the real thing, the sequence of motion and fact that made the emotion . . . was beyond me and I was working very hard to get it." [31] The journalistic habit of close dispassionate observation was to be kept, but it would be controlled by an aesthetic demanding even more stringent precision.

Certainly Hemingway discovered the principal components of that aesthetic in the colloquial tradition. In *in our time* we can observe him testing techniques even as he does voices. Gradually he evolved a synthetic style that fixed a group of related and carefully tested elements into a new and brilliant mosaic. Ford Madox Ford once described Hemingway's words as being like "pebbles fetched fresh from a brook. They live and shine, each in its place. So one of his pages has the effect of a brook-bottom into which you look down through the flowing water. The words form a tessellation, each in order beside the other." [32] Ford's metaphor is an apt one, for by stressing the colloquial emphasis upon the word, Hemingway brought his prose to a point of unparalleled verbal individuation.

This concentration upon the word was made possible by Hemingway's modifying his diction, adjusting and paring his qualifications, and varying his rhythm so that attention was focused on the separate verbal units in the sentence. And furthermore, unlike Anderson, Hemingway paid the strictest attention not only to the units as devices for telling a story, but also to the relations and patterns existing among them.

As the first step in outlining the verbal tesserae on his page, Hemingway resolutely eliminated abstractions. He depended almost completely on concrete objects for the body and movement of his prose. If there was meaning, the thing, the object, the image had to supply it. No meaning existed apart from this world of particulars. This was matched by the rigorous exclusion of all but the most essential qualification. Even the minimally used adjectives and adverbs were sometimes translated into active dependent clauses. Given this bareness, Hemingway found it useful to introduce emotional overtones into his prose. For this reason he retained that laconic narrator whose understated reactions were paradoxically expressed by colloquially overstated adverbs — "very nice," "very funny," "awful," and "plenty." If the scene was devilishly horrid, as in the executions, then evaluative comments became extraneous. But sometimes a slight touch of the brush humanized the scene. The talk with the Greek king is "very jolly." The brave, naïve revolutionist is "a very nice boy." This restraint reminds us of Huck crying "a little" over the body of Buck Grangerford, "for he was mighty good to me." Similar as the understatement may be, however, a wide web of experience intervenes between the two examples. Huck's boyish earnestness invests his restraint with sincerity. He cannot and need not be more explicit. Hemingway's laconism on the other hand is the result of rigorous control. He will not be more explicit. Although the formal appearance in *Huckleberry Finn* and Hemingway may be similar, the emotions covered by the simple expressions come from quite different sources. When the narrator in Chapter 5 says of the barricade,

> They rushed it, and officers came out alone and worked on it,

the word "alone" conceals yet admits the narrator's professional knowledge that because the barricade was so good, the soldiers would refuse to rush it again. This obliged the officers to emerge. Behind that technical knowledge is elation over the success of the barricade coupled with admiration for the officers.

Even as he creates dynamic contrasts between the spare substance of his prose and his occasional emotional interjections — "Their officers were very fine" — so Hemingway deliberately alternates specific names, titles, foreign words, and exotica, and very ordinary nouns and pronouns. This passage drawn from Chapter 13 shows him handling both Spanish and English words. The italics here are Hemingway's.

> Finally the bull was too tired from so much bad sticking and folded his knees and lay down and one of the *cuadrilla* leaned out over his neck and killed

> him with the *puntillo*. The crowd came over the
> barrera and around the torero and two men grabbed
> him and held him and some one cut off his pigtail
> and was waving it and a kid grabbed it and ran
> away with it.

The insistent use of the nomenclature of the bull ring here threatens self parody, but we can see that Hemingway's intention is to variegate the prose surface. "Puntillo" is italicized and "barrera" is not. "Pigtail" is one word, but in the same clause "some one" is made two. And the vagueness of "crowds," "men," "kid," and "it" is set next to the specificity of "knees," "neck," and "torero." Simple as the words themselves are, their relationships and increments are intricate. Evidence of similar tinkering is visible in the verbs. Chapter 10 begins,

> They whack whacked the white horse on the legs
> and he knee-ed himself up.

After this initial experimentation the chapter proceeds with perfectly commonplace verbs: "twisted," "pulled," "hauled," "swung," and "hung." When the scene was republished in *In Our Time* Hemingway dropped one "e" from "knee-ed" as well as the hyphen, and added a hyphen to "whack whacked." His conservatism reduced the force of the original sentence:

> They whack-whacked the white horse on the legs
> and he kneed himself up.

(Much later, in *Across the River and into the Trees,* a book marked by a desperately radical style, Hemingway reversed himself once more, referring to a soldier's "puttee-ed legs." [33]

These examples of variation in treatment of words are the key to the durability of Hemingway's style. Rather than depend on a mechanically simplified diction and syntax, he created a dynamic complex of words in which the various elements were determined quite as much by reference to one another as they were by reference to some observed reality off the printed page. Chapter 1 shows this very well:

> Everybody WAS DRUNK. The whole battery WAS DRUNK GOING ALONG THE ROAD IN THE DARK. We WERE GOING to the Champagne. The lieutenant KEPT RIDING HIS HORSE OUT into the fields AND SAYING to him, "I'm drunk, I tell you, mon vieux. Oh, I am so soused." We WENT ALONG THE ROAD all night IN THE DARK and the adjutant KEPT RIDING UP alongside my kitchen AND SAYING, "You must put IT out. IT is dangerous. IT will be observed. We were fifty kilometers from the front but the adjutant worried about the fire in my kitchen. It was funny GOING ALONG THAT ROAD. That was when I was a kitchen corporal. (capitals added)

The repetition, while useful here as a binding device and as ironic commentary, is not obtrusive, nor is it merely a reminder of the speaker's lack of sophistication or a rhetorical trick of emphasis. Here the lieutenant will keep riding out and talking to his horse, the adjutant will keep riding up and talking to his kitchen corporal, and the formal similarity of their actions reminds us that a common condition of war causes both the lieutenant's erratic behavior and the adjutant's nervous fussing.

Other and different instances of repetition appear in other chapters, all inventive. In the execution of six ministers (chapter 6), we are told that they were shot "against the wall of a hospital." The soldiers futilely try to hold one of them, sick with typhoid, "against the wall," and while these efforts are being made, "the other five stood very quietly against the wall." In a scene described in some ten lines, this discreet repetition keeps both the impending execution and its incongruous location against the wall of a hospital before the reader. So too there is an inevitable cross-relationship set up between this chapter and the next, which begins, "Nick sat

against the wall of the church." He, soldiering, has been shot
in the spine. Civilian or soldier, hospital or church, men end
suffering against the wall. Hemingway's point is made quietly
with the signals of language.

Another favorite device of Hemingway's also appears in
Chapter 6 — the repetition of numbers with different
meanings.

> They shot the six cabinet ministers at half-past six
> in the morning. . . .

Chapter 9 begins similarly:

> At two o'clock in the morning two Hungarians got
> into a cigar store at Fifteenth Street and Grand
> Avenue.

The slightly off-center repetition is retained in the next sentence where "Fifteenth Street" is no longer a place, but an
adjectival specification.

> Drevitts and Boyle drove up from the Fifteenth
> Street police station in a Ford.

Prepositions are also repeated in proximity with shifting meanings. The repeated preposition, like the repeated
number, forces the reader alert, even as it furnishes a substra-
tum melody. In Chapter 4, a shot German "fell DOWN into
the garden. Then three more came over further DOWN the
wall." Down down the wall they came, twice and in two
senses. Chapter 8, the account of a soldier praying under fire,
contains a close parallel to this. After the deliberately uncapi-
talized plea for mercy, "please please dear jesus," the account
continues,

> The shelling moved further UP the line. We went to
> work on the trench and in the morning the sun
> came UP and the day was hot and muggy and cheer-
> ful and quiet. The next night back at Mestre he did

> not tell the girl he went UPstairs with at the Villa
> Rossa about Jesus. (capitals added)

The simple distinctions in meaning of a word like "up" had
been lost in prose before this, lost in the flood of rhetoric; but
here they are seen, felt, and used, I think, consciously. Indeed, since elegant variation was possible in most of the
quoted instances, we must take Hemingway's repetitions to
be either deliberate or unusually careless. Believing the former, I argue their intention is to afford variety within the
severe limits of the simplest sort of syntax and diction. The
subtle success of the technique illustrates how Hemingway
applied what he had learned from Gertrude Stein about "the
abstract relationship of words."

Several other stylistic observations arise out of this same
paragraph. Hemingway has capitalized "Jesus" in the last
quoted sentence, to indicate, economically, that there the
name occurs outside the essentially disbelieving mind of the
soldier who prays "please please dear jesus." Also, by technical means he has contrasted the frenetic, jammed, tumbling
words of prayer under fire:

> Oh jesus christ get me out of here. Dear jesus get
> me out. Christ please please please christ.

with the relaxed and syntactically expansive details of the day
following the shelling:

> hot and muggy and cheerful and quiet.

Both procedures force the reader to proceed as deliberately as
a motorist on an unfamiliar detour. Stendhal, one of Hemingway's acknowledged favorites, once commented in this
connection: "I had the audacity to despise elegance of style. I
saw the young apprentice fully occupied in avoiding ugly
endings to sentences and strings of awkward sounding words.
On the other hand he constantly altered the details of circumstances that were difficult to express." [34] Although con-

sciousness of style is everywhere in *in our time,* Hemingway's first concern was to render "the way it was," that favorite expression of his, and first cousin to Gertrude Stein's (and Henry James's) "things as they are."

One more instance of repetition contrasts usefully with Sherwood Anderson's problem concerning apples and other round objects in "Paper Pills." In a work as short as *in our time* (eighteen chapters on thirty pages), some carry-over of images may be expected. Chapter 4 begins,

> We were in a garden at Mons.

There it is that, as the Germans come over the wall, they are shot. Chapter 18, on the other hand, begins,

> The king was working in the garden.

We are then introduced to a time-serving, good-natured cynic who "like all Greeks . . . wanted to go to America." There is a planned cross reference, I think, between the two scenes, not unlike that between the men standing with their backs to the hospital wall waiting to be shot, and the wounded soldier against the church. This is made possible by the brevity and simplicity of the book, and is cued by the evident resemblance of the phrases "in a garden" and "in the garden." Both phrases appear in the first sentence of their chapters. In one we find men at work, bodies thumping to the garden floor. In the other, a genial conversationalist is said to be "working," also in a garden; but *he* has time for a whiskey and soda. The implicit irony of this comparison I take to be central to Hemingway's understanding of the actual nature of our time.

Chapter 7 also plays a variation on repetition. With Nick seated and Rinaldi "face downward against the wall," Nick's head is described taking three different positions, each one part of a slow, pained movement. Between the moves of his head, the scene is elaborated, Nick's thoughts are rendered and Nick himself addresses a few words to Rinaldi. The varied repetitions occur this way:

> Nick looked straight ahead brilliantly.
>
> Nick turned his head carefully and looked down at Rinaldi.
>
> Nick turned his head carefully away smiling sweatily.

The fighting has moved on — "Things were getting forward in the town" — leaving this backwash of the battleline, a hot still pool of misery without movement except Rinaldi "still in the sun breathing with difficulty" and the slow, controlled head-turning of a man hit in the spine. Down to the side. Back again. Hemingway draws attention to this first by the slight oddness of the original adverb, "brilliantly," which is connected with the sun and heat but also has a thin wash of irony over it. Nick's head movement is then indicated by a phrasing repeated but slightly and pertinently varied. This verbal and syntactic care emphasizes the delicate, economical movement of a man injured and in shock.

Hemingway also learned to take full advantage of prepositions. Mark Twain's careful management of them created the impression of vivid directional movement in *Huckleberry Finn:* "I went straight out in the country as much as a mile, before I stopped; then I doubled back through the woods towards Phelps's" (ch. 31). A preposition points a direction or locates an object. At times Hemingway's prose became a series of arrows rhythmically pointing now this way, now that. He relied especially upon prepositional intensity for the difficult job of describing movement through towns and across landscapes. So in *The Sun Also Rises:*

> Down below there were grassy plains and clear streams, and then we crossed a stream and went through a gloomy little village, and started to climb

again. We climbed up and up and crossed another
high Col and turned along it, and the road ran down
to the right.[35]

Hemingway's poetic evocations of movement depend upon
the careful placement of his nouns, participles, and conjunctions. His reportorial accuracy is heightened by the purely
formal relationships of the words themselves, as in the first
sentence of Chapter 15:

I heard the drums coming down the street, and then
the fifes and the pipes, and then they came around
the corner, all dancing.

Euphony of sound — fifes, pipes, drums coming, they came
around the corner — and a subtle cadence supplements Hemingway's exposition. Significantly, *in our time* contains these
examples of rhyme and alliteration:

the bull only bumped him

he hung on to the horn

the bull rammed him wham

kids were in carts crouched

the flank had gone and we had to fall back

the picador twisted the stirrups straight

the horse's entrails hung down in a blue bunch

over the barrera and around the torero

the corridor of the county jail

the priest skipped back onto the scaffolding [36]

One cannot expect to find many more instances than this in
so short a book. Still, when the diction and syntax are simplified as far as they are in Hemingway, then these moments will
occur more often than in standard prose. And even if they
must often have arisen spontaneously during composition,

the new, important point is that they were retained during revision.

The Villalta chapter, 14, and especially its second paragraph, is the most successful and complex piece in *in our time*. It incorporates repetition, rhyme, alliteration, and assonance ("snarl," "charge," "curve," "roar," and "toro" are its central words), and a number of participles that culminate in a very fine final pose which is at once static, yet intensely active.

> If it happened right down close in front of you, you could see Villalta snarl at the bull and curse him, and when the bull charged he swung back firmly like an oak when the wind hits it, his legs tight together, the muleta trailing and the sword following the curve behind. Then he cursed the bull, flopped the muleta at him, and swung back from the charge his feet firm, the muleta curving and each swing the crowd roaring.
>
> When he started to kill it was all in the same rush. The bull looking at him straight in front, hating. He drew out the sword from the folds of his muleta and sighted with the same movement and called to the bull, Toro! Toro! and the bull charged and Villalta charged and just for a moment they became one. Villalta became one with the bull and then it was over. Villalta standing straight and the red hilt of the sword sticking out dully between the bull's shoulders. Villalta, his hand up at the crowd and the bull roaring blood, looking straight at Villalta and his legs caving.

The repetition is employed here for both harmonic and symbolic purposes. For example, following the command, Toro! Toro!, Villalta moves toward the bull and at that point his name takes over to dominate the remainder of the paragraph — just as in fact he dominates the bull. The deliberateness of this cannot be denied. Next, man and beast each charge in a separate clause, and with the stroke of death "they became one." A variation then: "Villalta became one with the bull" — and the act of killing is finished. Now the "roaring" of the crowd from the first paragraph is transferred to the bull's blood, and the bull that formerly "looked at him straight in front, hating," now is "looking straight at Villalta and his legs caving." In this moment when many complicated aesthetic forces successfully interact, the literary use of the vernacular and all its techniques is fully justified.

Hemingway's mode of stylistic attack changes too often and is too clearly signalled to be accidental. I do not mean that Hemingway followed a mechanical rhythm, or that such diversity was unique to him. But Sherwood Anderson, for example, had nothing like Hemingway's variety of effect, and indeed he was only intermittently aware of the necessity of relieving colloquial simplicity with contrast. He could rapidly bore or irritate with his stretches of declarative sentences bearing simple-minded images and ideas across the page. Similarly, the prose of Lardner and Stein, was too often of a piece, unrolling long ribbons of narrative without respite. Hemingway's style was eclectic, alert for the incipient monotony that dogs the colloquial style. Without lapsing into the stylistic vaudeville of a Saroyan, he enlivened his prose by means of formal variety, and he polished his stylistic surfaces to reflect his meaning. His labor is there for all to see in that extraordinary little book, *in our time*.

IV

If all this simplification took place in narrative prose because, after decades of segregation, dialogue finally infiltrated it, then it is reasonable to assume that the dialogue of a dialogue-dominated narrative will change too, and it does. Again *in our time* furnishes us examples of a variety of possibilities in the treatment of dialogue, thus bringing us full circle.

*Three Stories and Ten Poems,* published earlier, showed evidence of the dialogue usually associated with Hemingway — clipped, repetitive, advancing incrementally. In "Out of Season" two men prepare to fish, and the repetition typically centers on *piombo,* an otherwise unemphasized foreign word whose definition is organically furnished.

> "Have you some lead?"
> "No."
> "You must have some lead." Peduzzi was excited. "You must have piombo. Piombo. A little piombo. Just here. Just above the hook or your bait will float on the water. You must have it. Just a little piombo."
> "Have you some?"
> "No." He looked through his pockets desperately. Sifting through the cloth dirt in the linings of his inside military pockets. "I haven't any. We must have piombo."
> "We can't fish then," said the young gentleman, and unjointed the rod, reeling the line back through the guides. "We'll get some piombo and fish tomorrow." [37]

The dialogue continues in this vein. It is still a little awkward, but it is new. This apparently artless kind of conversation evolved under the pressure of Hemingway's prose, and he made it his hallmark. But before he returned to work this vein, he conscientiously tried out a number of ways of recording conversations. In fact, *in our time* contains *no* instance of dialogue rendered in completely conventional form, with quotation marks and paragraph indentations. To examine the book's dialogue is to find still more deliberate experimentation, as well as to see the spoken word blending insensibly into the narrative.

The most normal arrangement of dialogue in *in our time* occurs in Chapter 17. During the moments before the hanging, a terse, unindented interchange takes place.

> "How about a chair, Will?" asked one of the
> guards. "Better get one," said a man in a derby hat.

In Chapter 1, a similar arrangement is used, but there it is
more highly formalized. The lieutenant keeps riding out into
the fields and saying to his horse, "I'm drunk, I tell you, mon
vieux. Oh, I am so soused," and the adjutant keeps riding up
to the kitchen corporal and saying, "You must put it out. It is
dangerous. It will be observed." Neither quote is indented,
both are approached over almost identical phrasing, and each
is dominated by repetition of subject: I, I, I, it, it, it.

In Chapter 7, the formal designation of the speaker and his
action is eliminated.

> Nick turned his head carefully and looked at Rin-
> aldi. "Senta Rinaldi. Senta. You and me we've made
> a separate peace." Rinaldi lay still in the sun breath-
> ing with difficulty. "Not patriots." Nick turned his
> head carefully away smiling sweatily.

Chapter 9 reproduces the conversation of two policemen
just after one of them has shot a pair of thieves. It combines
three different kinds of quotations: those with no formal introduction, those introduced by dashes, and those introduced
by indentation. The critical points are indicated by capitals.

> Drevitts got frightened when he found they were
> both dead. HELL Jimmy, he said, you oughtn't to
> have done it. There's liable to be a hell of a lot of
> trouble.
> — THEY'RE crooks ain't they? said Boyle. They're
> wops ain't they. Who the hell is going to make any
> trouble?
> — That's all right maybe this time, said Drevitts,
> but how did you know they were wops when you
> bumped them.
> WOPS, said Boyle, I can tell wops a mile off. (cap-
> itals added)

Chapter 15 depends upon indentation and commas alone to set off its quotations, but near the end it works into a stylized frenzy of bitterness, marked by the curious locution "we kills" and the colorful phrase *"riau-riau* dancers' bulls."

> Well, I said, after all he's just an ignorant Mexican savage.
> Yes, Maera said, and who will kill his bulls after he gets a *cogida?*
> We, I suppose, I said.
> Yes, we, said Maera. We kills the savages' bulls, and the drunkards' bulls, and the *riau-riau* dancers' bulls. Yes. We kill them. We kill them all right. Yes. Yes. Yes.

In Chapter 18 banal social observations are set off simply by commas.

> We walked through the garden. This is the queen, he said. She was clipping a rose bush. Oh how do you do, she said. We sat down at a table under a big tree. . . .

The brief shout Villalta gives for the bull is met in chapter 14 without fuss: ". . . and called to the bull, Toro! Toro! and the bull charged." In 13 even the comma has disappeared.

> He was very short with a brown face and quite drunk and he said after all it has happened before like that. I am not really a good bull fighter.

In Chapter 8 too one enters the mind of the shelled soldier without formal warning.

> He lay very flat and sweated and prayed oh jesus christ get me out of here.

No one of these instances is in itself of any great moment, but significantly they are all different. They provide an uncommonly clear view of how Hemingway publicly tested

various techniques. After working out these exercises he returned to the traditional way of enclosing dialogue, and
began to change reported speech from within. The strategy
of revolutionizing not its presentation but its constitution
turned out to be a wise one, for Hemingway needed a dialogue to match his prose. He simplified conversations, length-
ened them, and extended them vertically — that is, a characteristic Hemingway dialogue is a long, often thin, vertical
rectangle, rather than a square Hawthornian block. And he
economized so that the very briefest statements were forced
to bear his meaning, to *be* his meaning, in fact. In this respect
Hemingway resembles Henry James, whose characters invested a surprising amount of feeling in innocuous-sounding
chats. Carlos Baker has discussed the similarity of the two
writers' dialogue, saying that "if one tries the experiment of
lifting a Jamesian conversation *verbatim* from its framework,
and substituting 'he saids' and 'she saids' for James's more
complicated directions, the dialogue proceeds in a manner
scarcely distinguishable from Hemingway's." [38] Two passages from which only brief prose parts of the framework
have been excised, one from *The Portrait of a Lady* and the
other from *The Sun Also Rises,* prove Baker's point:

>    "Well now, there's a specimen," he said to her.
>    "A specimen of what?"
>    "A specimen of an English gentleman."
>    "Do you mean they're all like him?"
>    "Oh no; they're not all like him."
>    "He's a favourable specimen then, she said, "be-
> cause I'm sure he's very nice."
>    "Yes, he's very nice. And he's very fortunate." [39]

>    "Doesn't anything ever happen to your values,"
> she asked.
>    "No. Not any more."
>    "Never fall in love?"

"Always," he said. "I am always in love."
"What does that do to your values?"
"That too has got a place in my values."
"You haven't any values. You're dead, that's all."
"No, my dear. You're not right. I'm not dead at all." (p. 63)

As it happens, Hemingway has on several occasions testified to his admiration for James. In *Green Hills of Africa* he wrote, "The good writers are Henry James, Stephen Crane, and Mark Twain. That's not the order they're good in. There is no order for good writers" (p. 22). Some years later in an interview with Harvey Breit, he repeated his sentiments, although he dropped Crane from the list: "As a Nobel Prize winner I cannot but regret that the award was never given to Mark Twain nor to Henry James, speaking only of my own countrymen." [40] In that statement Hemingway links the two men who I think must be linked in order to make any real sense of the genesis of modern American prose style.

It is particularly in dialogue that Hemingway emulates James. Baker has referred to a "hovering subject" as being characteristic of both men's dialogue. Their characters normally talk around, or below, or above, or beside their real subject. One convenient index of the stylistic and cultural distance between Hemingway and Mark Twain exists in Mark Twain's criticism of Fenimore Cooper's dialogue. The trouble with it, Mark Twain thought, was that "the talk wandered all around and arrived nowhere. . . . Conversations consisted mainly of irrelevancies, with here and there a relevancy, a relevancy with an embarrassed look, as not being able to explain how it got there." [41] But the use of irrelevancies in speech as a means of revelation is part of Hemingway's stock in trade. He recognized that in spoken banalities lay much of the inchoate drama of human life, and as we read his dialogue, we are always looking through it to meaning. Probably the indirect influence of Freud's work had something to

do with this, but it also arose out of the habit of close observation cultivated in this century. Pedestrian exchanges were
forced to represent more complicated emotional states. In
"Cat in the Rain" the wife reveals her discontent by the repeated, "Anyway, I want a cat . . . I want a cat. I want a cat
now. If I can't have long hair or any fun, I can have a cat." [42]
And in Hemingway's later story "Hills like White Elephants"
occurs perhaps the most famous instance of what F. O. Mat-
thiessen called one of Henry James's special gifts, "the ability
so to handle a conversation that he keeps in the air not
merely what is said, but what isn't — the passage of thoughts
without words." [43] By means of conversational trivia and
without ever being directly broached, the idea of an abortion
is proposed, discussed, objected to, and finally accepted.

The nature of Hemingway's dialogue also bears out the
earlier contention that he wrote a style based on deliberate
diversification. Unlike the highly specific narrative, his dialogue is often vague, ambiguous, indirect. It is even more
truncated and narrowed than the prose. Indeed, the epitome
of inexpressiveness between quotation marks is reached in
the account of a Montmartre dance in *The Sun Also Rises:*

> The drummer shouted: "You can't two time — "
> "It's all gone."
> "What's the matter?"
> "I don't know. I just feel terribly."
> ". . . . . ." the drummer chanted. Then turned
> to his sticks.
> "Want to go?"
> I had the feeling as in a nightmare of it all being
> something repeated, something I had been through
> and that now I must go through again.
> ". . . . . ." the drummer sang softly.
> "Let's go," said Brett. "You don't mind."
> ". . . . . ." the drummer shouted and grinned at
> Brett.
> "All right," I said. (pp. 66–7)

The drummer is understood still to be making sounds, however unintelligible they may be; but at times Hemingway's dialogue reaches a point of explicitly noted silence.

> Her husband did not answer.
>
> His wife was silent.
>
> I don't know what to say.
>
> I did not say anything.
>
> Cohen said nothing.
>
> Krebs said nothing.
>
> Nick said nothing.
>
> I said nothing.[44]

Hemingway's talk, pared, splintered, and adrift, marked by inarticulate emotional flareups and the verbal blur behind six dots, at last falls into silence, and a long cycle is completed. With his dialogue this study, which began with dialogue, has come full circle to discover all has changed.

The cycle began as nineteenth-century American writers sought to naturalize fictional talk, either by imitating dialects or by loosening literary representations of standard discourse. In the process they followed the bent of colloquial speech — gave it its head and let it assume its own hitherto unimaginable forms. As men like Mark Twain and Henry James learned to reproduce versions of American speech free from obtrusive regionalisms, they introduced elements of that speech into their narrative prose. Gertrude Stein extended their example. By exaggerating the characteristics of the vernacular she produced abstract patterns of words meant to cohere independently of rational meaning. Her work proved valuable, for other writers in the vernacular tradition had discovered that in using the vernacular, they were unable to free themselves from an acknowledged narrator. When they dropped the narrator, they also lost control of their prose. Guided, however, by Gertrude Stein's revelation of the underlying formal structure of the vernacular, Ernest Hemingway developed a subtle, intricate, and balanced narrative prose independent of a specific narrator. In response to the radical stylization of his narrative prose, Hemingway's dialogue then began contracting and kept on until at last it dwindled down to silence, the other side of speech. Having achieved this attenuated extreme, American prose style began to recomplicate itself, but now it possessed the considerable advantage of starting from a stabilized colloquial base.

To simplify the voluminous documentation that a stylistic study necessarily entails, I have observed the following procedures:

(1) Familiar works from which I draw numerous quotations and for which there are several editions easily available—i.e. *Huckleberry Finn, The Wings of the Dove*—I normally identify parenthetically in the text following the quotation *by chapter*. Unless otherwise noted, I cite the original versions of Henry James's novels rather than those prepared for the New York edition.

(2) Aside from such standard sources as Sut Lovingood and Josh Billings, I have drawn most of my examples of vernacular prose humor from three anthologies: *The Cyclopedia of Wit and Humor* which appeared in the middle of the nineteenth century; *The Humour of America* which appeared at the end of the century; and *Native American Humor* which was compiled in recent years. I did this partly for personal convenience, but also because I do not seek to compel the reader's assent by overwhelming him with numerous inaccessible quotations. As noted in the first citation of each, these anthologies are abbreviated as *Cycl., HA,* and *NAH.*

Since most of my quotations come from primary literary sources, I have not thought it necessary to provide a separate bibliography; rather, all sources are fully described in their first footnote entries and indexed by author. But a few stylistic studies — beyond the classic ones of Erich Auerbach, Ernst Robert Curtius, and Leo Spitzer — I have not had occasion to use directly in the text. Their value to me has been such that I would not wish them to go unmentioned. They are:

Croll, Morris W. "Attic Prose: Lipsius, Montaigne, Bacon," *Schelling Anniversary Papers*. New York, 1923, pp. 117–50.

Hatzfeld, Helmut. *A Critical Bibliography of the New Stylistics*. Chapel Hill, 1953.

Jones, Howard Mumford. "American Prose Style: 1700–1770," *The Huntington Library Bulletin*, No. 6 (November, 1934), pp. 115–51.

Levin, Harry. "Observations on the Style of Ernest Hemingway,"
   *Contexts of Criticism*. Cambridge, 1957.

Ohmann, Richard M.   *Shaw: The Style and the Man*. Middle-
   town, Connecticut, 1962.

Sebeok, Thomas A., editor. *Style in Language*. New York, The
   Technology Press of Massachusetts Institute of Technology,
   1960.

Williamson, George. *The Senecan Amble: A Study in Prose Form
   from Bacon to Collier*. Chicago, 1951.

Wilson, Edmund. "The Chastening of American Prose Style,"
   *Patriotic Gore*. New York, 1962.

# NOTES

## INTRODUCTION

1. The books referred to are Henry Nash Smith, *Virgin Land* (Cambridge: Harvard University Press, 1950); R. W. B. Lewis, *The American Adam* (Chicago: University of Chicago Press, 1955); and Harry Levin, *The Power of Blackness* (New York: Knopf, 1958).

2. "Prolegomena to the Analysis of Prose Style," *Style in Prose Fiction* (English Institute Essays, 1958), ed. Harold C. Martin (New York: Columbia University Press, 1959), p. 14.

3. The quotations are from (a) "Ethan Brand" (1850), (b) *The Sun Also Rises* (1925), (c) George Lippard, *The Quaker City* (1844), (d) Irwin Shaw, *The Young Lions* (1948).

4. *Green Hills of Africa* (New York: Charles Scribner's Sons, 1935), p. 22. The quotation goes on: "If you read it you must stop where the Nigger Jim is stolen from the boys. That is the real end. The rest is just cheating. But it's the best book we've had. There was nothing before. There has been nothing as good since." Nigger Jim was, of course, not stolen from the *boys* but from Huck alone.

5. "Credo," quoted in *Literature in America,* ed. Philip Rahv (New York: Meridian Books, 1957), pp. 300–301.

6. *Faulkner at Nagano,* ed. Robert A. Jelliffe (Tokyo: Kenkyusha Ltd., 1956), p. 88.

7. "America's Voice Is Mark Twain's, "San Francisco *Chronicle,* August 5, 1956, *This World* section, p. 20.

8. "American Literature and the American Language," *Washington University Studies, New Series, Language and Literature,* 23 (1953), p. 16.

9. Introduction to *The Adventures of Huckleberry Finn* (New York: Rinehart & Co., 1948), p. xvi.

10. *The Portable Mark Twain* (New York: Viking, 1946), p. 28.

11. "American Style," *Points of View* (New York: Charles Scribner's Sons, 1924), p. 159.

12. "The Vernacular Tradition in American Literature," *Studies in American Culture,* ed. Joseph J. Kwiat and Mary C. Turpie (Minneapolis: University of Minnesota, 1960), p. 109.

13. *Dissertations on the English Language* (Boston, 1789), p. 36.

14. Quoted in Mitford M. Mathews, *Beginnings of American English* (Chicago: University of Chicago, 1931, 1963), p. 131.

15. Thomas Chandler Haliburton, *Judge Haliburton's Yankee Stories* (Philadelphia, 1844), II, 8.

16. Jonas Barish, *Ben Jonson and the Language of Prose Comedy* (Cambridge: Harvard University Press, 1960), p. 19.

17. The integral relationship between the Southerners and the writers I am

discussing is suggested by Frank Baldanza in his acute and compact essay, "Faulkner and Stein: A Study in Stylistic Intransigence," *Georgia Review*, XIII, 3 (Fall, 1959), 274–86.

## ONE

1. *Adventures of Huckleberry Finn*, ed. with intr. by Henry Nash Smith (Boston: Houghton, Mifflin, 1958), p. 261.

2. Porter G. Perrin, *Writer's Guide and Index to English*, 3rd ed. (Chicago: Scott, Foresman & Co., 1959), p. 756.

3. John Neal, *American Writers: A series of papers contributed to* Blackwood's Magazine, *1824–1825*, ed. F. L. Pattee (Durham: Duke University, 1937), p. 186.

4. "Concerning the American Language," *Tom Sawyer Abroad, and Other Stories* (New York, 1896), p. 370.

5. "Linguistic Patriot," *The Kenyon Review* (Winter, 1946), VIII, 159–60.

6. "The Middle American Style," *The New York Times Book Review*, July 15, 1945, pp. 3, 14.

7. *The Well-Tempered Critic* (Bloomington: Indiana University Press, 1963), p. 21.

8. F. L. Pattee in the introduction to Neal's *American Writers*, p. 12.

9. *American Writers*, pp. 185–6.

10. *Wandering Recollections of a Somewhat Busy Life: An Autobiography* (Boston: Roberts Brothers, 1869), pp. 235, 261, 315, 44, 71.

11. James Hall, "Pete Featherton," *The Cyclopedia of Wit and Humor*, ed. William E. Burton (New York, 1870, originally 1858), p. 111. Hereinafter, *Cycl.*

12. "Mrs. Yardley's Quilting," in George Washington Harris, *Sut Lovingood* (New York, 1867), p. 134. Hereinafter, *Sut.*

13. *A Quarter Race in Kentucky and Other Sketches*, ed. William T. Porter (Philadelphia, 1846), pp. 182, 174, 46.

14. Ibid., pp. 186, 59, 14.

15. *Zury: The Meanest Man in Spring County* (Boston, 1887), pp. 2, 10, 21.

16. "Mrs. Yardley's Quilting," *Sut*, p. 134.

17. "Rare Ripe Garden-Seed," *Sut*, p. 231.

18. "Eaves-Dropping a Lodge of Free-Masons," *Sut*, pp. 115–16.

19. "Daisy Miller," *Selected Fiction*, ed. with intr. by Leon Edel (New York: Dutton, 1953), pp. 44, 40, 48.

20. "Sicily Burns's Wedding," *Sut*, p. 92.

21. Finley Peter Dunne, "On the Victorian Era," in Walter Blair, *Native American Humor* (San Francisco: Chandler Publications, 1960), p. 461. Hereinafter, *NAH*.

22. William Hall, *Cycl.*, p. 220. (Capitals added.)

23. "After the Storm," *The Short Stories of Ernest Hemingway* (New York: Modern Library, 1938), p. 472. (Capitals added.) Hereinafter, *Short Stories*.

24. *Huckleberry Finn*, ch. 13; and "The End of Something," *Short Stories*, p. 206.

25. Allen Drury, *A Senate Journal: 1943–1945* (New York: McGraw-Hill Book Co., 1963), p. 119.

26. *The Deer Park* (New York: Putnam, 1955), pp. 4, 257. In *Advertisements for Myself* (New York: Putnam, 1959), pp. 238–9, Mailer describes the writing of *The Deer Park:* "I worked by tricks, taking marijuana the night before and then drugging myself into sleep . . . benzedrine entered the balance."

27. *The Tale of Peter Rabbit* (New York: Warne, 1904), pp. 48, 49. (Capitals added.)

28. *The Humour of America,* ed. James Barr (London and New York, 1894), pp. 63, 69, 69. Hereinafter, *HA.*

29. *Mark Twain: The Development of a Writer* (Cambridge: Harvard University Press, 1962), p. 17.

30. "S——L" of Tennessee, "Dick Harlan's Tennessee Frolic," *Quarter Race,* p. 83. (Capitals added.)

31. W. T. Thompson, "The Fire-Hunt," *Cycl.,* p. 243. (Capitals added.)

32. J. M. Bailey, "Tempest in a Tub," *HA,* p. 128.

33. William Hall, "Mike Hooter's Bar Story," *Cycl.,* p. 219.

34. Donald Stanley, "The Sex Revolution," *People* in *The California Weekly,* San Francisco *Examiner,* June 28, 1964, p. 15.

35. Richard Ellmann, "In Lord Alfred's Camp," *The New York Review of Books,* II, No. 6 (April 30, 1964), 7.

36. "Song of Myself," sec. 13.

37. *Short Stories,* p. 295.

## TWO

1. William Cabell Bruce, ed., *Benjamin Franklin, Self-Revealed* (New York, 1917), II, 440

2. Mitford M. Mathews, *Beginnings of American English* (Chicago: University of Chicago, 1931, 1963), p. 69.

3. *American Writers,* ed. F. L. Pattee (Durham: Duke University, 1937), p. 26.

4. Letter to Dr. Staunton, June 1, 1762, quoted in Boswell's *Life of Johnson.*

5. *Modern Chivalry,* ed. Claude M. Newlin (New York: Hafner, 1962), Part One. Vol. I, Postscript, p. 78.

6. In Benjamin T. Spencer, *The Quest for Nationality* (Syracuse: Syracuse University Press, 1957), p. 62.

7. In Paul M. Angle, ed., *The Lincoln Reader* (New Brunswick: Rutgers University Press, 1947), p. 104.

8. In Spencer, *The Quest for Nationality,* p. 85.

9. *American Writers,* p. 25.

10. "James Fenimore Cooper" in *Essays from the North American Review,* ed. Allan T. Rice (New York, 1879), p. 376.

11. In Perry Miller, *The Raven and the Whale* (New York: Harcourt, Brace and World, 1956), p. 191.

12. Ibid., p. 125.

13. "Defense of Poetry" (July, 1832) in *Essays from the North American Review*, pp. 328–9.

14. Frederick S. Cozzens, "Living in the Country," *Cycl.*, p. 412.

15. Thomas Chandler Haliburton, *Judge Haliburton's Yankee Stories* (Philadelphia, 1844), pp. 31–2.

16. *The Question of Our Speech* (Boston, 1905), p. 38.

17. Haliburton, *Yankee Stories*, pp. 45–6.            ,

18. "Notions of the Americans," Letter 23, quoted in Louis D. Rubin, Jr., and John R. Moore, eds., *The Idea of an American Novel* (New York: Thomas Y. Crowell, 1961), p. 4.

19. Part Two, Vol. I, Bk. II, Introduction, p. 405.

20. "The Veil," *Essex Gazette*, Haverhill, Mass., November 24, 1827. Stanza is quoted in John B. Pickard. *John Greenleaf Whittier* (New York: Barnes and Noble, 1961), p. 10.

21. *NAH*, p. 18.

22. John Neal, "The Yankee Peddler," *Cycl.*, p. 79.

23. *The Biglow Papers*, Second Series (Boston, 1873), lxxiii.

24. *William T. Porter and the Spirit of the Times* (Baton Rouge: Louisiana State University Press, 1957), p. 97.

25. Letter to Hamlin Garland in *Roadside Meetings* (New York, 1930), p. 232.

26. George H. Hill, "A Yankee Card-Table," *Cycl.*, p. 180.

27. *Biglow Papers*, lxx.

28. Ibid.

29. The relative lack of American dialects has been remarked upon since at least the end of the eighteenth century, when John Witherspoon observed that "the vulgar in America . . . moving frequently from place to place . . . are not so liable to local peculiarities either in accent or phraseology" ("The Druid," no. 5 [1781] in M. M. Mathews, *Beginnings of American English*, p. 16). A generation later, John Pickering repeated the observation: "There is greater uniformity of dialect throughout the United States (in consequence of the frequent removals of people from one part of our country to another) than is to be found throughout England . . ." ("Essay," [1816] in ibid., p. 67).

More recently George Philip Krapp has commented: "American dialect literature rests upon a foundation of general informal colloquial speech, locally established by action and setting with its local character confirmed by a slight addition of local practices in speech" (*The English Language in America* [New York, 1925], I, 243). And finally, H. L. Mencken: "In place of the discordant local dialects of all other major countries, including England, we have a general Volkssprache for the whole nation . . ." (*The American Language*, 4th ed. [New York, 1938], p. 90).

It is true that a greater precision in the recording of dialects can distinguish numerous sub-categories, down to the individual "idiolect." But the fact remains that comparatively few distinct dialects have existed in the

United States, and this has, I believe, contributed importantly to the establishment of an accepted colloquial prose.

30. *Maggie,* Vol. X of *The Work of Stephen Crane,* ed. Wilson Follett (New York, 1926), p. 212.

31. John Neal, "The Yankee Peddler," *Cycl.,* p. 79.

32. "The Novel of Dialect; W. D. Howells," *The American Essays of Henry James,* ed. Leon Edel (New York: Vintage Books, 1956), p. 253.

33. The fictional names come from Joseph Neal, *Charcoal Sketches; or Scenes in a Metropolis* (Philadelphia, 1840).

34. C. F. M. Noland, " 'Old Sense' of Arkansas," in *Tall Tales of the Southwest,* ed. Franklin J. Meine (New York: Knopf, 1930), p. 133.

35. Henry P. Leland, "The Dutchman Who Had the 'Small-Pox,' " *Cycl.,* p. 451. Kenneth Lynn usefully discusses the "frame" device which placed "a *cordon sanitaire* between the morally irreproachable Gentleman and the tainted life he described" in *Mark Twain and Southwestern Humor* (Boston: Little, Brown & Co., 1959), p. 64.

36. T. B. Thorpe, "A 'Hoosier' in Search of Justice," *Cycl.,* p. 372.

37. B. R. Hall, "A Breakfast in a Log Cabin," *Cycl.,* p. 390.

38. George H. Hill, "A Yankee Card-Table," *Cycl.,* p. 180.

39. George Wilkes, quoted in *Tall Tales,* ed. F. Meine, xxviii.

40. Thomas Wentworth Higginson, *American Orators and Oratory* (Cleveland, 1901), p. 59.

41. Anonymous, "A Western Lawyer's Pleas Against the Fact," *Cycl.,* p. 124.

42. Frank R. Stockton, "Pomona's Novel," *HA,* p. 119.

43. Artemus Ward, "The Showman's Courtship," *HA,* pp. 292-3.

44. Henry W. Shaw, "The Feathered Ones," *Everybody's Friend, Or; Josh Billings's Encyclopedia* (Hartford, 1874), p. 179.

45. *NAH,* pp. 413-17, and Artemus Ward, "Interview with President Lincoln," *NAH,* p. 403.

46. *Sut,* pp. 49, 48, and Henry Shaw, "What I Kno About Pharming," *Everybody's Friend,* p. 65.

47. *Sut,* "Preface," p. ix.

48. Letter to Hamlin Garland, *Roadside Meetings,* p. 107.

49. Anonymous editorial in *The Nation,* VI (January 9, 1868), quoted in *The Idea of an American Novel,* p. 30.

50. *Literary Essays, The Works of Mark Twain,* Definitive Edition, ed. Albert Bigelow Paine, 37 vols. (New York: Harper, 1922-5), XXII, 62. All references to Mark Twain's work, except *Huckleberry Finn,* hereinafter are keyed to the *Works.* They will be cited by volume title, number, and page.

51. "The Dialect of Cooper's Leather-Stocking," (1927) in *Selected Writings of Louise Pound,* ed. Lowry C. Wimberly (Lincoln: University of Nebraska Press, 1949), pp. 174, 166.

52. Vintage Edition (New York, 1956), p. 116.

53. The adjective "return" fails here, because, although it animates the scene by serving as a stage direction to remind us that the buckets are moving both ways as in a fire line, the overspecification jars in context.

54. "The Middle American Style," *The New York Times Book Review*, July 15, 1945, p. 3.

55. *Their Wedding Journey* (Boston and New York, 1890), pp. 211–12.

56. "William Dean Howells," *The Shock of Recognition*, ed. Edmund Wilson, 2 vols. (New York: Farrar, Straus, and Cudahy, 1955), I, 574. The article originally appeared in *Harper's Weekly*, June 19, 1886.

## THREE

1. (Norfolk, Conn.: New Directions, n.d.), p. 140.

2. Collected in *The Art of the Novel*, ed. R. P. Blackmur (New York, Charles Scribner's Sons, 1934), p. 106–7.

3. Henry James, "Gustave Flaubert," in *The Future of the Novel*, ed. Leon Edel (New York: Vintage Books, 1956), p. 160.

4. "Summer's Day," *Selected Short Stories of John O'Hara* (New York: Modern Library, 1956), p. 87.

5. "No Mistakes," *Selected Short Stories of John O'Hara*, p. 168.

6. *Hawthorne*, reprinted in *The Shock of Recognition*, ed. Edmund Wilson, 2 vols. (New York: Farrar, Straus, and Cudahy, 1955), I, 430.

7. "Fenimore Cooper's Literary Offenses," reprinted in *The Shock of Recognition*, I, 583.

8. *A Treasury of Damon Runyon*, intr. by Clark Kinnaird (New York: Modern Library, 1958), p. 44.

9. There is a strong resemblance between James's technique and one Flaubert is famous for having originated, called "free indirect discourse." For a discussion of the subject, see Stephen Ullmann, *Style in the French Novel* (Cambridge, Eng.: Cambridge University Press, 1957), ch. II, "Reported Speech and Internal Monologue in Flaubert."

10. *Instigations* (New York: Boni and Liveright, 1920), p. 122.

11. (Paulton, Eng.: John Lehmann, 1947), p. 21. (Spacing added.)

12. *The Literary Apprenticeship of Mark Twain* (Urbana: University of Illinois Press, 1950), p. 199.

13. "Cooper's Offenses," in *Shock of Recognition*, I, 586–7.

14. *A Tramp Abroad*, X, 115 n.

15. Ibid., Appendix D, p. 281.

16. "Tom Sawyer Abroad," XIX, 86.

17. *Mark Twain's Letters*, XXXIV, 258–9.

18. *Europe and Elsewhere*, XXIX, 341.

19. *The Art of the Novel*, p. 69.

20. *The Method of Henry James* (Philadelphia: Albert Saifer, 1954), pp. 76–7.

21. "Twain's Method and Theory of Composition," *Modern Philology*, LVI, No. 3 (February, 1959), 176.

22. Ch. 25. Knowing Twain's propensity for concealed bawdiness, one may easily make something out of the American slang term "jism" meaning "semen" — see the *Dictionary of American Slang*, ed. Harold Wentworth and

Stuart B. Flexner (New York, 1960). Then there is the joining of the king's two words: *orgojeesum.*

23. Ch. 43. The title of Wright Morris's book of criticism, *The Territory Ahead,* distorts the phrase, making "ahead" qualify "territory" rather than "light out."

24. Frank Baldanza has suggested that similar thematic and episodic repetitions give *Huckleberry Finn* its coherence. See "The Structure of *Huckleberry Finn*," *American Literature,* XXVII (November, 1955), 347–55.

25. *Mark Twain at Work* (Cambridge: Harvard University Press, 1942), p. 93.

26. Frances G. Emberson, "Mark Twain's Vocabulary," *The University of Missouri Studies,* X, No. 3 (July 1, 1935), p. 11.

27. Sydney Krause, "Twain's Method and Theory of Composition," p. 175.

28. "About Magnanimous-Incident Literature," *Tom Sawyer Abroad,* XIX, 330. On the other hand, Twain found adjectives useful in *Huckleberry Finn* as substitutes for adverbs. Functioning unconventionally, they too drew attention to themselves as individual words. If the feminine ending in poetry is weaker than the masculine, then the signal for the adverb, "-ly," can similarly be said to reduce the power of the adjective to which it is attached. Because of Huck, Twain could use adjectives adverbially, as in these examples: "Reverend Hobson opened up, slow and solemn"; "him and the duke . . . walked slow and solemn"; "painted up gaudy"; "we woke him up gentle and gradual"; and "a-spinning downstream soft, but quick" (chs. 27, 25, 17, 36, 7).

29. Ch. 22 (capitals added). Huck normally does use participles more than is the case in traditional literary prose, but the less involved he is in an episode, the fewer participles there are.

30. Ch. 8 (capitals added). Note that there is something distinctive about each of these familiar fruits. The idiom "plenty of" is halved before the strawberries; a neologistic specification is made of "summer" grapes; raspberries is colloquially spelled; and there is a paradoxical clash of colors in "green blackberries." Twain sometimes gives emphasis to both the object and its qualities by placing the qualification after the noun, as he does here —"ripe and prime." See also "the wreck, dim and dusky" (ch. 13).

31. Ch. 18 (capitals added). Col. Grangerford's hair turns from black to grey in succeeding editions of the book. Also, he wears the same coat the king does. See "He had an old long-tailed blue jeans coat with slick brass buttons" (ch. 19).

32. *Mark Twain's Autobiography,* XXXVI, 172.

33. Ch. 9. See also ch. 20, "the thunder would go rumbling and grumbling away. . . ."

34. *In the Cage,* ed. with intr. by Morton D. Zabel (Garden City: Doubleday Anchor Books, 1958), p. 321, 324.

35. *The Portable Mark Twain* (New York: Viking Press, 1946), p. 20.

36. *The Art of the Novel,* pp. 145–6. Even as James consciously rejects the adolescent voice, his dictated prose betrays the unconscious promptings of association. The whole intricate statement is held together by the assonance

of "at any moment . . . at all . . . amusing . . . as it might be . . . as well as . . . at once . . . attempt . . . attends . . . amplifies." And that is not to mention "conclusions . . . commentary . . . constantly."

FOUR

1. *The Portable Mark Twain* (New York: Viking Press, 1946), p. 28.
2. *The Street I Know* (New York: Lee Furman, 1935), p. 52.
3. See *My Several Worlds* (New York: John Day Co., 1954), p. 62; *Sacred and Profane Memories* (New York: Alfred A. Knopf, 1932), p. 19; *A Child of the Century* (New York: Simon and Schuster, 1954), pp. 67–8; *I Wanted To Write* (Garden City; Doubleday & Co., 1949), p. 58; *A Peculiar Treasure* (New York: Doubleday, Doran & Co., 1939), pp. 36–7; *The Books in My Life* (Norfolk, Conn.: New Directions, n.d.), p. 41.
4. *Homecoming* (New York: Farrar & Rinehart, 1933), p. 81.
5. "A Cat Tale," *Concerning Cats,* ed. with intr. by Frederick Anderson (San Francisco, 1959), p. 13.
6. "Mark Twain," *Mark Twain, Selected Criticism,* ed. Arthur L. Scott (Dallas: Southern Methodist University Press, 1955), p. 79.
7. *Mammonart* (Pasadena, Calif.: By the author, 1925), pp. 90–91.
8. Ch. 17.
9. Brander Matthews, *Tom Paulding* (New York: Century, 1917), p. 37; Stephen Crane, "Lynx-Hunting," *Twenty Stories,* intr. Carl Van Doren (New York: Alfred A. Knopf, 1940), p. 466; and *Penrod,* in *The Gentleman from Indianapolis,* ed. John Beecroft (Garden City: Doubleday & Co., 1957), p. 306.
10. Hervey Allen, "A Great American," *The Magazine of Sigma Chi,* George Ade Memorial Issue (October–November, 1944), p. 12.
11. Fred G. Kelly, *George Ade, Warmhearted Satirist* (Indianapolis: The Bobbs-Merrill Co., 1947), p. 32.
12. *The New York Times Magazine,* March 25, 1917, quoted in Donald Elder, *Ring Lardner* (New York: Doubleday and Co., 1956), p. 137.
13. *The New York Times,* April 22, 1910, p. 2.
14. Ibid.
15. James Woodress, *Booth Tarkington* (Philadelphia: J. B. Lippincott Co, 1954), p. 86.
16. *Fables in Slang* (Chicago, 1899), p. 17.
17. Ibid., pp. 196, 158, 64, 71.
18. "The Development of Style in Nineteenth-Century American Fiction," *Style in Prose Fiction,* English Institute Essays (New York: Columbia University Press, 1959), p. 132.
19. Otto Jespersen, quoted in Harold C. Martin, *The Logic and Rhetoric of Exposition* (New York: Rinehart and Co., 1958), p. 148.
20. *Twenty Stories,* pp. 409–10.
21. *Fables in Slang,* p. 64.
22. "W. H. Hudson — Some Reminiscences," *The Little Review Anthology,* ed. Margaret Anderson (New York: Hermitage House, 1953), p. 292.

23. Quoted in Frances G. Emberson, "Mark Twain's Vocabulary," *The University of Missouri Studies*, X, No. 3 (July 1, 1935), p. 11.

24. *Pudd'nhead Wilson*, XVI, 12.

25. Uniform Edition (New York, 1889), p. 86.

26. *Twenty Stories*, p. 83.

27. "The Monster," *Twenty Stories*, p. 246.

28. Quoted in Albert Bigelow Paine, *Mark Twain*, II, 949.

29. Uniform Edition (New York, 1896), p. 36.

30. *The New York Times Book Review*, February 18, 1912, p. 82.

31. (Garden City: Doubleday and Co., 1912), p. 184.

32. "A Successor to Mark Twain," *Michigan Alumnus Quarterly Review* (July 24, 1937), p. 603, 604.

33. *Style in Prose Fiction*, pp. 166, 167.

34. *Ring Lardner*, pp. 81, 81, 138.

35. *You Know Me Al* (New York: Charles Scribner's Sons, 1925), p. 222. All page numbers for Lardner quotations refer to this edition.

36. *The Selected Writings of Gertrude Stein*, ed. with intr. by Carl Van Vechten (New York: Random House, 1946), p. 437.

37. *Three Lives* (New York: Modern Library, 1936), p. 212

38. May Arbuthnot, *Children and Books* (Chicago: Scott, Foresman & Co., 1947), p. 370.

39. *Three Lives*, pp. 212–13.

40. Elder, *Lardner*, p. 287.

41. *The Portable Sherwood Anderson*, ed. with intr. by Horace Gregory (New York: Viking Press, 1949), p. 554. This was written in 1919 for the *New Republic*.

42. *A Literary Chronicle: 1920–1950* (Garden City: Anchor Books, 1956), p. 40.

43. "Ring" in *The Crack-Up*, ed. Edmund Wilson (New York: New Directions, 1956), p. 36.

44. See Elder, *Lardner:* "He and Kendall talked over drinks, Ring asking him if Kendall thought him as good a writer as Finley Peter Dunne, George Ade, or Harry Leon Wilson, or finally, Mark Twain; and Kendall would tell him that he was the greatest of humorists" (p. 131).

45. *Letters of Sherwood Anderson*, ed. with intr. by Howard Mumford Jones, in association with Walter B. Rideout (Boston: Little, Brown & Co., 1953), p. 3.

46. *Sherwood Anderson's Memoirs* (New York: Harcourt, Brace and Co., 1942), p. 246.

47. For this particular correspondence see either Anderson's *Letters*, or the collection in *The Shock of Recognition*, II, 1258–90. Anderson was always alert for an injured fellow author. No other American writer seems to have felt such a deep sense of a brotherhood of artists as Anderson did. His comments on Lardner are typical. "I daresay that the tragedy of Ring Lardner . . . that gorgeous talent of his so often smeared . . . is our common tragedy, the tragedy of every creative man, big or little, in our day. No one of us escapes it. How can he?" "Meeting Ring Lardner," *The Sherwood*

*Anderson Reader,* ed. with intr. by Paul Rosenfeld (Boston: Houghton, Mifflin Co., 1947), p. 302.

48. *The Modern Novel in America* (Chicago: Henry Regnery, 1951), p. 109.

49. *Hello Towns!* (New York: Horace Liveright, 1929), p. 294.

50. *Sherwood Anderson's Notebook* (New York: Boni and Liveright, 1926), p. 195.

51. *Letters,* p. 33. Walter Blair's *Mark Twain and Huck Finn* (Berkeley: University of California Press, 1960) will disabuse anyone sharing Anderson's notions of the spontaneous writing of *Huckleberry Finn.*

52. *Letters,* p. 31.

53. Ibid., p. 53.

54. (New York: Viking Press, 1919), pp. 19–20.

55. Irving Howe, *Sherwood Anderson* (New York: Sloan, 1951), p. 95.

56. *Letters,* p. 88.

57. (Boston: Four Seas Co., 1922), p. 8.

58. *Hello Towns!,* p. 325.

59. "Not Sixteen," *Sherwood Anderson Reader,* p. 843.

60. *Anderson Reader,* p. 70.

61. Ibid., p. 236.

62. (New York, 1920), p. 3.

63. *Sherwood Anderson,* p. 154.

64. *Horses and Men* (New York: Viking Press, 1923), p. 16.

65. The title is misleading. An adolescent has the experience. Anderson again fails to make the age and the tone correspond, for although the narrator seems quite young and indeed is mistaken for a girl, he says that he was "nineteen years old then" (p. 185).

66. *The American Earthquake* (Garden City: Doubleday and Co., 1958), p. 127.

67. *On Native Grounds* (Garden City: Doubleday and Co., 1956), p. 170.

68. "Homage to Hemingway," *After the Genteel Tradition,* ed. Malcolm Cowley (New York: W. W. Norton & Co., 1937), p. 192.

69. *Letters,* p. 300.

70. "Paper Pills," *Winesburg,* pp. 18, 20.

71. "Loneliness," *Winesburg,* p. 206.

72. *On Native Grounds,* p. 167.


FIVE

1. In 1913 Ezra Pound was counseling the apprentice writer to fill his mind with cadences from the finest poetry, "preferably in a foreign language so that the meaning of the words may be less likely to divert his attention from the movement." "A Few Don'ts by an Imagiste," *Poetry* (March, 1913), p. 202.

2. *Art by Subtraction* (Norman: University of Oklahoma Press, 1958), p. 155.

3. *Malabar Farm* (New York: Harper and Brothers, 1947), p. 103.

4. "Steinese," *The New York Times Book Review,* November 3, 1946, p. 6.

5. *Gertrude Stein: A Biography of Her Work* (New Haven: Yale University Press, 1951), p. 9. On the concluding page of the book the publishers note that "The title was changed to a phrase used by Gertrude Stein in this novel. . . ." That phrase appears in the next to the last sentence: " 'Can't she see things as they are and not as she would make them if she were strong enough as she plainly isn't' " (p. 87).

In this connection see Henry James's "The Author of Beltraffio" (1884), where the following appears: " 'Moreover, I care for seeing things as they are; that's the way I try to show them in any professed picture. But you musn't talk to Mrs. Ambient about things as they are. She has a moral dread of things as they are.' " — *In the Cage,* ed. with intr. by Morton D. Zabel (Garden City: Doubleday Anchor Books, 1958), p. 59.

6. "Steinese," p. 6.

7. *Journey into the Self,* ed. Edmund Fuller (New York: Crown, 1950), p. 120.

8. In a letter from Alice B. Toklas to Jerry Allen, author of *The Story of Mark Twain.* The quotation was transcribed by Miss Allen in a presentation copy of her book given to Miss Isabel Lyon.

9. *Everybody's Autobiography* (New York: Random House, 1937), p. 92.

10. (New York: Random House, 1933), p. 59.

11. *Lectures in America* (New York: Random House, 1935), p. 53.

12. *Things As They Are* (Pawlet, Vt.: The Banyan Press, 1950), pp. 15–16.

13. In any case we now suspect that association is not "free" at all. In her writings Gertrude Stein made perhaps as many contributions to psychology as she did to art. But no one so far as I am aware has availed himself of her record of the mind operating.

14. *Lectures in America,* p. 215.

15. *Autobiography of Alice B. Toklas,* p. 96.

16. *Being Geniuses Together* (London: Secker and Warburg, 1938), p. 139.

17. *The Third Rose* (Boston: Little, Brown, and Co., 1959), p. 45.

18. *Gertrude Stein,* p. 47.

19. Brinnin, *The Third Rose,* p. 46.

20. P. 44. See also p. 6, "You have a foolish notion that to be middle-class is to be vulgar, that to cherish the ideals of respectability and decency is to be commonplace and that to be the mother of children is to be low." The passage continues in this highly formalized vein.

21. *Art by Subtraction,* p. 72.

22. For a full discussion of the transformation, see R. Bridgman, "Melanctha," *American Literature,* XXXIII, No. 3 (November, 1961), 350–59.

23. In *The Autobiography of Alice B. Toklas,* Gertrude Stein says that she and Leo had purchased "a portrait of a woman" by Cezanne, and that "it was an important purchase because in looking and looking at this picture Gertrude Stein wrote Three Lives. She had begun not long before as an exercise in literature to translate Flaubert's Trois Contes and then she had this Cezanne and she looked at it and under its stimulus she wrote Three

Lives" (pp. 40–41). She adds that when Picasso was painting her portrait, she walked daily to his Montmartre studio, and "she was then in the middle of her negro story Melanctha Herbert . . . and the poignant incidents that she wove into the life of Melanctha were often these she noticed in walking down the hill from the rue Ravignan" (p. 60).

Alice Toklas in a taped interview with Roland Duncan said that Gertrude Stein "never made up her mind that she was going to be a writer, never expected to be one, and she started writing by translating the — what is it, of Flaubert. And then she started it — I think it's at Yale — she did the first paragraph and said, 'I'm not interested in somebody else's writing — I'm going to do a story myself.' " (Typescript at the Bancroft Library, University of California, Berkeley, p. 35.)

The first paragraph of "Un Coeur Simple" is one short sentence: "Pendant un demi-siècle les bourgeoises de Pont-l'Evêque envièrent à Mme Auban sa servante Félicité." James Joyce, master logodaedalist, also noted this paragraph, once pointing out that the verb should be *enviaient* because the envious feelings were continuous. See Richard Ellmann, *James Joyce* (New York, 1959), p. 506.

24. *The Future of the Novel*, ed. with intr. by Leon Edel (New York: Vintage Books, 1956), p. 161.

25. *Three Lives* (New York: Modern Library, 1936), p. 132.

26. See also "sweet appearing," and "sweet-appearing" (p. 90); "tender-hearted" and "tender hearted" (p. 186); "may-be" and "may be" (pp. 196, 198).

27. The following unsimple words do appear in "Melanctha": resentment, endurance, sodden, docile, demean, reproach, abandonment, abomination, complicated disillusion, promiscuous immorality, submissive, negligent, repression, unendurable, resolution, unimpassioned, sympathetic, tumultuous, and pungent.

28. Gertrude Stein was always shrewdly aware of the distinctions between words. In *Wars I Have Seen* (New York: Random House, 1945), for example, she commented, "One might not be very free in the unoccupied [zone of France] but we were pretty free and in the occupied they were not free, the difference between pretty free and not free at all is considerable" (p. 87).

29. *Gertrude Stein*, p. 48.

30. *Collected Essays*, ed. with intr. by Edmund Wilson (New York: Charles Scribner's Sons, 1948), p. 41. Bishop also noted (and this view is close to my own) that "if the problem was to combine Mark Twain and Gustave Flaubert — to convert a common American speech to the uses of the French tradition — it could hardly be doubted that Miss Stein had done it" (p. 41).

31. Her brother Leo thought Gertrude repeated because of psychical illness. "Gertrude never could use words with precision and force," he wrote in a letter to Mabel Weeks in 1933, "and she was always terribly addicted to repetition. I can't see anything else than a case of Adler's deficiency and compensation." — *Journey into the Self*, p. 134.

32. *Lectures in America*, p. 184.

33. *Selected Writings of Gertrude Stein*, ed. with intr. by Carl Van Vechten (New York: Random House, 1946), pp. 455–6.

34. *Gertrude Stein*, p. 64.

35. *How To Write* (Paris, 1931), pp. 57, 57, 55, 56, 73, 101, 58, 59, 58.

36. *Selected Writings*, p. 265 (italics added).

37. *Lectures in America*, p. 138.

38. *Wars I Have Seen*, p. 63.

39. *A Pluralistic Universe* (New York, 1928), p. 258.

40. *Lectures in America*, p. 139.

41. "A Propos du 'style' de Flaubert," *Nouvelle Revue Française*, XIV, No. 1, 73–4.

42. *Lectures in America*, p. 174.

43. *The Tragic Muse* (Boston, 1890), III, 811.

44. *Lectures in America*, p. 175.

45. "Introduction to Metaphysics," *Selections from Bergson*, ed. with intr. by Harold A. Larrabee (New York: Appleton-Century-Crofts, 1949), p. 22. Allegra Stewart in her article, "The Quality of Gertrude Stein's Creativity," *American Literature*, XXVIII, No. 4 (January, 1957), notes that "Gertrude Stein attended Bergson's lectures in Paris in the winter of 1908 just before she began to write portraits, and it may well be that the impact of those lectures turned her attention from the problem of time in narrative to the problem of objectifying purely qualitative perceptions" (pp. 498–9).

46. *Lectures in America*, p. 210.

47. *Selected Writings*, pp. 420, 415.

48. *Selected Writings*, pp. 437, 436, 434.

49. Ibid., p. 437.

50. Ibid., pp. 439, 438, 437.

51. II, No. 3 (October, 1924), 305.

52. *Selected Writings*, p. 437.

## SIX

1. Quoted in Charles Fenton, *The Apprenticeship of Ernest Hemingway* (New York: Farrar, Straus & Young, 1958), p. 59.

2. Quoted in Carlos Baker, *Hemingway, The Writer as Artist* (Princeton: Princeton University Press, 1956), p. 4 n.

3. Fenton, pp. 33, 34, 187.

4. *Death in the Afternoon* (London: Jonathan Cape, 1950), p. 10.

5. *Ernest Hemingway* (New York: Rinehart & Co., 1952), p. 160.

6. See Fenton, p. 196, and Baker, pp. 11-12, for the story.

7. Fenton, p. 149.

8. Fenton, p. 118.

9. *Collected Essays*, ed. with intr. by Edmund Wilson (New York: Charles Scribner's Sons, 1948), p. 40.

10. Fenton, p. 104.

11. "The Soul of Spain (In the Manner of Gertrude Stein)" in *Der Querschnitt* (Herbst, 1924), reprinted in *The Collected Poems of Ernest Hemingway*, "Number One of the Library of Living Poetry" (n.p., n.d.), no pagination.

12. "The Art of Fiction XXI," *The Paris Review* (Spring, 1958), 73.

13. Quoted in Edmund Wilson, *A Literary Chronicle: 1920–1950* (Garden City: Anchor Books, 1956), p. 44.

14. (New York: Charles Scribner's Sons, 1964), p. 17.

15. *The Hemingway Reader,* ed. with intr. by Charles Poore (New York: Charles Scribner's Sons, 1953), pp. 74–5.

16. *The Short Stories of Ernest Hemingway* (New York: Modern Library, 1938), p. 179 (capitals added). Passage analyzed in Fenton, pp. 152–4.

17. Ibid., p. 266 (capitals added).

18. Ibid., p. 245 (capitals added).

19. "Homage to Hemingway," *After the Genteel Tradition,* ed. Malcolm Cowley (New York: W. W. Norton & Co., 1937), p. 193.

20. *Shakespeare and Company* (New York: Harcourt, Brace and Co., 1959), p. 26.

21. *The Letters of Ezra Pound 1907–1941,* ed. D. D. Paige (New York: Harcourt, Brace and Co., 1950), p. 38.

22. Note that Pound remarked in 1937 "It should be realised that Ford Madox Ford had been hammering this point of view into me from the time I first met him (1908 or 1910) and that I owe him anything that I don't owe myself for having saved me from the academic influences then raging in London." *Letters,* p. 49. Hemingway too was closely associated with Ford, especially during the life of the *transatlantic review,* but he is not mentioned in this study because I am necessarily compressing influences into a few representative figures.

23. Letter to Iris Barry, July 1916, ibid., p. 90.

24. *Pudd'nhead Wilson,* epigraph to chapter XI; *Letters,* p. 49; *Lectures in America* (Boston: Beacon Press, 1957), p. 211.

25. *in our time* (Paris, 1924), p. 13. Hereinafter identified in the text by chapter.

26. "The Middle American Style," *The New York Times Book Review,* July 15, 1945, pp. 3, 14. Cowley never makes it clear whether he intended to designate a social, geographic, or rhetorical "middle style." But he does point out the necessity of developing this style as "a literary instrument. In a sense, Mark Twain had apologized for using it, by putting it into the mouth of an illiterate hero; it was not at all his fashion of speaking for himself." As Cowley intimates, the convention of an illiterate narrator imposes serious limitations upon the writer. He shrewdly suggests that the way out of the dilemma is "for an educated author to use this style when writing ordinary third-person narrative. That was the step taken by Gertrude Stein in her first book, *Three Lives.*" This is true, if we add the important qualification that Gertrude Stein took that step with no support from Mark Twain. It was in fact the discovery of how difficult it was to establish any meaningful

connection between Gertrude Stein and Mark Twain that gave the present work its final direction.

27. *The Torrents of Spring* is parody, and the chapter-end conversations of *Death in the Afternoon* are mordantly good-humored. A slight dialect (one of educational deficiency) is used in *To Have and Have Not,* and there is some imitation in it too, in "Albert Speaking."

28. Wilson, *A Literary Chronicle,* p. 48.

29. Quoted in Fenton, p. 18.

30. See Fenton, pp. 229–36 for a discussion of the story's gradual transformation.

31. *Death in the Afternoon,* p. 10. See his letter to Gertrude Stein in November 1923: "I am going to chuck journalism I think. You ruined me as a journalist last summer. Have been no good since." — Fenton, p. 160.

32. Quoted in introduction to *The Hemingway Reader,* p. xiv.

33. (New York: Charles Scribner's Sons, 1950), p. 59.

34. *On Love,* tr. H. B. V. under direction of C. K. Scott-Moncrieff (New York: Anchor Books, 1957), p. xix.

35. (New York: Charles Scribner's Sons, 1926), p. 95. By the 'thirties Hemingway had begun to press very hard on his mechanics, so that in *Green Hills of Africa* there appeared this extreme version of the same technique.

> So in the morning, again, we started ahead of the porters and went down and across the hills and through a deeply forested valley and then up and across a long rise of country with high grass that made the walking difficult and on and up and across, resting sometimes in the shade of a tree, and then on and up and down and across, all in high grass, now, that you had to break a trail in, and the sun was very hot. (p. 68)

36. The quoted phrases come from chapters 16, 2, 2, 3, 5, 12, 13, 17.

37. *In Our Time,* p. 134.

38. *Hemingway,* p. 183.

39. *The Portrait of a Lady,* intr. by Fred B. Millett (New York: Modern Library, 1951), p. 90. This passage is taken from the revised edition which is somewhat more colloquial and hence more to the present point. In the third chapter of this study, however, I have consistently quoted from the original versions, because I was discussing James's gradual movement *toward* the colloquial.

40. *The Writer Observed* (New York: The World Publishing Co., 1956), p. 276.

41. "Fenimore Cooper's Literary Offenses," *The Shock of Recognition,* ed. Edmund Wilson, 2 vols. (New York: Farrar, Straus, and Cudahy, 1955), I, 592.

42. *In Our Time,* p. 123.

43. *Henry James, The Major Phase* (New York: Oxford University Press, 1944), p. 169.

44. Lines quoted appear in "The Doctor and the Doctor's Wife," *In Our Time,* p. 29; ibid., p. 30; "The End of Something," *In Our Time,* p. 40; "The Revolutionist," *In Our Time,* p. 106; *The Sun Also Rises,* p. 47; "Soldier's Home," *In Our Time,* p. 99; "The Battler," *In Our Time,* p. 74; *The Sun Also Rises,* p. 48.

All page numbers in the Index over 230
should be increased by two.

# INDEX

Page references in boldface type indicate the major discussions of the subjects.

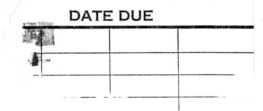